Torture Porn

Torture Porn

Popular Horror after Saw

Steve Jones
Northumbria University, UK

First published 2013 by
PALGRAVE MACMILLAN

Palgrave Macmillan in the UK is an imprint of Macmillan Publishers Limited, registered in England, company number 785998, of Houndmills, Basingstoke, Hampshire RG21 6XS.

Palgrave Macmillan in the US is a division of St Martin's Press LLC, 175 Fifth Avenue, New York, NY 10010.

Palgrave Macmillan is the global academic imprint of the above companies and has companies and representatives throughout the world.

Palgrave® and Macmillan® are registered trademarks in the United States, the United Kingdom, Europe and other countries

ISBN: 978–0–230–31941–7 hardback

This book is printed on paper suitable for recycling and made from fully managed and sustained forest sources. Logging, pulping and manufacturing processes are expected to conform to the environmental regulations of the country of origin.

A catalogue record for this book is available from the British Library.

A catalog record for this book is available from the Library of Congress.

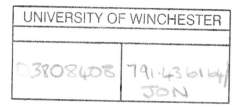

Contents

List of Figures

Acknowledgements

Although I do not have the space here to name every individual that I would like to, I offer my heart-felt gratitude to my family, friends, and colleagues for their support, and not only in the writing of this book. I am sure those individuals know who I am referring to: I hope they also know how much they mean to me.

Project-specific thanks are due to the editorial team at Palgrave Macmillan for their help and support in constructing this book. Particular thanks to Felicity Plester, who suggested compiling a monograph on torture porn in the first instance. My appreciation is offered to Peter Hutchings, John Armitage and the anonymous reader who kindly offered constructive feedback on the proposal for this book. My thanks also go to those at Northumbria University who enabled me to take a sabbatical to draft the monograph.

Above all, I wish to thank my partner, Lydia, whose patience and support know no bounds. This book is dedicated to you, as am I.

Introduction: 'Welcome to Your Worst Nightmare'[1]

'Revolting...repellent' (N.a. 2008b), 'poisonous' (Sarracino and Scott, 2008: 219), 'perverse' (Slotek, 2009a), 'terrible...ugly' (Phelan, 2011), 'vile...distasteful' (Graham, 2009a), 'rancid...joyless' (Hornaday, 2008a), 'salacious' (Kinsella, 2007), 'mean, dingy' (Lacey, 2007), 'grim' (Kendall, 2008), 'nasty' (Cochrane, 2007), 'queasy...nauseating' (Bradshaw, 2007), 'woeful...despicable' (Tookey, 2008b), 'repugnant' (Holden, 2008), 'spirit-sapping' (Booth, 2008), 'astonishingly depraved' (N.a. 2007b), 'deplorable...tasteless...sleazy and gratuitous' (Puig, 2008).

These are some of the hyperbolic terms used to describe 'the 21st century's vilest new genre: torture porn' (N.a. 2007a). It is hard to imagine that fictional films could warrant the loathing instilled in these adjectives, and resultantly in the term 'torture porn' itself. Following David Edelstein's 2006 *New York* article 'Now Playing at Your Local Multiplex: Torture Porn',[2] the label has been applied (often retroactively) to more than forty horror films made since 2003. Based on critical responses, one might mistakenly believe that torture porn is wholly irredeemable rather than being 'one of the major cultural cornerstones of the decade', as Tara Brady (2010a) has it. How torture porn came to be characterised as unacceptable and whether the subgenre deserves the remonstration it has received are key questions that this book will address. Taking stock of what 'torture porn' signifies is crucial, since the trend and the term continue to impact on how contemporary horror-fiction is understood more broadly.

Although it will be argued that torture porn films have been unfairly dismissed in press discourse, this book does not seek to erase 'torture porn'[3] or 'rescue' films from that category. 'Torture porn' is a shorthand label that brushes over the subgenre's diversity, but numerous productive tensions emanate from collecting texts together under a single banner. Labelling texts 'porn', for example, is a process of demarcating the border-line between what is 'acceptable' and 'unacceptable' in popular culture. Since torture porn films are both illegitimated by reviewers and yet also legitimated by their relative financial success, 'torture porn' discourse highlights confusions regarding how taboo is defined at present. Rather than using 'torture porn' to dismiss these films as critics predominantly have then, this book engages with torture porn, exploring wider concep-tual meanings that spring from grouping these films together.

The vast majority of torture porn's detractors have failed to adequately engage with the subgenre's content. Some of the subgenre's most prof-itable films have been addressed, but those responses are commonly superficial. Rather than dealing with torture porn itself, the subgenre's belittlers instead tend to replicate various prejudices about popular violent cinema, duplicating established rhetorical paradigms. 'Torture porn' misrepresents the films themselves then, but the label has also been utilised to incriminate the subgenre's filmmakers and fans. These imbalances will be redressed by analysing 'torture porn' discourse, torture porn films, and the broader contexts implied by referring to horror movies as 'extreme' or 'pornographic'. The book is divided into three parts that correspond with these aims. Part I is diachronic. The category 'torture porn' will be explored by probing how torture porn is situated within critical and generic contexts. Press responses to the subgenre will be inspected in these chapters. Part II is theoretical. 'Torture' provides a primary focus for this part, and moral philosophy will be used to illu-minate aspects of torture porn's narrative content. In these chapters, the films themselves will be analysed. Part III is synchronic. Here, the term 'porn' is examined via an investigation into the subgenre's sexual content. Chapters 8 and 9 will then contextualise that evaluation, illus-trating how extremity manifests in contemporaneous pornographic and non-mainstream horror films, where sex and violence are blended much more literally than they are in torture porn.

Chapters 1 to 3 will outline what is meant by 'torture porn', exploring issues that arise from using a category-label as the primary means of understanding these films. 'Torture porn' discourse discloses less about the films themselves than it does about critical responses to popular horror more generally. Chapter 1 will investigate torture porn's generic lineage. Critics and filmmakers alike directly compare torture porn to the slasher subgenre, for instance, but do so for very different purposes.

Torture porn's filmmakers regularly refer to slasher films to demonstrate their genre knowledge, making favourable comparisons between their films and earlier famous horror movies. Pundits have used the same comparisons to denigrate torture porn, painting torture porn as inferior to past 'classics'. The latter term is not only utilised to refer to influential movies, but also to broadly distinguish between contemporary horror and genre films made more than 30 years ago. This mode of argumentation duplicates the same rhetorical devices that critics employed when disparaging contemporaneous popular horror films in the 1960s and 1970s.

Resultantly, torture porn's opponents present the subgenre as wholly different to 'classics', and yet the films are also presumed to be identical enough that paradigms established to denigrate earlier horror movies can be applied to torture porn. This confusion derives from a failure to distinguish between (a) continuities within the horror genre, and (b) continuities within critical reactions to horror. Derogatory responses remain remarkably consistent, despite the genre's continual evolution. Torture porn clearly inherits traits from its generic predecessors, but critical narratives do not adequately account for torture porn's particular configurations and attributes. A tangential paradigm ('porn') has been applied to expound changes within horror, but the resulting amalgam is undermined by its imprecision. 'Torture porn' discourse is inconsistent because objectors have utilised the porn-horror combination to fit various conflicting agendas and diverse propositions about what makes horror 'pornographic'. Despite these idiosyncrasies, several dominant trends emerge consistently within 'torture porn' discourse. Those commonalities descend from conceptual presumptions about what porn and/or horror are, rather than from the films themselves.

Thus, Chapter 2 will appraise press reviews and commentary in order to decipher torture porn's alleged characteristics and the terms on which the subgenre has been illegitimated. Torture porn is surmised to lack substance because the films are putatively constituted by violence. Of particular affront to these reviewers is the mainstream acceptability of such depictions. Critics bemoan torture porn's presence in the multiplex, suggesting that these films should be marginalised. Their complaints about torture porn ultimately express unease not about filmic content, but about how taste boundaries are regulated.

Referring mainly to press articles, DVD commentaries, and briefly to online fan forums, Chapter 3 will explore another off-screen factor that has shaped 'torture porn': how filmmakers and fans have been addressed in and have responded to complaints about the subgenre. Filmmakers have primarily defended their films by distancing themselves from 'torture porn', or by vindicating their violent imagery. This is unsurprising given that reviewers tend to deride torture porn filmmakers by branding them untalented, irresponsible, and even deviant. Horror fans have similarly been dubbed immature, unintelligent, or perverse for watching torture porn. Fans have also therefore typically dissociated themselves from 'torture porn'. Many horror fans have co-opted 'torture porn' to refer to films that they dislike, consolidating the label's pejorative connotations. Others concur with pundits' shared, nostalgic view that liking torture porn amounts to not understanding what authentic, 'classic' horror (and horror fandom) is. Fan, filmmaker, and critical discourses converge on the point that torture porn qua 'torture porn' is contemptible, supporting the notion that 'torture porn' is a consistent category, even though these films, fans, and filmmakers have been brought together by an artificial rubric. Surface coherence masks the inconsistencies within 'torture porn' discourse, and those tensions are Part I's nucleus.

In Part II (Chapters 4 to 6), the films themselves will be examined with the intention of challenging the presumptions outlined in the opening chapters. Chapter 4 will redress two common critical suppositions. The first derives from defences that treat torture porn as an allegory for the Bush Administration's War on Terror. Numerous scholars have used the allegory interpretation to prove that torture porn films are politically charged cultural artefacts. However, that reading has been reiterated to the extent that the approach ties torture porn into a very specific politico-historical juncture. Cumulatively, those allegory interpretations imply that torture porn is stimulating chiefly – or perhaps *only* – because of the immediate political context. To read torture porn merely as a reflection of its contemporaneous context is to divest the subgenre of its potential long-term meanings. Subsequent chapters in Part II will counter those restrictions, and moral philosophy is used to expand the debates.

The second assumption addressed in Chapter 4 is narratological. Detractors have claimed that torture porn is sadistic, alleging that the films are mainly focused on torturers' pleasures. This supposition again arises from pre-established discursive narratives. Slasher films, for instance, have stood accused of fostering sadistic pleasure because they regularly include camera shots that emulate antagonists' first-person perspectives. Numerous critics have vilified horror films for encouraging audiences to 'identify' with killers, suggesting that first-person camerawork facilitates sadistic attitudes. This established critical paradigm has been transposed onto torture porn without examining the subgenre's content. As Chapter 4 will illustrate, torture porn narratives are aligned with sufferers' perspectives much more consistently than they are with torturers'.

Leading from these discussions regarding torture's narrative contextualisation, character positions will be deliberated in Chapter 5. Torture is typically imagined to be a two-party struggle involving a torturer and a tortured individual. Torture porn's violence is consistently less clear-cut, involving a third participant: a witness. Moreover, characters slip between these three positions: tortured protagonists become torturers, witnessing itself becomes torturous, and so forth. Concentrating on morality, the analysis will demonstrate that torture porn is not constituted by mindless sadism. Complex ideas such as justice, choice, innocence, guilt, blame, and retribution are dramatised and scrutinised via torture porn's representations of violence. This discussion will be developed in Chapter 6 by exploring the relationships between diegetic space, power, and morality. Torture porn's torture occurs in circumscribed vicinities. The characters' power-relations are revealed via their grappling for spatial control as much as they are by torture itself. Abductees' commitments to moral principles are impugned as a result of their imprisonment. In order to survive, prisoners must resist their captors and attain control over their circumstances. However, doing so customarily involves hostages becoming violent aggressors or forsaking others in order to ensure their escape from the torture-space. The slippages discussed in Chapter 5 are thus implicated in characters' contestations over spaces.

Despite prevailing assumptions to the contrary then, torture porn's character dynamics are intricate. The narratives disturb the dichotomous logic that underpins pejorative responses to torture porn, whereby torture is envisaged as a two-party interrelation in which positions (tortured and torturer) and intentions (innocence and sadism) are fixed. Binarism is equally evident in responses to gender and sexual violence in 'torture porn' discourse. Torture porn's men are customarily presumed to be sexually violent agents who victimise women. This supposition again stems from a lack of detailed engagement with the films themselves. There is, for example, far less nudity and sexual violence in films that have been dubbed 'torture porn' than the label connotes. Accordingly, in Part III (Chapters 7 to 9) torture porn's complex representations of sexual violence and gendered power will be scrutinised, as will implications that arise from casting mainstream horror films as 'porn'.

'Torture porn' implies generic hybridity and so cannot be deciphered by looking to the horror genre alone. Edelstein coupled 'torture' with 'porn' to posit that violent multiplex horror-fiction had become obscenely gratuitous. However, this view does not account for collusions of horror and pornography outside of the multiplex setting. In Chapter 8, two branches of pornographic film that more overtly fit the complaints levelled at torture porn will be discussed. Khan Tusion's *Meatholes* films are utilised as a case study via which to explore manifestations of degradation, sex, and violence in extreme porn, a subgenre that also peaked in popularity during the 2000s. In the chapter's latter stages, films such as *Texas Vibrator Massacre* and Zero-Tolerance's *Saw*-based porn-spoof will be used to exemplify how horror motifs and candid sexual depictions comingle in contemporary horror-porn. Parallel amalgamations of genitally-explicit imagery and violence will be probed in Chapter 9. Torture porn may have stolen the limelight, but hardcore horror filmmakers have bridged the gaps between pornography and horror more literally than their mainstream foils by merging the narrative facets and aesthetic practices of both genres. Torture porn directors such as Eli Roth have declared that their portrayals of graphic violence 'push the envelope', but numerous micro-budget horror filmmakers have utilised sex–violence combinations to maintain their status as more 'extreme' than their commercially profitable counterparts. Despite having received virtually no scholarly attention to date, this concurrent movement sheds light on torture porn's ostensible 'extremity', and the meanings of 'torture porn' as a categorising term.

The book's three parts are focused on three respective key concepts: category, morality and extremity. It might initially appear as if applying these concepts entails marking out dichotomous separations. Categorisation involves differentiating between items that are included or excluded from a category. Ethical evaluation is similarly underpinned by an ostensibly oppositional separation between 'right' and 'wrong'. Assessing extremity is a matter of distinguishing between 'extreme' and 'non-extreme' or 'acceptable' and 'unacceptable'. These binary models are constituted by entirely separate poles. However, the overarching concepts reveal that these apparently distinct binaries share commonalities. For example, although categorising torture porn involves distinguishing torture porn movies from other films and other forms of culture, that process equally requires *comparing* torture porn to those other cultural forms. Without such comparisons, it is not possible to distinguish what belongs to the category.

Hence, the concepts (category, morality, extremity) articulate relationships between seemingly dichotomous poles. Morality, for instance, encompasses both 'right' and 'wrong', bridging between the two.

Attempting to engage with dichotomies without considering relationships at the conceptual level is to risk (a) eliding the broader commonalities that define the dichotomy, (b) over-emphasising the apparent differences between objects, and (c) failing to understand how apparently dichotomous relationships are formed and change over time.

Consequently, unless overarching conceptual frameworks are accounted for, distinctions become too sharp. Dynamic relations are reduced to seemingly unchanging, fixed binaries. Torture porn's detractors commonly neglect the conceptual, relational mode. Resultantly, 'torture porn' criticism is mainly focused on the immediate present and fails to adequately account for torture porn's organic development over time. Moreover, torture porn's hecklers also tend to universalise their evaluations about the films and their worth, but offer little detail to substantiate claims. The outcome is a series of confused, ill-founded accusations that do not portray the subgenre accurately. To counter those flaws, torture porn's content must be attended to in greater detail. Particularities will be related to the conceptual frameworks to assess torture porn's wider, long-term meanings. Those meanings are dynamic. The analysis herein is submitted with the proviso that the conceptual terrain is ever-shifting, and the meanings evoked here cannot be final. Some generalisation is involved in such analysis in order to flag patterns. The act of describing equally entails fixing meaning in the present. The dissection of torture porn offered in this book is a snapshot of fluctuating meanings and fluid conceptual relations.

Having established what is to follow, some caveats are necessary. Imposing subgenre labels risks lapsing into spiralling distinctions that quickly become impracticable. For instance, in his attempt to discuss sex-horror blending, Thomas Sipos (2010: 26–8) refers to 'splatter porn', 'erotic horror' and 'non-horror splatterporn' as distinct subgenres. While some delineation is necessary when handling (sub)genre, such hyper-specialised distinctions are usually unproductive: new, increasingly specialised micro-categories must be created when films do not quite 'fit' existing labels or when movies traverse subgenre boundaries. Torture porn is not a fully discrete subgenre, even according to the press's limited usage. Torture porn intersects with other genres including the thriller (*Unthinkable*), and art-drama (*Antichrist*), as well as other horror subgenres such as rape-revenge (*I Spit on Your Grave*), home-invasion horror (*Cherry Tree Lane*), and the slasher (*The Watermen*). Hence, categorisation itself is queried in this book rather than seeking to impose criteria that encapsulate torture porn's facets. The analysis thus begins with properties shared by films that have already been dubbed 'torture porn'. When widespread traits are discussed, they are so (a) to handle these texts in a productive manner by opening up debate, (b) to connect torture porn to its genre lineage, and (c) to understand the contexts that situate 'torture porn'.

The chapters will detail those common traits. To retain the popular sense of what constitutes 'torture porn', three pivotal qualities are utilised as indicators for grouping these diverse texts. Torture porn films (a) were made (roughly) after 2003, (b) centralise abduction, binding, imprisonment, and torture (mental or physical), and (c) broadly belong to the horror genre. The latter is most problematic, since discerning the difference between 'horror' and 'thriller' or even 'drama' is no simple matter. Here, the term 'horror' is used with the assumption that the category cannot be perfectly delimited. Horror, as the genre-label is utilised in this book, implies that the narrative under inspection thematically prioritises protagonists' fear and/ or suffering for emotive affect. That is, torture porn's protagonists overtly respond to torment with terror, outrage, or disgust, and the emphases placed on those emotional states suggest that the narrative is encoded to inspire trepidation, tension, or revulsion for the audience.

Torture porn's key attributes derive from commonalities found within 'torture porn' discourse. Those same facets equally apply to dozens of films that have not been dubbed 'torture porn' by the popular press, many of which are also discussed in this book. Major theatrical releases (including *Saw*, *Hostel*, and *The Texas Chainsaw Massacre: The Beginning*) will be analysed alongside lower budget non-theatrical features (*Flesh*, *TX*, *Dark Reality*, and *Stash*, for instance). The 45 films the press have (to date) regularly labelled 'torture porn' are included, but so too are more than 90 additional films that have been neglected in critical appraisals of torture porn. Any discussion of torture porn in this book refers to the extended subgenre definition. References to the press's 45-film torture porn canon will be explicitly distinguished.

Torture porn initially gained attention from the mainstream press due to its relative success in the multiplex. Non-multiplex films have been included in order to reflect the subgenre's continued proliferation on the DVD market since 2007. Numerous DVD distributors have clearly aligned their films with the subgenre. Even if the term 'torture porn' is avoided, comparisons to box-office hits are commonplace, manifesting in the DVD packaging of *The Tortured* ('[f]rom the producers of *Saw*'),[4] *The 7th Hunt* ('[f]ans of the *Saw* movies will love this!'),[5] and *Live Feed* ('*Hostel*... with snakes!').[6] These marketing strategies feed from torture porn's popularity. Therefore, such DVD releases should be accounted for in attempting to understand torture porn.

Other provisos regarding what this book does *not* aim to do are necessary. Torture porn's global, transnational nature is not probed here. The majority of films referred to are American, because Anglo-American press critics – who coined and propagated the term – mainly dub American films 'torture porn'. Scholarly responses to torture porn are equally biased towards American production and reception. No distinctions are made between films of different national origins in this book. Movies filmed in and co-produced between Asian, Australian, European, North American and South American countries are included since these countries have all produced horror films that fit the 'torture porn' paradigm. Additionally, it is important to recognise that torture porn is not only the product of American concerns. Roth has contended that *Hostel* was a response to Abu Ghraib, yet the transnational dialogue evident among torture porn's filmmakers demonstrates that *Hostel* is not just relevant in the US context. Pascal Laugier has perspicuously presented his film *Martyrs* as a response to *Hostel*,[7] indicating that *Hostel*'s themes resonate in European torture porn. Furthermore, Takashi Miike's cameo in *Hostel* attests to the influence of pre-9/11 Japanese horror on *Hostel*. The transnational flow is multi-directional. *Saw* is evoked in the Japanese marketing for many UK and US torture porn films, including *Broken* (renamed *Jigsaw: Dead or Alive*), *Steel Trap* (*Jigsaw: Tower of Death*), and *Are You Scared?* (*Jigsaw: Game of Death*), for instance. Thus, it is insufficient to think of torture porn as an American subgenre per se. However, that complex topic will not be dwelt upon here, since exploring torture porn's global shape would itself require a monograph-length study.

Similarly, it is beyond this book's scope to dissect distinctions between horror, porn and 'art' film. 'Torture porn' has been applied to non-English language 'art' dramas such as *The Passion of the Christ* and *The Stoning of Soraya M.*, as well as the work of European auteurs Lars von Trier (*Antichrist*), Michael Winterbottom (*The Killer Inside Me*), and Michael Haneke (*Funny Games*). Critics' attempts to decide if these films count as torture porn have inspired lengthy debates over directorial intention and artistic merit in the press.[8] The terms 'art' and 'torture porn' have been used respectively to defend or vilify these films. The same discussions are absent from press reviews of horror genre-pictures such as *The Devil's Rejects* or *Turistas*, which have been roundly dismissed. The disparities between Anglo-American reviewers' treatment of popular American horror and 'world cinemas' – despite similarities in content – speak volumes about the presumed cultural value of these texts. 'Torture porn' discourse concretises the double standards in operation, and would benefit from in-depth analysis in that respect. In order to debunk the hierarchical bias present in those press discussions, films that straddle 'art' and 'torture porn' – such as *The Book of Revelation*, *Irreversible*, and *Senseless* – are included as examples of torture porn.

Although this book briefly touches on torture porn fandom by utilising press articles and printed interviews, it is beyond this book's purview to offer empirical research. To assess consumption with enough validity would again require a separate, devoted study. Torture porn films are primarily discussed as narratives in this book in a bid to counter the dearth of detailed filmic analysis in 'torture porn' discourse. The analyses offered are informed by deontology and feminism, which are respectively harnessed to grasp themes that are integral to the debates surrounding torture and porn: morality and gendered power. While this book does some work to investigate these films outside of the prevalent War on Terror allegorical interpretation then, dozens of other angles remain untouched. Detailed explorations of new redneck-cannibal torture porn crossovers, or of class in British 'hoodie' torture porn films are just two approaches to the subgenre that would prove fruitful. This book can only scratch the surface of the material available for evaluation. The central aim here is to stimulate debate regarding this rich subgenre.

Part I
'Torture Porn' (Category)

1
'The Past Catches Up to Everyone':[1] Lineage and Nostalgia

The aim of the following three chapters is to establish how 'torture porn' has been constructed as a category, outlining characteristics that have become associated with the subgenre. Part I will establish what 'torture porn' means, and the conditions under which those meanings are defined. The aim of examining 'torture porn' discourse is to clarify what the subgenre 'is' according to the critics who have propagated the term. As a starting point, this chapter addresses a paradox that arises within 'torture porn' discourse. 'Torture porn' appears to refer to a coherent category formed by films that exhibit mutual conventions and values. By providing a point of similarity, the label brushes over numerous discrepancies.

At the most basic level, torture porn films have been conceived as sharing a root commonality: torture porn is a sub-category of the horror genre. Yet, by distinguishing this subgenre as a unique grouping, the label contradictorily fosters the sense that torture porn is different to other horror subgenres. So, on one hand reviewers have overtly compared torture porn to earlier horror subgenres, such as slasher and splatter films, conceiving of torture porn as part of horror's generic continuum. On the other hand, such comparisons have generally been unfavourable, painting torture porn as inferior (that is, entirely *different*) to past horror 'classics'. The result is tension, which stems from the implication that both 'torture porn' and 'horror' are delimited, static categories, when they are more accurately hazy gestures towards imperfect, fluid, ever-evolving sets of conventions. Delineating a subgenre perfectly is impossible since both the subgenre and the overarching genre it belongs to are in constant states of flux. The relationship between torture porn and horror will be investigated in this chapter by probing the press's conflicting treatments of 'torture porn'.

Rather than accepting 'torture porn' as a label that simply encompasses a particular body of films then, the objective of this chapter is to examine the difficulties that arise from journalists' uses of the label as if it signifies a fixed, delimited category. The inadequacy of 'torture porn' in that regard is evident. For example, although the label seems to encompass all torture porn films, in practice, the discourse fails to do so. At the time of writing, 45 films have been dubbed 'torture porn' by three or more separate articles in major English language news publications.[2] Almost all of those films received theatrical releases in both the US and the UK.[3] The many direct-to-DVD films that fit the 'torture porn' paradigm have thus far been neglected in 'torture porn' discourse. Theatrically released films have been scapegoated, meaning that the category has been mainly composed around a distributional context – the multiplex – rather than mutual conventions.

Torture porn's content has been largely disregarded in press discourse. Consequently, the subgenre is characterised as having 'sprung up' from nowhere (Tookey, 2011), being constituted by films that are wholly distinct from earlier, 'better' horror movies. In actuality, the charges levelled at torture porn are uncannily similar to the scorn bestowed upon those 'classic' horror films torture porn has been unfavourably compared to. The desire to separate past from present reveals more about critics' resistance to change than it does about torture porn. The segregation strategy – attacking torture porn while also defending 'classic' horror – fails to explicate continuities within the genre, or precisely what is allegedly wrong with torture porn. Deciphering the similarities between torture porn and earlier horror – in terms of filmic content and the discourses that surround horror film – illuminates both what torture porn putatively is and is not. Torture porn neither simply replicates nor overturns prior genre attributes. The subgenre has organically evolved from its generic precursors. By mapping out problems that arise from categorisation, this chapter establishes the groundwork for the remainder of Part I, which will be devoted to factors other than filmic content that influence how torture porn is understood.

'Every Legend Has a Beginning':[4] shared facets and influences

Since 'torture porn' collects films under an umbrella term, it is necessary to grasp how the label itself speaks for and shapes responses to the films classified under that rubric. Understanding torture porn as 'torture porn' necessarily limits how each film is construed relative to that category.

A cyclic logic is at play in such categorisation. Torture porn films are torture porn because they have been brought together under the banner 'torture porn'. The label itself arose as a response to the films, and presumptions about their content. However, once in motion, 'torture porn' imbues any film categorised as such with meanings that do not belong to the individual film itself. Labelling any film 'torture porn' also entails washing over its idiosyncrasies, instead emphasising the presumed similarities it shares with other torture porn films.

Torture porn is conceived as a subgenre fixated on sex ('porn') and violence ('torture'). This coalescence manifests in four contentions that will recur in various guises throughout this book. First, some objectors claim that torture porn is constituted by violence, nudity, and rape. Second, violence is read as pornographic. Critics allege that torture porn's violence is depicted in such prolonged, gory detail that its aesthetic is comparable to hardcore pornography's, since the latter is renowned for its close-up, genitally explicit 'meat shots'. Third, the 'porn' in 'torture porn' is interpreted as a synonym for 'worthless'. Since the films are allegedly preoccupied only with 'endless displays of violence' (Roby, 2008), they are dismissed as throwaway, immoral entertainment. Finally, it is proposed that the films are consumed as violent fetish pornography: that viewers are sexually aroused by torture porn's horror imagery. Torture porn's disparagement begins with these undertones, which are inherent to the label rather than the subgenre's filmic content. The first two contentions portray torture porn as sexually focused. As Chapter 7 will demonstrate, this misrepresents the content of the films that have been dubbed 'torture porn'. The latter two contentions are based on unsubstantiated assumptions about reception, which, as Dean Lockwood (2008: 40) notes, conform to the 'limiting...logic of media effects'. Such attempts to understand the subgenre favour paradigms that pre-exist torture porn over filmic content. As this chapter will evince, that strategy is ubiquitous in 'torture porn' criticism.

For the moment, it is worth contemplating what exactly torture porn films do have in common. The four contentions above do not necessarily harmonise, undermining the coherence implied by 'torture porn' and making it difficult to grasp why these films have been grouped together. However, critics have more consistently concurred about which films belong to 'torture porn' than they have about why these films should be denigrated. Stepping back from detractors' insinuations and looking to the films themselves offers a clearer sense of torture porn's root properties according to its opponents. Although diverse, the 45 films dubbed 'torture porn' by the press share two main qualities: (a) they chiefly belong to the horror genre and (b) the narratives are primarily based around protagonists being imprisoned in confined spaces and subjected to physical and/or psychological suffering. The subgenre's leitmotif is the lead protagonist being caged, or bound and gagged.

Critics' fleeting gestures towards filmic content can be utilised to refine those foundational commonalities. For example, although he is preoccupied with a contextual issue – audience reaction – Kim Newman's (2009a) reference to torture porn's 'deliberately upsetting' tone is worth considering. His grievance is surprising given that horror films intentionally foreground perilous situations, and so are customarily 'deliberately upsetting' in tone. It is unclear why torture porn should be singled out on those grounds. Newman's complaint regarding the character of torture porn's violence becomes more obvious when considering why some films have *not* been dubbed 'torture porn'. Adam Green's *Frozen* concentrates on three protagonists who are imperilled by their entrapment on a ski lift. The film has not been labelled 'torture porn' in major English language news articles despite (a) being marketed as a horror film, (b) prioritising entrapment themes, (c) setting the narrative in a restrictive diegetic space, and (d) focusing on protagonists' suffering. Indeed, Green (in Williamson, 2010b) has posited that the film is *anti*-torture porn. There are two reasons why *Frozen* has not been dubbed 'torture porn': gore is kept to a minimum, and suffering is not inflicted by a torturer. In *Frozen*, the teens are accidentally rather than *intentionally* trapped.

Human cruelty and bloodshed are key triggers that influence opponents' decisions about which films do or do not fit into the subgenre, and help to clarify what Newman means by torture porn's 'deliberately upsetting' tone. The same implication is evident in Luke Thompson's (2008) sweeping definition of torture porn as 'realistic horror about bad people who torture and kill'. Graphic gore ('realistic...torture') is paramount. By proposing that torture porn narratives are *about* 'bad people', Thompson equally alleges that torture porn narratives are invested in the calculated infliction of human cruelty.

Thompson's assessment that torture porn is 'realistic horror' is another point of consensus among critics. Jeremy Morris (2010: 45), for instance, declares that torture porn is 'never supernatural'. However, *Somebody Help Me*, *Farmhouse*, and *Wicked Lake* are among those contemporary horror films in which supernatural elements are mixed with abduction, imprisonment, and intentionally exacted torture. Such generic 'slippage' might mean that these texts fall out of the 'torture porn' category for many critics. Indeed, these hybrid texts have rarely been termed 'torture porn' in press reviews. It is equally telling that supernatural horror films such as *Paranormal Activity* and *1408* have been critically lauded specifically because they are *not* torture porn. John Anderson (2007a) and Kevin Williamson (2007b) both valorise *1408* because, in contrast to torture porn, the film lacks gore and is driven by ghostly forces rather than human intentions. Williamson's and Anderson's views confirm that torture porn is understood as a subgenre constituted by brutal spectacle. As is typical of such argumentation, both reporters assume that torture porn is gory, but do not evince that point with reference to torture porn's content. They thereby connote that violent spectacle itself is not worth scrutinising. Since torture porn is reputedly constituted by such superficial violence, it too is denigrated.

Content is also eschewed in favour of context where torture porn is delineated via its roots. This is a popular method for determining the meanings of 'torture porn' in press discourse, yet the subgenre's origins are again subject to disagreement. Assorted pundits peg torture porn's progenitor as *Hostel* (Maher, 2010a) or *Saw* (Lidz, 2009; Floyd, 2007). Others cite the 2003 films *Wrong Turn* (Gordon, 2009), *House of 1000 Corpses* (Johnson, 2007), *The Texas Chainsaw Massacre* (Fletcher, 2009: 82), and *Switchblade Romance* (Newman, 2009a) among torture porn's originators. One difficultly in pinning down torture porn's starting-point is that the horror genre is replete with torture-themed films. Vincent Price vehicles such as *Pit and the Pendulum* (1961) and the uncannily *Saw*-like *The Abominable Dr. Phibes* (1971) are only two examples that pre-date 'torture porn'. Torture-based horror is clearly not the 'radical departure' some disparagers have claimed (Fletcher, 2009: 82; see also Di Fonzo, 2007). Ergo, torture themes and genre-affiliation are not enough to distinguish torture porn as a horror subgenre, since that combination pre-exists 'torture porn'. The category-label was coined in response to a critical mass of torture-horror production at a particular moment.

A further defining factor is thrown into relief by the candidates for torture porn's progenitor then: 'torture porn' is conceived as referring to torture-based horror films made after 2003. It is likely that pre-21st century horror movies will remain omitted from such analysis since they are anachronistic to the term itself. That torture porn is partially defined by era underscores the extent to which context is privileged over content in 'torture porn' discourse. Lockwood's (2008: 41) question 'how should we specifically distinguish torture porn from earlier horror cinema?' is telling then, insofar as it underscores that the practice of labelling films 'torture porn' is precisely a distinguishing strategy: the aim is to separate torture porn from its generic past rather than examining what that lineage reveals about the subgenre. Fencing torture porn in this manner is a way of closing off rather than opening up meaning.

Although the majority consensus is that torture porn belongs to the 21st century, not all critics so sharply deny torture porn's relationship to earlier horror. Some have rooted torture porn in late 19th century Grand Guignol (Anderson, 2007c; Johnson, 2007). In other cases, torture porn has been linked to previous subgenres such as the splatter film (Fletcher, 2009: 81; Benson-Allott, 2008: 23), to specific filmmakers including Herschell Gordon Lewis (N.a. 2010c; Johnson, 2007), Lucio Fulci (Kermode, 2010), and Dario Argento (Hornaday, 2008b), or to 'classic' horror touchstones such as *Peeping Tom* (Huntley, 2007; Kendall, 2008), and the original *The Texas Chainsaw Massacre* (Felperin, 2008; Safire, 2007). Numerous torture porn filmmakers explicitly concur with these correlations in their DVD commentaries,[5] since doing so allows them to appropriate the cultural reputation those earlier horror films and filmmakers carry. Torture porn's filmmakers and critics customarily share a respect for horror's past, then. That similarity notwithstanding, 'torture porn' discourse is constituted by opposing attitudes to torture porn's relationship with earlier horror. On one hand, decriers have dismissed torture porn by separating it from 'classic' horror. On the other, since torture porn is a horror subgenre and is compared to these past 'classics', its lineage cannot be evaded. These tensions become apparent when torture porn is compared to its predecessors.

'I've seen a lot of slasher flicks'[6]

In seeking to establish what 'torture porn' is, critics recurrently use the slasher subgenre as a point of reference. Some have cited the slasher as a primary influence on torture porn filmmakers (Hulse, 2007: 17; Kendrick, 2009: 17; Safire, 2007). Others have referred to torture porn films *as* slashers (see Platell's (2008) review of *Donkey Punch*, for instance). Furthermore, some torture porn films such as *The Texas Chainsaw Massacre* (2003) are remakes of slasher originals. These correlations are apt given that torture porn shares aspects of the slasher formula. Slasher narratives typically entail killers stalking teenagers in a specific locale such as Camp Crystal Lake in *Friday the 13th*, or the town of Haddonfield in *Halloween*. Torture porn's imprisonment themes distil that formula by making it harder for protagonists to evade threat. Since they are often confined, escaping their tormentor is more difficult for torture porn's captives than it is for the slasher's teens. Torture porn's adaptation of slasher films' stalking conventions thus

Figure 1.1   Yasmine's freedom is hard won in *Frontier(s)* (2007, France/Switzerland, dir Xavier Gens)

amplifies tension. When one character survives in torture porn – Wade in *Invitation Only*, or Yasmine in *Frontier(s)*, for example – their freedom is even more hard won than it was for the slasher's survivors. Torture porn increases the stakes by levelling the field. In torture porn, it is rare to find lead protagonists who are unambiguously destined to survive.[7] Torture porn adapts established slasher conventions to augment the horror, since it is unclear whether any characters will still be alive when the end-credits roll.

Such continuities elucidate ways in which torture porn's traits have grown organically from their generic predecessors. Evolution within the slasher subgenre must also be accounted for. Scholars distinctly contrast torture porn to later 'postmodern', ironic *Scream*-style slasher films (Lockwood, 2008: 41; Prince, 2009: 283; Murray, 2008: 1). Many torture porn filmmakers – including Alexandre Aja, Marcus Dunstan, and Rob Schmidt – concur, characterising their films as a return to scary horror and a reaction against *Scream*'s self-conscious humour.[8] Although such comments acknowledge torture porn's relationship with earlier horror, these scholars and filmmakers seek to separate the two subgenres. That ethos is embodied within *Scream 4*. In the film's opening sequence, one character explicitly rejects torture porn, stating, 'it's gross. I hate all that torture porn shit'.

Such segregation is too blunt, negating evident continuities. The murder-mystery horror films that followed in the wake of *Scream*'s success are not as starkly different to torture porn as has been claimed. The *Saw* series' progressing plot revolves around a game-playing narrative style that echoes post-*Scream* whodunit slashers. As movies about making movies, *The Hills Run Red* and *Callback* are among several torture porn films that encompass the kind of metacommentary *Scream* was famed

Figure 1.2   The Human Centipede 2 (Full Sequence) (2011, Netherlands/USA/UK, dir Tom Six)

Figure 1.3   Paying tribute to horror classics: Martin claws at a car window in *The Human Centipede 2 (Full Sequence)* (2011, Netherlands/USA/UK, dir Tom Six), a nod to the first zombie attack in *Night of the Living Dead* (1968, USA, dir George Romero)

for. Filmmakers' and critics' interpretations of torture porn as a reaction against *Scream*-style generic self-consciousness fail to account for Roth referring to his torture porn films as exploitation pastiche (McCartney, 2007a); Aja's homage to *Maniac* in *Switchblade Romance*'s toilet stalking sequence; or Quentin Tarantino and Robert Rodriguez's *Grindhouse* project, which emulates the aesthetics of exploitation cinema from an era before digital filmmaking. Torture porn filmmakers use genre referentialism to delineate their indebtedness to earlier horror film, just as Wes Craven does in *Scream*.

The development from earlier stalk'n'slash films to *Scream*-style slashers to torture porn is also revealed by uses of humour. *Scream's* comedic self-referentialism is not a unique innovation. Rather, it advances the jokey catchphrases and self-consciousness found in the later *Friday the 13th* and *A Nightmare on Elm Street* sequels, for instance. Moreover, Rob Zombie's postulation that 'horror and comedy have nothing to do with one another' (in Zinoman, 2007) – his defence for torture porn's movement away from *Scream's* jokey style – overlooks not only the continuing popularity and pervasiveness of horror-comedy (particularly in the zombie subgenre),[9] but also Rob Zombie's own uses of humour. Captain Spalding in *House of 1000 Corpses* is an overtly comedic character, while Zombie's mock-trailer for *Werewolf Women of the SS* – filmed as part of the *Grindhouse* project – is also horror-comedy. Although torture porn is generally believed to be 'grindingly humourless' (Leith, 2010), that notion needs to be explicated with greater care than is usually offered in 'torture porn' discourse.

Such comparisons evince that without attention to detail, subgenres may be erroneously perceived as entirely distinct categories. Horror subgenres are further bracketed by their association with the specific decades in which they became most prominent. Linnie Blake's (2008: 139) observation that torture porn filmmakers 'pay stylistic and conceptual homage to their *1970s* predecessors' is indicative of that tendency (emphasis added; see also Hays, 2010; Lovece, 2010; Brady, 2010b). 1960s horror (Aftab, 2009; McEachen, 2010) and 1980s horror (Anderson, 2007; Hill, 2007; Cole, 2007) have similarly been cited as points of comparison via which to define torture porn. Opponents' allusions to decades as a means of demarcating shifts in tone verify that the discourse of cycles is shorthand. The implication that there are unequivocal breaks between subgenres – that torture porn is 'a different breed of film entirely' compared to its precursors (Robey, 2007b) – bypasses generic development.

'Torture porn' discourse thus offers polarised views on the subgenre's lineage. Cumulatively, these responses are paradoxical, since torture porn is portrayed as both like and unlike earlier horror. Torture porn cannot aesthetically and narratologically resemble earlier horror whilst also being entirely 'new'. That tension makes the subgenre label problematic for Lockwood (2008: 47). The same awkwardness is apparent in Carmen Gray's (2008: 68) disdain for *Frontier(s)*'s 'stylistic jumble'. These rifts are not unique to 'torture porn'. It is a customary critical response to contemporaneous popular horror. For example, Kate Egan (2007: 31) notes that similar objections were raised to the slasher cycle, which was vilified for its lack of artistry and tradition. These two aspects are coupled, insinuating that pastness ('tradition') connotes credibility and creativity ('artistry'), in contrast to commerciality and transient pleasure. Torture porn filmmakers frequently flag their genre credibility via homage to slasher films particularly. That tendency exacerbates the tensions Egan identifies. Torture porn filmmakers' homages canonise the slasher: a subgenre that has been dismissed for its lack of artistry and tradition thereby becomes part of an artistic tradition. The slasher film's traditionlessness becomes a tradition. Additionally, torture porn's detractors replicate past critical complaints when they segregate the subgenre from its generic predecessors. Ironically then, reprimanding contemporary horror for its lack of tradition is itself something of a tradition.

Categorising films via imprecise shorthand labels – category-banners or decades – results in cyclic argumentation. With time, those cycles will smooth over confusions and paradoxes. Conventions and generalisations will remain, to the detriment of detail. 'Torture porn' will become increasingly coherent, leaving the kind of sweeping précis that Kevin Johnson (2007) uses to encapsulate the slasher subgenre: 'large body counts, quick killings by superhuman bogeymen, and…the sex-means-death equation'. Such summation is unsatisfactory, but ubiquitous. In her retrospective discussion of the 'video nasty', Egan (2007: 26) remarks that generic labels are '"reductive, descriptive" categories' that allow 'critics to make brief, and predominantly negative judgments without the need for lengthy discussion or debate'. Rather than seeking to understand torture porn, the shorthand label allows critics to eschew in-depth analysis in favour of prejudicial notions that pre-exist films. Inspecting discursive inconsistencies is one way to counter that leaning towards generalisation. These details uncover more about what 'torture porn' means than brushing over those tensions can.

'Perhaps I am getting old, but…':[10] nostalgia and generic decline

The press's responses to 'torture porn' illustrate how instituted discursive patterns impact upon critical responses. Torture porn has organically developed out of existing genre conventions. When those characteristics evolved to the extent that the resulting films no longer precisely fitted into pre-existing diagnostic paradigms, reporters appear to have become frustrated. Torture porn's denigration may stem from its failure to adhere to established critical models. Indeed, the discursive paradigm established to make sense of these films – 'torture porn' – is reactionary, being formulated to rebuke individual films and the entire category that they are assigned to. Accordingly, depreciators have customarily exaggerated torture porn's uniqueness, characterising the subgenre's 'new' properties as evidence that torture porn has changed the horror genre for the worse. The latter is evident in pejorative responses to torture porn, which range from mild accusations – such as Newman's (2009a) proposal that 'the vision of the horror film is narrowing' – to over-reaction. Torture porn has been envisaged as defiling (Maher, 2009b), afflicting (Slotek, 2009b), blighting (Ide, 2008b), devolving (Terrell, 2009), and dumbing down (Conner, 2009) the horror genre, for instance.

Delimiting torture porn as a closed category rather than a progression from previous genre movements, the subgenre's opponents have cited horror 'classics' to exemplify what has been forsaken. Kaleem Aftab (2009), for example, denigrates torture porn's 'sick gore-fests' by comparing them to 'the great horror films' such as *Rosemary's Baby*, *Psycho*, and *The Exorcist*. Numerous other pundits follow suit, unfavourably comparing torture porn to films from the 1960s–80s to verify generic decline (Robey, 2007b; Monahan, 2010). Similarities between torture porn and earlier horror are downplayed, or are interpreted as inadequacies in such commentary. Torture porn is consequently characterised as indicating that horror has 'lost all its edge and ability to scare' (Slaymaker, 2008), being deemed unworthy of critical attention because it is shallow or lacks artistry (Gatiss in N.a. 2010a, and Romero in Anderson, 2008). Older films, in contrast, are painted as 'complex ... philosophical, and ... idiosyncratic' (LaBruce in Hardy, 2010), 'transgressive' (Patterson, 2010), or plainly 'good' (Aftab, 2009; Robey, 2007b). Earlier horror films are considered to demonstrate 'restraint ... taste and intelligence' (Monahan, 2010), because characterisation is emphasised over 'gruesome acts' (Thomson, 2008a), because the films have 'a point' (Anderson, 2008), and because they are 'about something' (Newman, 2009a). Torture porn films, it is asserted, have none of these qualities.

Justifying this presumed difference between 'then' and 'now' is vital so that critics can defend the former while attacking the latter. That necessity, however, results in hypocritical argumentation. For instance, John Patterson (2010) shuns torture porn's violence but celebrates the 'orgasmic fusillade of machine-gun fire climaxing *Bonnie and Clyde*', which 'was as much sexual as brutal'. Similarly inconsistent is Liam

Lacey's (2007) vision of the 1970s as a 'golden age', which 'saw film-makers pushing to one-up each other in more dramatic, splashy, graphic, sublime, and ugly violence', coupled with his rejection of torture porn on the same grounds. Furthermore, when citing the original *The Texas Chainsaw Massacre* as a 'classic' and rebuffing its remake as too violent, David Kehr (2003) forgets that the original *The Texas Chainsaw Massacre* was itself banned in the UK for exactly the same reasons. The only difference these detractors offer to distinguish torture porn from 'classic' horror is that one set of films is older than the other. Although intended as derogation, their disputations make a more convincing case that torture porn should be valorised for precisely the same reasons 'classic' horror is.

Many contentions regarding torture porn's supposed inferiority are undermined by critics' artful misremembering of past 'classics' and what they signified for contemporaneous reviewers. Carla Di Fonzo's (2007) complaint that torture porn is not exciting because protagonists are 'tied down on a table or handcuffed to a radiator' is flawed because she does not address the continuities between slasher films and torture porn. Di Fonzo identifies that stalking (rather than slashing) is the slasher films' main source of terror, and yet misremembers how slasher victims were habitually depicted. Apart from the final girl (to use Carol Clover's (1993) terminology), the slasher's targets were conventionally doomed from the outset, meaning chase sequences prolonged their deaths rather than offering hope that they might escape. Lacey Terrell (2009) similarly suggests that 'original [1980s] slashers, at least, had characters to root for', while dismissing torture porn's protagonists: '[w]ho's next? Who cares[?]'.[11] This statement uncannily echoes Jonathan Lake Crane's (1994: 148) incrimination of 1980s slashers: '[h]ow did they live? Who cares?...How did they die?' Terrell forgets that slasher films were also known as 'slice-em-up' movies, and that teens in slasher films were often perceived as 'inconsiderate, unpleasant people' (Hutchings, 2004: 200). Jenny McCartney's (2008) unease regarding torture porn's audience is equally telling. 'My generation' she professes, 'was terrified by the Child Catcher in *Chitty Chitty Bang Bang*'. McCartney's evocation of a nostalgic, subjective past to evidence declining standards is unconvincing, because she favours anecdote over direct comparisons between torture porn and horror of the era she refers to.

These strategies reveal little about changes in genre or audiences and much about critics' subjective biases. President of Picturehouse Films Bob Berney's hypocrisy (in Gordon, 2006) summates the issue. On the one hand, he opines that 'these newer [torture porn] movies are purely sadistic'. On the other, he nostalgically recalls his 'parents saying stuff like this, and [he] ignored it. They wouldn't let [him] see *A Clockwork Orange*, and [he] went 25 times'. Berney's comment flags two problems with the 'past versus present' position. First, horror tends to be marketed primarily towards young adults. Second, pundits frequently respond more favourably to horror they saw in their youth than to horror they encounter later in life. This certainly elucidates why there have been few positive responses to torture porn in print media, while younger online reviewers, as McCartney (2007a) observes, 'are significantly more enthusiastic' about the subgenre.

The same attitudinal problem haunts Edelstein's (2010) realisation that torture porn poses a 'dilemma' for those who 'grew up loving horror and exploitation films...because what attracted us in the first place was the flouting of taboos'. Rather than explaining the differences, he simply denounces torture porn: 'I'm not sure I want to live in a world that would embrace [*The Human Centipede*]'. Newman's (2009a) rationalisation is equally flawed. He discloses that 'twenty years ago...I was already beginning to see the horror films of [the day]...as a lesser, meaner breed than the works I valorised in [*Nightmare Movies*]'. 'Even then', he continues, 'I saw this as a subjective inevitability – we prize the discoveries of our youth and defend them.' It is startling that Newman then condemns torture porn, irrespective of his brief reflection. By Newman's own admission, the problem is his own developing attitude towards violent horror, not changes in violent horror itself.

Other opponents have raised the same age-related anxieties. Liaguno (in Zoc, 2008) admits that his nostalgia indicates his age, stating '[y]ou know you're getting older when you find yourself saying... "Remember those great old slasher films?"'. Less self-critical is Gatiss's recognition that he 'risk[s]...sounding like an old curmudgeon' in divulging that he has 'little appetite' for contemporary horror.[12] Di Fonzo (2007) uses 'going soft' or being 'lame-o' rather than 'older', but her justification shares Gatiss's and Newman's strategy of spurning torture porn outright despite briefly contemplating that her shifting perspective might be the problem. Statements about age are followed by defensive reversals that aim to validate the reviewer's opinion. Some pundits explicitly use their age to endorse their anti-torture porn stance. For instance, Patterson (2007) refers to himself as 'a veteran of the gore-wars', asserting that his opinion should be respected rather than rejected as out-of-touch.

Many of torture porn's belittlers employ this rhetorical device, yet few recognise that they have become the oppressors they rallied against in their own youths. By failing to reflect on their personal biases, these detractors propagate a general unwillingness to critically engage with whichever forms of horror are popular in the present moment. It is unsurprising that despite some micro-level changes, the wider arguments against popular horror have remained remarkably consistent over time. For example, discussions of contemporaneous horror becoming gorier and therefore 'worse' are evident in interviews with Forrest J. Ackerman and John Goodwin in the documentary *Shock Cinema Vol. 2* (1991). That is, the same pejorative rhetoric found in 'torture porn' discourse was being utilised by authorities on horror 20 years ago. Such patterns suggest that torture porn is not the marker of generic decline its detractors have suggested.

This chapter has begun to sketch out how and why torture porn has been characterised in conflicting ways that do not clearly or consistently represent torture porn's content. The discourses' shortcomings partially stem from classifying films under a banner that absolutely separates torture porn from other subgenres. Categorisation necessitates generalisation, overlooking differences and augmenting commonalities. Yet, as complaints levelled at torture porn demonstrate, categorisation may also curtail understanding of torture porn's relationship to the past. Without a foundational comprehension of torture porn's origins and 'torture porn' discourse's inheritances, responses to torture porn are likely to remain reactionary and neglect the lessons the past has to offer. As the next chapter will illustrate, the hyperbolic charges against torture porn overcompensate for the discourse's unstable foundations, inappropriately characterising torture porn as cause for immediate alarm.

2
'Bend to Our Objectives':[1]
'Torture Porn' as Press Discourse

Critics' judgments directly shape the meanings of 'torture porn'. As Newman (1996: 134) notes, it is 'usually film critics' who label films, and this is certainly true of 'torture porn', a term that was coined and propagated by journalists. The press's responses to torture porn are culturally powerful, gaining gravitas from the mode of dissemination. Not only are such evaluations inter/nationally distributed, but the news context also situates such commentary in a context that intimates factuality. That context lends an impression of authority to print press reviews that other forms of criticism – such as internet-distributed opinion pieces and fan responses – do not necessarily share. Ergo, it is vital to grasp how torture porn has been represented in the press in order to explicate what 'torture porn' means.

The aim of this chapter is to examine the connotations of 'torture porn', exploring the complications that arise within press reporters' discussions about the subgenre. This involves detailing what qualities have been associated with 'torture porn' and the subgenre's films. The attributes that derogators point towards in order to disparage torture porn typically spring from off-screen contexts rather than on-screen content. Torture porn's depreciators predominantly universalise their objections to and assumptions about the subgenre, interpellating their readers and masking their personal biases. Such obfuscation also veils the fact that their individual complaints are symptomatic of the press's tendency to illegitimatise popular horror film more broadly. By rejecting the films outright, depreciators naturalise the lack of textual detail in their responses: the films are presented as unworthy of investigation. In sum, press critics directly shape the connotations of 'torture porn', but their complaints are seldom made about torture porn's content alone.

In order to collate press responses to torture porn, searches were conducted across major English language news articles for the terms 'torture porn', 'torture horror', 'horror porn', 'blood porn', 'gore porn', 'gorno' (as well as derivatives thereof) via LexisNexis UK. While these terms are used somewhat interchangeably in such criticism, 'torture porn' is the most ubiquitous of these labels. These searches provided an expansive base of articles from which to ascertain 'torture porn' discourse's chief patterns. Indicative examples have been selected to illustrate dominant trends. The most pertinent statements have been opted for rather than, for instance, quoting from news sources with the largest distribution reach. The chapter itself is structured around the recurring contentions uncovered by this study of more than 1200 articles. The prevalent suggestions within press discourses are that torture porn (a) is constituted by violence, (b) is a fad, (c) is problematic because it is mainstream entertainment, and (d) affronts critics' sensibilities. These trends reveal inconsistencies within 'torture porn' as a category. This chapter's closing sections inspect those discrepancies, evaluating their impact on 'torture porn'.

'Every Ten Minutes One Must Die!':[2] centralisation of violence

Foremost, torture porn is characterised as a subgenre constituted by graphic, realistic violence (see McClintock, 2006; Zinoman, 2007; Anderson, 2009). Since violent horror films have been classified as 'torture porn' according to that property, it is self-fulfilling that torture porn films are primarily concerned with physical threat, rather than supernatural/spiritual peril. However, some caveats are necessary. The notion that torture porn is made unique by its goriness is over-pronounced in this discourse, as are allegations concerning the amount of violence displayed in each torture porn film. The idea that 'levels of horrific violence on show at the multiplexes…have gone through the roof' (Cochrane, 2007), is hyperbolic. As Blair Davis and Kial Natale (2010: 44) demonstrate, although torture porn films are bloody, 'the average number of on-screen acts of gory violence [in successful multiplex horror] has not increased since 2001', and in fact declined between 2003 and 2007. Since this era is torture porn's theatrical boom-period, claims regarding torture porn's violence levels are evidently exaggerated.

Two factors feed that critical misperception. First, films are categorised as torture porn because they are violent, leading decriers to over-stress the level of violence each film contains. That is, the *idea* of what 'torture porn' is influences this view more than filmic content does. Second, R-rated or 18 certificated horror's increased multiplex presence in America and the UK in the mid-2000s followed a period in which the genre's most financially successful outputs were PG-13 or 15 certificated supernatural films such as *The Sixth Sense* (1999), or remakes such as *The Ring* (2002).[3] Both lower certification and supernatural themes are traits associated with less explicitly violent content, so the shift in the opposite direction led to the conclusion that the genre was becoming increasingly violent and graphic. Consequently, reviewers may have over-inflated their estimations of how gory torture porn's content is because the genre context pre-disposed critics to perceive gore as difference – as a means of comparing torture porn to less visceral horror – rather than judging each film's content individually. Measuring change by bloodshed accentuates the gore offered in torture porn films, and that may have led critics to over-emphasise the amount and significance of torture porn's violence.

Kevin Maher's (2007) précis of torture porn's formula – 'lots of screaming, yada yada yada...Ultraviolence overkill' – exemplifies how torture porn is conceived: as an unsettling cumulative trend rather than as a series of discrete films that contain disturbing themes or imagery. Detractors tend to embellish the amount of violence in individual films because each belongs to the category 'torture porn'. The quantity of violent films in the subgenre augments the impression that individual films are exceedingly bloody, because each film labelled 'torture porn' stands for the whole subgenre. Since the connotations of 'torture porn' are prioritised over filmic content in this discourse, critics often link films to one another when passing judgment. Samuel Wigley (2007), for instance, makes comparative assertions such as 'each entry in this brutal cycle is obliged to outdo the last'. Wigley's statement submits that film-makers conceive of their films as belonging to the subgenre, positing that 'torture porn' is a movement created by filmmakers rather than the press. The notion that filmmakers seek to out-do each other's depictions of violence is prevalent in 'torture porn' discourse (see Johnson, 2007; Orange, 2009; Puig, 2009). The common parlance for this idea is 'pushing the envelope' (Hulse, 2007; Ide, 2009), a phrase that implies both graphic escalation and filmmakers' shared desire to offend normative sensibilities via their violent imagery.

Highlighting violence in this way insinuates that torture porn's pleasures are one-dimensional, consisting of 'test[ing] how much gore you can watch before throwing up' (Zane, 2010; see also Ide, 2009). Those disdainful judgements about content are complimented by estimations of violence's effect on the audience. Descriptions of violence as 'repellent' (Phillips, 2010), 'nauseating' (Ordona, 2010a), 'stomach-churning' (Lowe, 2010), 'disgusting' (McEachen, 2010) and 'excruciating' (Anderson, 2009) all involve a leap from portrayals to presumed reactions, which are loaded with value-judgments. This rhetoric interpellates, proffering that most readers will (and should) agree that torture porn's images are disdainful.

'Torture porn' discourse situates torture porn's violence, imbuing it with connotative meaning. It is melodramatically professed that violence is *all* torture porn offers (see Muir, 2010a; Slotek, 2009a; Bowles, 2009), thereby painting the subgenre as vacuous. Moreover, torture porn is indicted with including 'gore for gore's sake' (Kermode, 2008a), 'nasty things...for the sake of nastiness' (Fox, 2007), and 'violence for the sake of violence' (Ketchum in Kirkland, 2008b). These sentiments are corroborated by the six 'gr-'adjectives habitually used to describe torture porn: 'gratuitous' (Hill, 2007; Phelan, 2011); 'gruesome' (Hunter, 2010; Tookey, 2007a; Lidz, 2009), 'graphic' (Ordona, 2010a; McEachen, 2010; Williamson, 2007c) 'grisly' (Dalton, 2009a; Kendall, 2008), 'gross' and 'grotesque' (N.a. 2010b; Kermode, 2010; Gordon, 2006: 60). Each intimates that torture porn's violence is excessive or – as Claire Hill (2007) has it – 'unnecessary'.

'When You Think the Worst has Happened... Think Worse':[4] torture porn as a fad

Torture porn's violence is subsequently perceived as replacing narrative depth and characterisation. As Aftab (2009) inveighs, '[n]arrative development is a mere inconvenience in these films' (see also Slotek, 2009a; Dalton, 2009b; Tookey, 2008a). Such supposition is typically utilised to verify torture porn's cultural illegitimacy: it is claimed that torture porn is 'pointless' (Cumming et al., 2010; Muir, 2010b) and 'meritless' (Ordona, 2010b). Cashmore (2010), for example, describes the subgenre as a 'sheer, ruptured-sewage-pipe deluge of gore, mutilation, and general unpleasantness'. The term 'sewage-pipe' underscores that violence is equated with worthlessness. The same tactic is apparent where torture porn is described as 'excrementous' (Williamson, 2007a), 'garbage' (Robey, 2007a), 'trash' (Phillips, 2010; Booth, 2008), 'junk' (Conner, 2009), and 'low' (Robey, 2007a; N.a. 2010e; Lim, 2009). Other adjectives such as 'daft' (Edwards, 2007), 'puerile' (Maher, 2009b; Tookey, 2008d), 'infantile' (N.a. 2007b), 'crass, silly' (Bradshaw, 2010), 'wrongheaded' (Phelan, 2011), 'cretinous' (Cashmore, 2010), and 'mindless' (Hunter,

2010; Patterson, 2010) consolidate that ethos. These judgements insinuate that anyone who produces or willingly consumes these films is mentally deficient and culturally undiscerning.

In this view, torture porn is indefensible per se. Where positive traits *are* noted, they are immediately qualified. For instance, Nigel Kendall (2008) states that *Untraceable* 'has a surprising amount to recommend it', his 'surprise' arising from the idea that any torture porn film *can* be recommended. Indeed, enjoying *Untraceable* is enough to prove its dissimilarity to '*Saw* and *Hostel*' for Kendall: the film cannot be both recommended *and* be torture porn. Kendall's qualifying statements attest to torture porn's ostensible worthlessness then, despite evidence to the contrary. Similarly, Shea Conner (2009) decries the subgenre, and then cites *Saw* – a film ubiquitously associated with 'torture porn' – as one of 'the few gems this decade [2000–9] had to offer'. 'Torture porn' discourse is constituted by such contradictory statements. The label has been widely applied to films that critics do not enjoy, and so if hecklers appreciate individual films, those films become exceptions to 'torture porn'. Another pundit (N.a. 2010c) sustains the critical narrative that torture porn is valueless in her/his evaluation of the *Saw* franchise. Rather than defending torture porn against accusations of one-dimensional narrativisation, the reviewer dismisses *Saw*'s narrative complexity as 'baffling', which implies incoherence rather than sophistication.

Other disparagers declare that torture porn is passé, thereby debunking the subgenre rather than addressing its popularity. Hence, torture porn is presented as a fleeting fad by some detractors (Kenny in Johnson, 2007; Monahan, 2010). To the same ends, others announce that torture porn is 'over', or verging on imminent collapse (Barnes, 2009; Safire, 2007; Mundell, 2008). In many articles, the theatrical success of films belonging to other horror subgenres is utilised as evidence of torture porn being 'replaced' (see N.a. 2010d; Wloszczyna, 2009; Newman, 2008). This was especially pronounced when *Paranormal Activity*'s sequels were scheduled for annual October releases, because the *Saw* franchise explicitly claimed ownership of the October multiplex horror slot. As *Saw III*'s tagline denoted, '[i]f it's Halloween, it must be *Saw*'. *Paranormal Activity* has been heralded as toppling that monopoly (see Schwartz, 2010: 51; Miska, 2012). Many pundits deem that the release of *Paranormal Activity 2* alongside *Saw*'s 'Final Chapter' in 2010 also marked torture porn's 'Final Chapter'.

The same point is made by citing disappointing returns made on *Hostel: Part II* in June 2007 (Wloszczyna, 2007; Leydon, 2007; Williamson, 2007b; Middleton, 2010: 2). Thomas Riegler (2010: 27) pegs the subgenre's demise even earlier, asserting that 'by the end of 2006 [torture porn] showed signs of beginning to wane'. Less than a year after the subgenre was named, it was said to be 'finished'. Such repudiation continues (see Killingbeck, 2011; Middleton, 2010), illustrating that reviewers were premature in pronouncing torture porn's death in 2007. In fact, the popularity of 'torture porn' in the press peaked in 2009, with 308 English-language articles employing the term.[5] Although usage has declined since 2009, the label has been utilised more times per year in the period 2008–11 than it was in 2007, when only 205 English-language articles used the term. Press discourse itself evinces that torture porn was far from moribund in 2007.

Such arguments may have aimed to facilitate rather than report the subgenre's decline. This rhetorical strategy – declaring that torture porn is 'over' – consolidates the established critical narrative that torture porn is superficial entertainment. Derogators predicted that torture porn was doomed to faddishness because violent escalation is unsustainable in the long-term (see Zinoman, 2007; Purcell in Zoc, 2008). Such arguments insinuate that the subgenre is not worth becoming too anxious about because it is doomed to transience. The latter assurance is belied by the near-hysterical tone that pervades the press's denunciation of torture porn, an inconsistency that exposes the flawed logic and reactionary impulses that underpin 'torture porn'.

Contrary to critics' persistent proliferation of 'torture porn' and torture porn films' continued production, the impression that torture porn has all-but died out since 2007 is prevalent. That idea is inherent to the 'torture porn' paradigm in two ways. First, since 'torture porn' is a theatrically-biased discourse, torture porn's shift to DVD releasing may appear to signal a decline in production, despite an increase in the quantity of torture porn films produced between 2007 and 2010. Torture porn's reduced theatrical presence has meant its cultural visibility has also diminished. Second, after 'torture porn' was established as a category, its characteristics were instituted and became predictable. Grouping these films based on repeated facets and shared attributes may have led audiences and pundits to perceive the material as less exciting than it was initially. That is, torture porn may have become less noticeable because critical discourses defined torture as a standard convention.

Box-office 'gross': the mainstream context

The subgenre's continuing success on DVD post-2007 is of little concern to those detractors who have eagerly proclaimed torture porn's demise.

Even if not explicitly stated, torture porn's box-office performance is a central problem for press reviewers, and there is more at stake in depreciators' vitriol than simply an objection to torture porn's apparently 'gimmicky' nature (N.a. 2010b; see also Di Fonzo, 2007). Filmmaking is a commercial industry. Nevertheless, decriers have limned torture porn's profitability as particularly noteworthy, contending that lucrative entertainment should not be based on violent spectacle. This is not primarily a moral protest against unsuitable filmic content. Rather, opponents take exception to torture porn's popularity itself. For instance, Rob Driscoll (2007) foregrounds economics over ethics by complaining that Roth 'mak[es] a mint from producing amoral entertainment'. Similarly, Williamson (2007a) compares Roland Joffe to a 'pimp' for directing Captivity (see also Skenazy, 2007), submitting that the director's greed is immoral. Feeding the critical narrative that torture porn offers vacuous, transient entertainment, it is alleged that torture porn production is driven by superficial motives; '[t]here's a reason for all this torture porn: [i]t makes money' (Lacey, 2009; see also Fern, 2008; Collins in Di Fonzo, 2007).

Resultantly, disparagers often amalgamate fleeting descriptions of torture porn's content with comments about finance. Frank Lovece (2010), for example, interrupts his sparse recap of the Saw franchise's plot to impart combined box-office figures for the series: 'The story so far – as some $370.2 million worth of domestic ticket buyers and a total $738.5 million worldwide know – involves a serial-killer mastermind'. Spuriously mentioning box-office gross in this manner is pervasive (see Schembri, 2010; Anderson, 2007c), sometimes manifesting in terms such as 'moneyspinning' (Vaughan, 2007) and 'cash in' (Phelan, 2011; Tookey, 2006; Kermode, 2007). Economic success is a focal point that usurps what little content-based consideration is available in journalistic discussions regarding torture porn.

Elsewhere, derogators spotlight that profit comes from movie-goers (Dalton, 2009b). The public are characterised as victims of filmmakers' 'vulgar opportunism' (Kermode, 2007) in such arguments. Framing torture porn as a kind of exploitation cinema allows critics to draw on another pre-existent critical paradigm to scornfully marry torture porn's 'vulgar' content with its financial performance. In this view, the public are duped into spending their money, and filmmakers willingly exploit audience naivety by supplying 'cheap thrills' (Gray, 2008). Disparities between production costs and profits are also flagged (Murray, 2008: 1; Kinsella, 2007), corroborating that torture porn is motivated by avarice, and portraying each ticket purchase as part of a cumulative dynamic.

Movie-goers are rendered culpable for torture porn, and so are asked to '[v]ote with [their] feet and [their] wallets': 'don't go to see [torture porn]' (Heal, 2007). Such suggestions are futile inasmuch as they appeal to those readers who are sympathetic to the authors' anti-torture porn position. Torture porn fans are unlikely to be persuaded by the belittling tone these pundits adopt, and readers who agree that torture porn is worthless are not likely to be among the ticket purchasers being addressed. The instruction is rhetorical rather than persuasive, contributing to the overarching proposal that torture porn should be hindered.

In order to support this case, some opponents interpellate even those press-readers who have not seen any torture porn films. Several of the subgenre's movies – such as *Mum and Dad*, *wΔz*, and *Donkey Punch* – were funded by the UK Film Council. Numerous reporters point this out, announcing that the British public unwittingly 'helped pay for...pointlessly unpleasant torture porn' (N.a. 2008b; see also Tookey, 2008b; Platell, 2008). Such argumentation rhetorically holds the entire populace – even non-movie-goers – accountable for torture porn. Doing so creates a sense of majority resistance to torture porn. The strategy holds film funders liable to public-pressure, tacitly stifling torture porn at the root by discouraging funders from becoming involved in torture porn production.

These economically-focused complaints are thus geared towards pushing torture porn out of the multiplex. The word 'mainstream' is habitually interjected into commentary regarding money, pointing to torture porn's theatrical exhibition as a source of apprehension (see McCartney, 2008; Gordon, 2009; Cochrane, 2007; Hunt, 2007). However, these allusions do not specify why torture porn's mainstream presence is problematic: it is just self-evidently worrying. Pointing out that '[t]orture porn movies play in multiplexes everywhere' (Johnson, 2007) has a similar effect, underlining that prevalence is a problem without stipulating why. Such observations are undermined by assertions regarding torture porn's decline elsewhere in the press. Much like detractors' over-inflation of torture porn's violent content, torture porn's multiplex presence is also typically exaggerated. As a horror subgenre, torture porn performed well at the box-office, but that is not to suggest that torture porn films are comparable to summer blockbusters in terms of profitability, for instance. When critics such as Driscoll (2007) and Pamela McClintock (2006) express anxiety over *Hostel* usurping the family film *The Chronicles of Narnia: The Lion, the Witch and the Wardrobe* at the top of the American box-office, it should be noted that *Hostel*'s success does not typify torture porn's performance as an entire subgenre, particularly given that torture porn has been more widely proliferated on the DVD market.

That few objections are raised over torture porn's continued production in the direct-to-DVD context elucidates that theatrical exhibition is a particular problem. For example, more than 80 English language articles in major world publications covered *Hostel: Part II*'s release in 2007. Most of these consisted of depreciatory opinion. Diametrically, only three short articles (Longsdorf, 2011; Bentley, 2011; and Miller, 2012) – mainly constituted by plot synopsis – immediately followed *Hostel: Part III*'s direct-to-DVD release. Notably, only one of these articles was printed in a major world publication. Furthermore, these disparities evince that disputes about torture porn are not ultimately concerned with filmic content. Torture porn DVDs are commonly packaged as 'unrated' or 'extreme', implying that the DVD version contains more explicit violence than the theatrical cut.[6] If content were the primary issue, then these expressly uncensored DVDs should alarm reporters more than the cinematically released, R-rated versions. However, the opposite is true in 'torture porn' discourse.

Torture porn's disparagement exposes much about the multiplex's significance as a site of cultural power. Critical unease is fixated on torture porn being 'accepted as the norm' (Hill, 2007), and horror's potential to move from the sidelines of film culture into its commercial centre. Most plainly, Aftab (2009) rejects torture porn by complaining that 'at least [splatter] films knew their place in B-movie theatres' (see also Lovece, 2010). His explicit reference to location reveals that the torture porn 'problem' can be resolved via what amounts to cultural gentrification.

' ... like some sort of epidemic':[7] the 'need' for restriction

Critics' affront stems less from torture porn's content than it does the structures via which they are exposed to that content. That is, reviewers frequently object to having to deal with these films. That sentiment is clear in Vicki Brett's (2007) admittance that 'my stomach isn't strong enough for [torture porn]. I'm the one who comes out screaming like the bloodied victims'. Various critics echo her apprehension, positing that they are directly – even physically – affected by their encounters with torture porn. Anna Smith (2010) declares that she 'would have given anything for release from the gratuitous torture porn of *Wolf Creek*', for instance (see also Platell, 2008; McCartney, 2007a). Such personal responses illustrate that reporters find torture porn's success problematic because they are 'forced' to sit through films they dislike. Journalists have a patent reason for defaming theatrical torture porn, then. If ghettoised to DVD, press-based film reviewers – who primarily concentrate on cinematic releases – will no longer 'be tortured' by the subgenre's presence.

This implicit subjective bias is masked by the outward focus adopted in 'torture porn' criticism. Reviewers customarily make the case that violent entertainment should not be permitted to occupy a medial cultural position per se. Torture porn's presence in the mainstream is cited to warn of broader problems, such as the ineffectuality of censorial bodies (see Kirkland, 2008a; Heal, 2007; McCartney, 2007a). Couched in this suggestion that the MPAA and BBFC have failed to protect the public from violent spectacle is the connotation that torture porn genuinely endangers the populace. It is unsurprising that this discourse flourished in the British press particularly, since numerous previously banned or heavily cut 1970s–80s films such as *Cannibal Holocaust* were re-released in the UK in less censored versions from the mid-2000s onwards, tallying with torture porn's boom-period.[8] Rather than perceiving this trend as evidence that films once considered worthy of banning lose their propensity to shock over time, torture porn's opponents have characterised these shifts as confirming that horror films are more violent than they once were, and that censorial bodies have become too liberal (see Tookey, 2011; Beckford, 2008; Bor, 2007; Gordon, 2009). Similar arguments are found in the American press, where critics have expressed concern that the MPAA's ratings categories are incapable of encompassing torture porn's content and should be more restrictive (see Zeitchik, 2010; Rechtshaffen, 2010; Goldstein, 2010). Contra to numerous torture porn directors – including Zombie, Zev Berman, and Aja – recounting how inflexible the MPAA is,[9] the press have emphasised instances in which censorial decisions have been appealed and overturned to propound censors' lack of authority (see McCartney, 2008).

The desire to classify and hence contain these films is as palpable in such discussions as it is in the practice of labelling films 'torture porn'. Torture porn is thus commonly dubbed 'extreme' (see Hill, 2007; Graham, 2009b; Macnab, 2011), verifying censors' failure to control the subgenre's content. Postulating that they know better than the censors, many critics position themselves as cultural guardians, a 'line of defence' between the public and torture porn's filmmakers, who are painted as greedy and irresponsible. These pundits thus advise that if filmmakers are not deterred, horror will continue its alleged decline. Jason Zinoman (2007), for instance, asks '[a]fter you blow up someone's head, rip people in two or burn off their faces, where do you go from there?' The question remains unanswered, intimating that although it is beyond Zinoman's and the reader's capacity to imagine what might follow, worse is surely to come. Contradicting another anti-torture porn argument – that torture porn is a fad because its representations of violence cannot escalate ad infinitum – here it is assumed that filmmakers will continue to provide increasingly shocking material.

Lenore Skenazy (2007) is particularly foreboding about what torture porn's 'extremity' might indicate: '[i]f we start accepting this kind of movie as just "extreme" horror, the baseline will change...If that's the world you want to live in...[i]t's coming. But if you'd like a different future, you've got to act'. Skenazy hyperbolically heralds torture porn's box-office performance as a symptom of impending social downfall. At this spectrum's most hysterical end, some proponents have urged that the advertising campaign for *Captivity* is 'a literal sign of the collapse of humanity' (Whedon in Cochrane, 2007), and that the *Saw* films are 'a sign of the apocalypse' (Beale, 2009). The rhetorical mechanisms at work here point outwards – away from critics' subjective affront and torture porn's content – towards unimaginable threat. Opting for abstract fear over tangible detail is illustrative of this discourse's central flaw. Detractors condemn torture porn for being spectacle without substance, yet their complaints are so often founded on unsubstantiated, salacious rhetorical gestures.

Similar strategies are utilised to prove torture porn's potential harm by connecting the subgenre to much broader socio-political problems. Although such arguments point to concrete events, they are usually undercut by the failure to explicate torture porn's connection to those incidents. Torture porn has been correlated with moral ambivalence issuing from Ghana's independence (Danquah, 2010), and 'the dramatic rise in sexually transmitted diseases among 16 to 24-year-olds' (Platell, 2008), for instance. These associations remain remarkably vague, since the reporters avoid making direct cause–effect statements while affirming that the films reflect social decline.

Despite predictions of societal meltdown, 'torture porn' discourse has not escalated into moral panic. Unlike recent responses to extreme porn (which will be discussed in Chapter 8), or past responses to the video nasties, torture porn has not prompted any legal modifications. Appeals are made directly to film-goers in 'torture porn' discourse, yet its disparagers' vitriolic reactions are so over-compensatory that the public have little impetus to respond. Torture porn's relative mainstream success confirms that the subgenre is not as controversial as the majority of objectors have exaggeratedly claimed. The critical discourse itself dispels much of torture porn's potential to offend. Labelling films 'torture porn' makes them knowable, diffusing their propensity to shock by categorising them. Contrary to opponents depicting torture porn as a stepping-stone towards social degeneration, torture porn's failure to launch as a moral panic is indicative of hegemonic stability.

'How can I disprove a false accusation?':[10] confusion and incoherence

Less stable is the category 'torture porn' itself. As a discursive paradigm, 'torture porn' is riddled with inconsistencies. The label masks divergences and tensions that are inherent to collecting diverse films together. Although initially aimed at multiplex horror, all manner of popular cultural objects have subsequently been called 'torture porn', further undercutting the category's coherence. 'Torture porn' has been applied to films outside of the horror genre, including comedies such as *Jackass Number Two* (Tookey, 2006) and action films such as *Casino Royale* (Schneller, 2008; Driscoll, 2007). This move undercuts one of torture porn's chief properties: that it is a horror subgenre. It is not just genre that is diversified, but also medium. Television crime-dramas *24* (Riegler, 2010: 32; Williamson, 2007c), *Dexter* (Mangan, 2007), and *Wire in the Blood* (McLean, 2007) have been dubbed 'torture porn'. The same is true for novels – including crime fiction authored by Jonathan Littell (Wilhelm, 2009), Scott Bakker (McKie, 2008), and Patricia Cornwell (Teeman, 2010) – and videogames such as *Manhunt 2* (Schiesel, 2009; see also Lacey, 2009). Therefore another point of coherence – that 'torture porn' refers to horror *film* – is undermined. While intended jokingly, *Sex and the City 2* (Leupp, 2010; Harlow, 2011), and *Shrek the Third* (Andrews, 2007) have also both been referred to as 'torture porn'. These gags treat 'torture porn' as a synonym for 'meritless'. In doing so, 'torture porn' is exposed as a discursive framework that has little to do with an object's content: it is merely an epithet in these cases. That treatment alone speaks volumes about what 'torture porn' means when applied to horror film.

One further factor weakening the consistency of 'torture porn' as a categorising term is the existence of similar labels before Edelstein coined 'torture porn' in reference to a body of horror films made after 2003. 'Horror porn' has been used to describe David Cronenberg's films (Vera, 2002) and hentai anime (Antonucci, 1998). Between 2001 and 2004, a number of authors used 'gore porn' to describe violent cinema, including the 2003 remake of *The Texas Chainsaw Massacre*, a film that would later be referred to as 'torture porn' (see N.a. 2001; Schneller, 2003; Nelson, 2004; Shoard, 2004). 'Torture porn' itself was used by one reporter in the 1980s to describe fetish imagery (Goldberg, 1989). These pre-2006 occurrences reveal that 'torture porn' is not a discrete, closed category. Extended uses and earlier forms undermine detractors' attempts to frame torture porn as a recent multiplex fad. Like the films that have been dubbed 'torture porn', the term has a lineage that shapes its meaning. The idea that 'torture porn' finally encapsulates a group of 21st century horror films is an illusion. Labelling a film 'torture porn' is not enough to separate it from other cultural objects. As the term's broadening elucidates, understanding what 'torture porn' represents necessitates being aware of the tensions raised by those other objects and the implications of the label's usage.

'Torture porn' is enriched by these slippages, which divulge much about how and why particular horror films have been demarcated as 'torture porn'. Responses to the subgenre are nonetheless shaped by 'torture porn' discourse, and in common parlance 'torture porn' (however imperfectly) still outlines a body of horror films that share similar themes. Although 'torture porn' will be utilised as a label in the remainder of this book, these limitations are implied within that usage. 'Torture porn' is in motion. It is intertwined with wider conceptual networks that impact on its various meanings. Torture porn's objectors have typically used the term to denunciate the subgenre, but also to delimit texts and fix their meanings. The two endeavours are incompatible, as the inconsistencies outlined in this chapter demonstrate.

'Torture porn' can instead be utilised as a starting point to stimulate engagement by connecting filmic content to the concepts that underpin the term. While the films themselves will be addressed in Part II, the next chapter will take stock of other off-screen contextualising factors that inform what 'torture porn' signifies. Since Edelstein's article was published, filmmakers and fans have responded to the label's pejorative connotations. The press may have situated the subgenre in the cultural zeitgeist, but these latter groups – torture porn's creators and primary consumers – are most affected by 'torture porn' discourse, and also shape what 'torture porn' means.

3
'No-one Approves of What You're Doing':[1] Fans and Filmmakers

Critics may have been pivotal in establishing the cultural meanings of 'torture porn', but filmmakers and audiences – particularly horror fans – are also rebuked via that discourse. Regularly, such derogation is indirect, conflating characters' actions with audiences' responses and/ or with filmmakers' intentions. For instance, Ben McEachen's (2010) grievance over 'violent films that appear to get off on their disturbing deeds' is loaded against either filmmakers, fans or both. McEachen's pernicious rhetorical strategy obscures its target by blaming the film (an object). Since films cannot 'get off', McEachen implicates some unnamed party who responds to the diegetic action, or who neglects their responsibility to create 'appropriate' representations. More directly, reporters such as Killian Fox (2007) complain that since the dawn of cinema, 'critics have abhorred the depravity of ... film-makers, and audiences have ignored the critics by trampling one another in a rush to see the films'. Fox's exasperation exaggerates both critical wisdom and audiences' defiance of pundits' acumen, implying that the reviewer's task is futile. Such statements disclose that although critics speak from an authoritative position, their ability to fix meaning is not final.

Filmmakers and fans also contribute to and shape 'torture porn' discourse. In interviews and on DVD commentaries, filmmakers have explicitly responded to the term. In blogs and online forums, horror fans have examined and debated what 'torture porn' signifies. While these outlets do not have the same distribution reach or cultural authority as the print press, they shape what 'torture porn' means for producers and consumers, two groups who claim ownership over the films in question. Torture porn's legacy is contingent on how horror fans and filmmakers use the term beyond the initial furore in the press. That is not to suggest that fans and filmmakers simply resist critical opinions as Fox suggests. The press's anxieties about torture porn are frequently replicated in fans' and filmmakers' responses.

This chapter is divided between those groupings, first dealing with filmmakers and then moving onto fans. Principally, the chapter's analysis is focused on how the press have characterised fans and filmmakers, and various contributions those groups have made to 'torture porn' discourse. This brief dissection utilises interviews from print media, DVD commentaries and some devoted online forum debates to investigate these positions.

'You don't make film, you live film':[2] filmmakers

Once films are gathered alongside one another under a subgenre banner, their commonalities take on a retroactive character. Collectivising films connotes that they have been intentionally created with shared values in mind. Those ideals and intentions belong to the films' creators, and so 'torture porn' groups filmmakers along with their films. Most plainly, Eli Roth, Greg McLean, Alexandre Aja, Darren Lynn Bousman, James Wan, Neil Marshall, and Rob Zombie – directors of high-profile torture porn films – have been branded as 'the splat pack' (Jones, 2006).[3] Separating torture porn filmmakers from other horror directors in this way consolidates the idea that torture porn *is* an intentional movement. Accordingly, McClintock (2006) describes the splat pack as a 'cadre', a 'closely knit...team' with a group manifesto: a 'dedication to the genre, which they say has been hijacked by watered down PG-13 fare'. McClintock's assertion has been confirmed by filmmakers such as Roth (in Driscoll, 2007) proclaiming that PG-13 movies are not 'proper' horror.

Roth has been singled out as the splat pack's progenitor (see O'Sullivan, 2009), perhaps because Edelstein name-checked *Hostel* specifically,[4] but also because Roth has been most vocal about the label.[5] Roth (in McClintock, 2006) has validated the term 'splat pack', stating that the group of directors 'all have the same agenda: to bring back really violent, horrific movies'. Roth's oxymoronic statement that 'what [the splat pack] all have in common is that everybody is...different from each other'[6] illustrates that grouping individual filmmakers together results in conflict. Just as 'torture porn' generalises about filmic continuities, 'the splat pack' places emphasis on similarity – that these filmmakers create torture porn – but does not convey anything about directorial distinctiveness.

Figure 3.1   The image of a typical Eli Roth fan? Poppy in *Storm Warning* (2007, Australia, dir Jamie Blanks)

Other filmmakers have been less vocal about such collectivisation or have actively distanced themselves from 'torture porn' and 'the splat pack'. Tom Shankland, for example, insists that *wΔz* was written before *Saw* and *Hostel*, and that although he enjoyed *Saw*, he finds the 'whole "torture porn" thing...quite dull...people have been tortured in drama since Homer. So, whatever'.[7] Jamie Blanks reveals that in the original script for his film *Storm Warning*, the torturers were Nazis – as if they 'weren't reprehensible enough' already – following up by facetiously imparting that they were also 'Eli Roth fans'.[8] Blanks thereby distances himself from Roth, and also from the excesses connoted by 'torture porn'. Laugier and Adam Mason have both used DVD extra features to distance themselves and their films from 'torture porn',[9] describing the subgenre as mean-spirited and gore-centric. In doing so, they replicate the press's fulminatory critical narratives. Moreover, their remarks demonstrate that 'splat pack' and 'torture porn' lack the ostensible coherence postulated via those labels. Many filmmakers are clearly uncomfortable about being associated with either term.

Their resistance is unsurprising given the pejorative overtones of 'torture porn'. The vast majority of reviewers who utilise 'torture porn' do so to disparage the films' cultural worth, and to belittle directors' abilities. As Bloody-Disgusting.com's editor Brad Miska (in Ventre, 2009) has it, '"torture porn" was coined basically to explain away poorly made films'. To be dubbed a 'torture porn' director is to be accused of: being 'inept' (Booth, 2008; Kern, 2008), or 'barely functional' (Lacey, 2007);

making 'shoddy...lazy' product (N.a. 2010b; see also Tookey, 2007b); not understanding their craft (that is, how to scare) (Phelan, 2009; Patterson, 2010); lacking creativity (Kenny in Johnson, 2007; Macabre in Zoc, 2008); failing to create human drama or flesh out characters (McCartney, 2007b; Slotek, 2009a); and being derivative (Monahan, 2010; Ide, 2008a). Even in the rare cases when directorial skill is acknowledged, the derogatory narrative is maintained. For instance, Zinoman (2007) admits that torture porn films are 'slicker' than earlier horror, but this observation is used to evidence a prejudicial punitive position. Zinoman inveighs that the films 'look like the work of maniacs...who've been to film school'. Such derision is ultimately used to dismiss the subgenre as undeserving of critical attention.

That attitude is verified by detractors who contend that torture porn filmmakers' collective motto is 'splatter, splatter, and we need more splatter' (Williamson, 2007b). Torture porn filmmakers' alleged aim – to deliver gore in increasing levels – is characterised as puerile. Additionally, in this view, directors even fail to produce *that* level of entertainment. Mark Monahan (2010) decries torture porn 'as a collective admission of crushing directorial defeat. Running low on imagination? Turn someone to mincemeat...in close-up! Like, cool!' The informal register of the last clause implies that torture porn directors are immature. Monahan's commentary concludes with an overt challenge to filmmakers: 'Can't you do better?' He intimates both that torture porn is deficient, and also that its creators have no excuse for not 'do[ing] better'. Monahan thereby hints that these directors fail because their aspirations are flawed.

The filmmakers' presumed intentions are of greater concern than gory content in such argumentation. '[G]raphic ferocity' is limned as a 'one-note' strategy, intended only 'to shock' (Holden, 2009; see also Thomson, 2008b; N.a. 2007a), connoting that the filmmakers only have superficial ambitions. Violence is characterised as 'a gimmick' (Di Fonzo, 2007), suggesting that torture porn filmmakers are driven by commercialism rather than creativity. Such arguments regularly incorporate directors' attempts to defend their films. Srdjan Spasojevic's declaration that *A Serbian Film* 'is not meant to be commercial...[or] popular' (Brady, 2010b), and Roth's promise that the 'end of *Hostel: Part II* will shock everybody' (Nelson, 2007), have been appropriated by their disparagers to prove that these filmmakers only aim to cause outrage, and have not thought carefully enough about the meanings of the representations they produce.

Given this tendency to adapt filmmakers' statements to fit existent uncomplimentary narratives, torture porn filmmakers have primarily responded to such accusations during DVD featurettes and commentaries

Figure 3.2 Life-affirming? Jean tortures Eddie in *wΔz* (2007, UK, dir Tom Shankland)

rather than in press interviews. Director DVD commentaries customarily address allegations regarding how carefully they have crafted their films and how violence is employed. For example, many directors defend their decisions by rooting violence in characterisation;[10] in his DVD commentary for *wΔz*, Shankland asserts that 'there is no sadistic pleasure ... [*wΔz's* antagonist, Jean] is looking for something much more affirmative about life'. Other filmmakers seek to justify violent content by stressing its thematic relevance or claiming that the story requires the level of violence portrayed. For instance, in *The Tortured's* DVD special features, both Erika Christensen (actor) and Rob Lieberman (director) comment that the narrative is based on 'moral dilemma' rather than spectacle, while Carl Mazzocone (producer) discusses how *The Tortured's* violence was carefully measured and controlled.[11] Directors such as Shankland and Zombie have also used DVD special features to state outright that they dislike violence, and take no pleasure in filming fictional bloodshed.[12] These defences demonstrate that the authors have appraised what is at stake in representing violence, directly addressing accusations levelled at torture porn's creators by the press. DVD special features provide a space in which directors can vindicate their choices without the negative mediation such explication is subjected to in the press.

The location of such defences also reveals power advantages the press have in shaping 'torture porn' discourse. Press criticism is widely distributed, and advance press screenings mean reviews are customarily printed before most readers have the opportunity to see the films themselves. DVD special features, in contrast, are ordinarily consumed by a limited audience, and only after they have seen the film. Even if it is the case that directors are principally interested in expounding their decisions to fans – the primary consumers of DVD special features – these defences are typically only heard by a sympathetically pre-disposed, specialised audience. Being mainly created *after* the film has been dissected by the press, and listened to *following* consumption of the film, directors' defences on DVD special features may come across as retrospective justi-fications. Press commentary has the advantage of setting the agenda, because critics' assessments are much more immediate.

Regardless of location, filmmakers' defences are not always successful, and sometimes validate their depreciators' averments. For example, by taking an erratic stance on 'torture porn' itself, Roth confirms the contention that torture porn filmmakers are confused. At first he rejected Edelstein's article, referring to 'torture porn' as 'insulting' (in McClintock, 2006). Less than a year later, Roth considered Edelstein's article 'terrific'.[13] Although Roth is entitled to change his mind, this inconsistency is representative of his tendency to verify his hecklers' criticisms. Roth's assertion 'I want lots of violence [in R-rated horror movies]. I want nudity. I want sex and violence mixed together' (Roth in Saner, 2007: 6), and his admittance that 'I usually have the biggest boner on set when we're shooting gore stuff'[14] are detrimental to Roth's case for *Hostel*'s cultural worth. His pronouncement supports the charge that his intentions are superficial, and the allegation that *Hostel* is mindless, visceral entertainment. Roth's remarks suggest that he has not carefully gauged how he represents himself by making such statements. It follows that *Hostel*'s representations may also be ill-conceived. Roth is not alone; other directors display that same confused logic in their DVD commen-taries, relishing violence while also protesting that these films are not 'about' bloodshed. Bousman's admission that he invented horror set-pieces 'on the fly', because he felt 'there was too much dialogue in [*Saw IV*], and not enough violence' fortifies his derogators' fears that *Saw*'s gore replaces characterisation and is not well-reasoned, for example.[15] Bousman's sentiments are echoed by Chris Smith and Steven Sheil in their DVD commentaries for *Creep* and *Mum and Dad*, respectively. Smith declares that he finds exposition scenes 'tiresome', and that the torture sequence is his 'favourite'. Sheil states that in his experience editing *Mum and Dad*, 'the more brutal we were, the better it worked'.[16] By the creators' own admissions, violence is central to both films.

Such proposals fuel the critical narrative that torture porn filmmakers are ignorant of or do not care about evaluating what their representations signify. Pundits often cite graphic violence when casting aspersions on filmmakers as well as their films, focusing on filmmakers' culpability for the images they create. Jack Ketchum (in Kirkland, 2008b), for instance, advocates horrific narratives, as long as 'they are told *responsibly*' (emphasis added), specifically pointing to *Saw* and *Hostel* as failing in this respect. Edelstein's remark (in Johnson, 2007) that Zombie is 'a sensationally good director' but lacks 'moral sense' gestures towards the same objection: that torture porn filmmakers are irresponsible and should be hindered.

Accordingly, when Roth (in Schembri, 2010) proffers that he is 'trying to make smart, intelligent movies', quoting Plato to illustrate his cultural credibility, his defences are mocked by objectors. McCartney (2007a) decries Roth's use of 'pseudo-intellectual[ism]' to justify his status as 'shameless pedlar of pain and gore'. More directly insulting is Mark Kermode's (2008a) opinion that Roth is a 'numbskull'. Kermode's slur is exemplary of another trend in anti-torture porn discourse. Direct personal attacks on filmmakers are commonplace in torture porn criticism, and sometimes become alarmingly literal. Ross Douthat (2007) claims that he would like to 'punch [Roth] in the face' because 'the sick bastard has it coming', for example. Reviews are meant to address the films themselves, but, as is typical of responses to torture porn, many critics are preoccupied with external factors. For instance, in his reviews, Chris Tookey repeatedly charges torture porn directors with having 'barmy ... morals' (2007b), or delighting in cruelty (2007a; 2008c). Since 'torture porn' is ubiquitously used to connote the subgenre's 'badness', it follows that torture porn films are presumed to be badly made. An off-shoot of that logic is the supposition that these films are made by 'bad' people. Roth again is scapegoated in such fulmination. The inference that 'Roth has a penchant for seedy sexual practices' (Catt, 2010; see also Nathan, 2010) epitomises the way in which Roth's personal life is implicated in attempts to censure his films.

More broadly, torture porn filmmakers are depicted as perverse to corroborate the sexual connotations of 'torture porn'. Within press discourse, pundits commonly portray themselves as more intelligent and morally staid than torture porn's filmmakers and fans. Jane Graham (2009a), for instance, posits that 'the general view among *grown-up* commentators is that the *Saw* movies represent an artistic and moral black hole' (emphasis added). Graham's condescending tone exposes her desire to present torture porn's creators and consumers as ignorant, contrasting with her own apparently mature view.

'You made me look like a degenerate monster':[17] fans

Divergences between reviewers' opinions and the target audiences' perspectives are unsurprising. Critics are professionally required to watch films, which is quite different to watching them of one's own volition. Even when press pundits self-identify as horror enthusiasts, they commonly use that status to disparage torture porn. For example, Tim Robey (2007b) declares that he 'was a fan of horror movies' before torture porn. Robey cites his fandom to reject torture porn with some authority, and to interpellate any other horror fans reading his article. In contrast, torture porn filmmakers also present themselves as fans, using their authority to support the subgenre. Roth (in Howell, 2009), for instance, describes his directorial role in terms of his devotion to the horror genre: 'I wanted to do *everything I could to help* bring back bloody R-rated movies' (emphasis added). In opposition to critics' outright dismissals of torture porn, Roth takes ownership of the genre, both as a producer and a consumer of horror.

Belittlers hold filmmakers culpable for creating torture porn, but fans too are condemned using that same ownership logic. Torture porn's audience is admonished for financially and symbolically supporting the subgenre. 'Torture porn' also collectivises fans via their shared interest in torture porn films. The negative qualities attributed to 'torture porn' by its detractors are thereby conferred onto fans. This move – 'turning an identification of the film's characteristics into a judgement on the film's supposed target audience' – is a standard press response to popular horror (Egan, 2007: 32–3; see also Hutchings, 2004: 83). That approach is equally evident in Carmine Sarracino and Kevin Scott's (2008: 161) proclamation that 'the most frightening' aspect of torture porn is not what 'occurs...on-screen, but [what occurs] in the audience'. This remark epitomises how reported audience attitudes are employed to substantiate the pejorative traits commonly assigned to both torture porn films and filmmakers.

Much of the critical discussion regarding torture porn's audience is concerned with youth, and manifests via two propositions. First, some depreciators allege that the subgenre 'harms' children. 'Harm' remains unspecified in such cases, but torture porn producers are nevertheless painted as degenerates who want to damage young people, or who do not care if their films do so (see Cieply, 2007; Hart, 2009; Cochrane, 2007). Second, torture porn fans are deemed naïve. This judgement is concretised by referring to the target-audience as 'sensation-hungry teenagers' or 'kids' (Driscoll, 2007). As Katy Hayes (2010) puts it, 'you may not have heard of [*Saw*] if you are over 23' (see also Graham, 2009b). This anti-youth sentiment is also iterated indirectly. Brady's (2010b) description of individuals 'aged between 19 and 25' as 'Generation Meh' in her response to *Saw 3D* connects on-screen cruelty with audience apathy. Brady depicts torture porn's audience as young, amoral, and dispassionate in order to explicate the subgenre's popularity. In Brady's view, torture porn could only be enjoyed by a younger generation who supposedly lack cultural awareness and enthusiasm, who neither know any better nor care to learn.

These detractors use youth as a rhetorical tool to signify their authority, explaining torture porn's success as symptomatic of the audience's 'erroneous' pleasures. Kendall (2008) limns the supposed dichotomy between teen fans and older audiences as an unassailable gulf. '[A] film that attempts to please both the teenage gorehound and the mature filmgoer', he posits, 'is doomed to disappoint' (see also Russell, 2007). The underlying suggestion is that reviewers are dissatisfied that young people enjoy contemporary popular entertainment instead of the 'classics' they valorise. That subjective taste judgment is projected as if the 'mature' view is empirically different to a teenagers'. This much is epitomised by debates over *Antichrist*'s status as torture porn or art film, which typically hinge on similar contrastive presumptions about critics' wisdom and audiences' lack of cultural knowledge. Williamson's (2010a) warning, '[r]un, torture-porn fan! Run! You don't know what you've stumbled into! It's an art film!' imagines that 'art' film's supposedly 'higher' intellectual and cultural pleasures are anathema to the torture porn fan (see also Hornaday, 2009). That distinction uses audience stereotypes to mark torture porn as 'lowbrow'. Again this strategy is typical of critical responses to popular horror cinema. An imaginary dichotomy is formed in this discourse whereby horror's audience is framed as 'vulnerable, impressionable', while pundits belong to a 'better and more mature audience' (Hutchings, 2004: 84). These reviewers coerce their readership into joining their 'mature' position by denigrating audiences who enjoy popular horror.

Torture porn fans' alleged immaturity is not only linked to cultural illiteracy in such arguments, but also to political unawareness. Driscoll's (2007) comment that 'the kids flocking to *Hostel* don't come out of the cinemas contemplating psychological undercurrents of revenge torture in Guantanamo Bay' makes sweeping, unfounded assumptions about who is watching torture porn and their reactions to the subgenre (see also Graham, 2009a). Other objectors similarly decry 'the public's *appetite* for *mindlessly* sadistic gore' (Dalton, 2009b, emphasis added), connoting that horror offers 'simple' visceral pleasures for 'stupid' people. These sentiments are prevalent in attempts to denounce torture porn (see Tookey, 2008a; Anderson, 2007b), although Monahan's (2010) certainty that torture porn will be dismissed by 'anyone with an IQ out of single-figures' stands out as a patently insulting example of such rhetoric.

Similarly pernicious is Angie Errigo's (2009) unpleasant declaration that 'anyone who would pay money to see torture porn this vile has a screw loose'. In such cases, 'perverse' fans are separated from an apparently normative majority audience. Michael Ordona (2010b) concurs with that position, assuming that 'some folks get their jollies from seeing a woman extensively brutalised', while that is not the case *'for most'* (emphasis added). Ordona characterises audience response to horror as visceral, aligning on-screen and off-screen physicality to proclaim that only a minority could enjoy such material. Furthermore, these pleasures are linked to gender inequality – that women are 'brutalised' – to evince that torture porn's themes are distasteful to the majority. Ergo, as Peter Debruge (2008) has it, only 'twisted auds' could enjoy the subgenre's 'blatantly "wrong" material'. Such insults are ubiquitous (see, for example, N.a. 2010b; N.a. 2008a) despite torture porn's box-office performance, which affirms that films such as *Saw* and *Hostel* were consumed by a crossover demographic, not a 'perverse' minority. In these cases, reporters' subjective responses are presumed to represent and therefore speak for the majority.

Another method of explaining the appeal of the subgenre's ostensibly unappealing films is to present consuming torture porn as a macho endurance test (Billson, 2008; Hare, 2010; Hill, 2007). This notion is bolstered by the twin deductions that PG-13 rated ('soft') horror attracted a female audience to the genre (Timpone in Tapper, 2006), and that R-rated horror appeals to males simply because those films are assumed to be more physically violent and invested in sexual aggression. Two intimations follow. First, it is supposed that torture porn aims *only* to shock, and this one-dimensionality precludes any need for further contemplation. The 'endurance' argument is a veiled strategy to disparage such texts along with their viewers. Since the appeal of extreme porn has also been understood according to the logic of macho fortitude (see Hardy, 2004: 7), the endurance argument also validates the porn-horror conflation implied by 'torture porn'. Second, torture porn fans are assumed to be male (see Graham, 2009b; Sandhu, 2009). The subgenre's association with pornography fosters the presumption that torture porn is a male-oriented subgenre, despite numerous individuals involved in producing and exhibiting torture porn – such as horror festival organiser Adele Hartley (in Roby, 2008) or Lionsgate's marketing team (Williams, 2006) – contending that torture porn's demographic is constituted by as many females as males. Again, critics tend to override such attempts to diverge from the dominant discursive narrative. Emine Saner (2007), for example, sceptically states that 'the movie industry wants us to believe women are more and more interested in' torture porn (see also Hill, 2007).

Having been portrayed in these ways, many horror fans have distanced themselves from the subgenre or have adopted 'torture porn' as a pejorative label. Both strategies bolster the popular discursive pronouncement that torture porn blights the horror genre. Since torture porn has been widely presented as irredeemable, horror fans may feel compelled to condemn torture porn in order to defend the horror genre and horror fandom itself against detractors' accusations. Iloz Zoc's (2008) question 'what does [promoting such movies] say about us, the audience[?]' is paramount, since reviewers have persistently asserted that torture porn's success *speaks for* the genre audience.

While this chapter's limited space is inadequate for a full empirical study into torture porn fandom, it is worth outlining some of the patterns that have emerged in online horror fan-forum discussions of torture porn. Much debate over 'torture porn' occurs in threads dedicated to individual films such as *Saw* and *Hostel*. However, several popular horror community sites – Bloody-Disgusting.com, HorrorDVDs.com, and *Rue Morgue* magazine's forum – have hosted discussion threads specifically dedicated to 'torture porn', provoking fans to deliberate what the term means to them. The resulting responses are remarkably consistent. The patterns briefly outlined here gesture towards indicative trends that are discernible in debates about torture porn on Fearnet.com, Dreadcentral.com, and other popular horror-based Internet discussion boards, sites populated by contributors who are connoted to be horror enthusiasts by their engagement with these forums.[18]

When the subgenre is broached as a topic for discussion in these forums, some users initially respond by closing-off debate, repudiating 'torture porn' as a 'stupid catchphrase', or requesting that the fan-community 'outlaw' the term.[19] These mechanisms overtly distance fans from the disdainful connotations of 'torture porn'. Where deeper engagement with the label occurs, conversations tend to gravitate towards (a) the relative quality of individual films, (b) torture porn's origins, (c) defining the term, (d) complaints regarding how 'torture porn' is applied, and (e) whether films have to contain sexual depictions to be classed as torture porn (see Miska, 2007 and 2009; N.a. 2008c). These debates are frequently cyclical in nature since users enter and leave threads as they evolve. Even horror fans – individuals who are presumably familiar with the genre – express confusion over what 'torture porn' means, thereby testifying to the term's woolliness.

HorrorDVDs.com's 'Great "Torture Porn" Debate Poll' (2009) may have only received 108 respondents, but that apparatus notably foregrounds fans' feelings about the label itself. 24 per cent of participants baulk at the term, finding it 'condescending to genre fans'. 51 per cent concur that they 'don't mind it', and 25 per cent agree with the phrase 'I love the term. The name fits'. While this suggests some ambivalence about the label, the conversations following the poll are more decisive. The participants justify their dis/like of certain films that have been dubbed 'torture porn'. Principally, users are not troubled by the label being applied to 'bad' films. That is, multiple respondents who like or do not mind the term elucidate that they also do not enjoy the subgenre's films in general, or accept the term when it is applied to specific films that they dislike. For these poll-voters, the label is far more problematic than the films themselves. Accordingly, participants who enjoy films that have been branded 'torture porn' by critics and their peers justify their stance by arguing that those particular films are not torture porn. Such participants do not refer to 'torture porn' as insulting them personally, since they do not identify with the subgenre, despite expressing their enjoyment of films commonly surmised to be torture porn.[20] Instances of horror fans willingly admitting that they enjoy torture porn qua 'torture porn' are scarce in these fan-forum contexts.

Another common topic addressed is how torture porn's denigration impacts on horror fandom. In such cases, users reflect on journalists accusing fans of being 'sickos'.[21] In some cases, contributors reveal that they have publically distanced themselves from horror fandom because of critical fulmination. One *Rue Morgue* user states 'I dont [*sic*] even tell people I like horror anymore', for instance.[22] The stigma felt by such fans is strangely at odds with the subgenre's relative financial success, which hints towards torture porn's popularity beyond a specific genre fan-base. Despite that broad appeal, reporters customarily hold horror fans accountable for torture porn's box-office performance, inasmuch as fandom implies devotion to, support of, and some ownership over the genre. Non-fan crossover audiences may approach torture porn films with a greater degree of detachment than fans can. Equally, some fan resistance to the label may arise from torture porn's crossover success insofar as torture porn may be perceived as a subgenre that is consumed by the general public rather than dedicated horror fans.

Replicating objectors' derogatory proposals, 'torture porn' is correlated with bad films or improper fandom in many forum discussions. Resultantly, 'torture porn' is subject to intra-community regulation: how a contributor uses the term is often treated as a benchmark against which the users' credentials as a horror fan are measured. This form of credibility evaluation is unsurprising in the forum context given that these communities are brought together by fandom. To illustrate, one user thus declares that '*casual* horror movie fans see too much gore and just categorise it into torture porn' (emphasis added), while another explodes '[h]ow long have you motherfuckers been watching horror movies? ... leave us alone about horror since you obviously dont [*sic*] get the purpose of the horror genre'.[23] This contributor suggests that 'real' fans understand what qualifies as torture porn. The question of 'how long' one has been watching horror avers that a degree of genre knowledge is required before one can accurately apply such labels. Using the label at all may signal a lack of subcultural capital in this context. Asking 'how long' one has been a fan also insinuates that torture porn is a passing fad, since the term carries overtones of fleeting or novice-level acquaintance with the horror genre. In rendering the label an indicator of genre knowledge, such comments distance horror fandom from torture porn fandom, and therefore from the scornful accusations offered in press responses to the subgenre. This strategy does not repudiate the films dubbed 'torture porn', but rather the negative discourse that surrounds the term.

Such online debates allow community members to collectively negotiate the connotations of 'torture porn', and the label's lasting meanings will eventually be forged in such discussion. 'Torture porn' was only employed in 213 articles in major English language world publications in 2011, the lowest number of articles to use the term since 2007. While that waning suggests high-profile public interest in the term is dissipating, horror fans continue to employ the category-label in online discussions, concretising 'torture porn' as part of horror's lexis. Press critics have instilled the term with assorted connotations, yet horror fans may eventually recoup 'torture porn' from those numerous pejorative associations. The terms 'slasher' and 'video nasty' were previously vilified by pundits in the same ways 'torture porn' has been, although it took over a decade for fans to embrace those labels as legitimate subgenre referents. It is not clear whether 'torture porn' will follow suit. Online forums expedite discussion amongst disparate fans in a way that was not available to previous generations of horror enthusiasts, for example. Online debates could allow horror fans to co-opt the label much more swiftly than the term 'slasher' was. Alternatively, the process may be stunted by the frequency with which established discursive prejudices are reiterated in discussions about 'torture porn'.

'No unnecessary violence. I've told you a hundred times':[24] conclusion

'Torture porn' is a site of discursive struggle. The category conflates films, filmmakers and fans, creating overlapping tensions, many of which originate with the label's fulminatory connotations. Torture porn's detractors have habitually sought to illegitimate the subgenre, railing against production and consumption of torture porn by insulting filmmakers and fans. However, characterising torture porn as illicit may have facilitated the subgenre's financial success. Since most torture porn films have not been subject to censorship, they are both 'forbidden' and yet highly obtainable. Torture porn's detractors may have inadvertently prolonged the subgenre's popularity by proclaiming that these accessible films are taboo.

Some horror fans' rejections of 'torture porn' may derive from that veneer of controversy. Torture porn films are not as outrageous as reporters have insisted. Horror fans' complaints regarding torture porn not being 'true' horror articulate that disparity between torture porn's content and its opponents' claims. Being more familiar with the genre than the casual consumer, horror fans are more likely to be aware of the numerous horror films that have been officially illegitimated (banned). If illicitness really is torture porn's predominant appeal, the multiplex is not where such films will be found. To consume torture porn *because* it is illicit therefore reveals one's unfamiliarity with the genre, and hence may explain why some self-identified fans correlate liking torture porn with genre ignorance. Press critics' concerns over torture porn are squarely focused on multiplex horror, drawing attention away from lower-budget, peripheral horror films. Some such films are included in the analysis that follows, and illegitimate horror films will be returned to in Part III once torture porn's content has been examined.

Despite outlining discursive complications and inconsistencies over the last three chapters, the objective has not been to entirely discredit the usefulness of 'torture porn' itself, or postulate that torture porn films are unworthy of investigation. 'Torture porn' provides ways of engaging with rather than disavowing the subgenre. Films that have been dubbed 'torture porn' share facets, and their categorisation imbues those commonalities with significance. In Part II, the focus will be on filmic content itself. In the chapters that follow, some of the patterns and meanings that emerge from torture porn's collectivisation will be illustrated.

Part II
'Torture' (Morality)

Introduction

Although 'torture porn' discourse is founded on pejorative press criticism, there have been some attempts to defend torture porn. Where defences do occur, they also frequently lean towards off-screen factors. Roth (in O'Sullivan, 2009) states that 'the people that [*sic*] watch [torture porn films]...actually think about them...analyse them', for example, defending the subgenre by referring to fandom rather than justifying the content of his films. Similarly, John Raybin (in Lidz, 2009) refers to *Saw* as a 'thinking man's horror movie', placing emphasis not on narrative content, but on the 'thinking' audience. Both validations make a case for 'alternative' perspectives on films that have otherwise been derided, intimating that torture porn merits analysis because the people who spend time with the films – the subgenre's fans – can perceive their value. It follows that the majority pillory torture porn because they fail to apprehend the subgenre's intrinsic worth. This strategy is often employed by those attempting to reclaim cultural objects that have been denounced as 'trash' (see Egan, 2007: 249). In the case of torture porn, the implication is that the subgenre's already present value has been buried under the 'damaging...and misguided' reputation of 'torture porn' (Hilden, 2007). By not detailing precisely what fans find interesting about torture porn, such defences connote that the subgenre self-evidently deserves attention, and that one could share the fan understanding of torture porn by laying prejudice aside. However, this mechanism thereby propagates the idea that torture porn films are 'obvious' or superficial and even risks implying that no detailed defence is offered because there is no substance to detect.

These films have been unfairly dismissed in the majority of critical responses since little attention is paid to the subgenre's content. Accordingly, Chapters 4–6 are organised around three principles. First, allegations levelled at torture porn will be tested by examining filmic content. Second, some of the patterns that emerge from collectivising these texts will be detailed, paying particular attention to commonalities that have been overlooked in critical discourse. These traits are not offered as taxonomic properties. Rather, they are prevalent attributes that stem from the subgenre's centralisation of torture. These features impact on and facilitate rumination on torture porn's meanings. Third, those textual details will be used to demonstrate why these films are more complex than has so far been accounted for in the vast majority of responses to the subgenre.

The 'torture' in 'torture porn' – violence and its narrative contextualisation – is the primary focus in Part II. 'Torture' itself therefore requires delineation. Various scholars' takes on torture will be alluded to throughout Part II, with Elaine Scarry's work being referred to most regularly. Scarry prioritises suffering rather than the politics of using torture as an interrogational technique. Her approach is apt for the study in hand since torture is very rarely inquisitorial in torture porn. Even in a film such as *The Horseman*, in which lead protagonist Christian tortures several men to uncover information regarding his daughter's death, the suffering he inflicts is chiefly motivated by a desire to avenge her demise and to resolve his own distress. Unlike interrogators, torture porn's torturers do not usually aim to crush a captives' will to attain information. There are torture porn films – such as *Breaking Nikki* and *Torture Room* – in which torture is inflicted to shape a captive's mind-set, yet these are exceptions. Torture porn's antagonists purposefully terrorise their prey. In some cases, the antagonist's goals remain unclear, although it is more common for antagonists to be motivated by personal gain or gratification. In torture porn then, torture is an expression of power insofar as sufferers are disempowered during their torment.

Because it is a social interaction that entails deliberately exploiting power, torture is inherently a moral issue. Frequently, ethical quandaries are explored in explicit and literal ways in torture porn films. The analysis in Part II is driven by moral theory, not only because of its appropriateness, but also because existing pejorative responses to torture porn are so inadequate in this regard. Torture porn's detractors frequently use terms such as 'immoral' without evincing how they have arrived at that conclusion, what exactly is immoral about torture porn, or what school of ethical thought they are drawing on to make such distinctions.

The analysis that follows draws on deontological ethics, and Kantian absolutism in particular. Immanuel Kant's moral philosophy is founded on principle-led moral decision-making.[1] Kant terms these principles categorical imperatives, denoting that they are inalienable. In accounting for how these imperatives come to be and how they are ensured to be correct, Kant proposes that principles are formed according to rational thought. Categorical imperatives must be universal in Kant's view: moral principles should be evaluated against the notion that everyone can and ought to do the same. Every person is responsible for their own actions, doing unto others as he/she expects others – having also deduced their principles via reason – to do unto her/him. In that sense, every individual is the author of their own morality. Consequently, subjects willingly adhere to imperatives rather than being slaves to them,[2] since the latter would infringe on one's autonomy. Moral principles are consequently bound into autonomous will, since the will that permits such thinking also defines the individual as a moral being (see Kant, 2000: 59–60).

These key notions inform the narrative analysis offered in Part II. In Chapter 6 the protagonists' difficult moral choices will be examined, contemplating how coercion, threat and suffering impact on the individual's ethical decisions. For example, imprisonment – one of torture porn's leitmotifs – prevents the captive from making free choices. Since incarceration infringes on the captive's autonomy, the abductee's capacity for moral decision-making is also brought into question. Moreover, as Chapters 4 and 5 will illustrate, narrative presentation shapes one's interpretation of the individual protagonist's moral righteousness.

Although Kantian theory provides an ethical framework for the analysis that follows, the version of deontology employed here is attuned to key shortcomings in Kant's absolutist position. Kant is assured that reasoned thinking will lead to correct moral principles because logic can only provide a single result. Other philosophers such as Arthur Schopenhauer (1909: 141–2) have critiqued that stance, claiming that Kant's emphasis on autonomous moral authors amounts to subjectivity – the particular individual's response to their immediate circumstances – disguised as universality. Kant certainly downplays the extent to which moral principles are based on normative standards that pre-exist the moral agent. When moral principles are referred to in the following chapters then, they will be treated as relational concepts that bridge between ideals and in situ particularities. Values that appear to be universal are ultimately relational. The ostensible universality of moral principle is a useful illusion, since it provides those values with meaning in any particularised context. Bridging between the particular and the ideal allows the moral agent to make choices in reference to broader social and discursive contexts, rather than responding to immediate pressures egoistically. Any references to moral principles in the following chapters are made with this proviso in mind. A second shortcoming is flagged by those who consider Kantian absolutism to be too devoted to principle to be practicable (see Ross, 2002: 28), especially under extraordinary circumstances (see Ginbar, 2008). Kant's (2003: 105) declaration that it is '[b]etter the whole people should perish' than it is to do injustice certainly feels powerfully counter-intuitive. However, the reactive stance is just as imperfect: abandoning moral principles in favour of self-interested instinct is not an ethically informed response to peril.

The latter tension demonstrates that in practice, it is seldom easy to do what one believes to be morally right. That discord is crucial to understanding torture porn's ethical struggles. When endangered, protagonists' moral principles are pitted against the immediate pressures of survival instinct. The *Saw* franchise's games incarnate this kind of dilemma, for example, by forcing captives to make choices about who will 'live or die'. *Saw*'s games epitomise a broader commonality among torture porn films: placing characters in exceptional, life-threatening circumstances, and embedding those moral quandaries in the narrative structure. Non-absolutists may accept that in perilous circumstances it is better to forsake principle than to give up one's own life, yet the resultant harm should be evaluated. Torture porn films do precisely that, dramatizing the costs of making hard ethical decisions. Choice-making is recurrently associated with suffering, underscoring how difficult those choices are.

The subgenre is replete with morally precarious situations, which test not only the characters, but the limits of moral duty. Although many of torture porn's characters commit immoral acts, that does not mean torture porn is an unethical subgenre. Such characterisation appraises the nature and usefulness of ethics. Zinoman's (2011) supposition that 'audiences don't see horror movies for moral improvement' is only correct inasmuch as it is not torture porn's place to preach. Zinoman overlooks how paramount moral dilemmas are to torture porn narratives, and how ethical meaning is intertwined with torture porn's empathic mechanisms. Jason Middleton (2010: 24) displays a similar attitude towards torture porn and its audience. Middleton asks whether torture porn's emphasis on human cruelty 'makes these films more or less scary (from a fan's perspective), or more or less ethically fraught (from a critic's perspective)', implying that fan enjoyment is primarily visceral ('scary'), while critical views are inherently more cerebral ('ethically fraught'). As Chapters 1–3 evinced, reviewers' responses to torture porn are often informed by gut-instinct rather than logical reasoning. Furthermore, separating 'scary' and 'ethically fraught' is problematic because, as the following chapters will elucidate, drama emotionally involves audiences in protagonists' circumstances. Watching torture porn entails not merely thinking about morality, but *experiencing* characters' moral dilemmas, then.

Torture porn narratives are, in these senses, comparable to the hypothetical thought-experiments moral philosophers customarily employ to test principles (such as Yuval Ginbar's (2008: 42–3) 'sadists torturing babies' example). In fact, numerous moral philosophers use fictional narratives to probe moral theory (see, for example, Govier, 2002: 6; MacAllister, 2003: 87). Torture porn's drama organically involves audiences in moral contemplation. The subgenre's narratives provoke such cogitation because the characters face emotionally challenging situations in which their intuitive responses clash with moral reasoning. Kant is devoted to non-negotiable principles, yet his insistence that one should adhere to categorical imperatives despite one's instincts to the contrary implies that there is a potential gap between emotional sway and moral duty. Kant resolves this breach by always opting for the imperative. Torture porn's drama instead explores that gap, routinely offering complex situations in which justice, innocence, guilt, blame, and retribution are brought into question via characters' experiences.

Torture porn narratives illustrate how and why moral standards are violated or maintained under a set of hypothetical conditions. Those conditions are portrayed as ordeals undergone by torture porn's protagonists. The lead characters' emotional arcs shape the narrative perspective, impacting on its moral coding. Contra to allegations that torture porn usually presents violence in a titillating manner and depicts narrative events from torturers' perspectives, Chapter 4 will establish that both in their uses of form – camera movement, sound, and so forth – and narrative structure, torture porn films chiefly engage with those characters who suffer rather than those who inflict pain.

This discussion will be developed in Chapter 5 via an exploration of character positions. While torture porn narratives are mainly aligned with sufferers' perspectives rather than torturers', those initial positions are regularly disputed as the narratives progress. Torture porn's moral dynamic is seldom a 'good' versus 'evil' dichotomy. In order to grasp torture porn's complexities, the notion that torture is a binary interaction must be revised. In torture porn, torture usually involves torturers, tortured, and witnesses. These relative positions are mutable rather than fixed. Characters shift between roles, meaning protagonists who initially seem to be tortured victims often themselves become torturers before the narrative closes, and so forth. Narrative alignment with sufferers means lead protagonists are typically encoded as 'heroes'. In cases where protagonists forsake their own moral principles, that conventional align-ment is placed under pressure, creating moral tensions.

Additional factors that complicate those moral dynamics will be considered in Chapter 6. Torture porn's characters negotiate their power relations by struggling to attain control over their immediate surround-ings. In torture porn, torture tends to occur in spaces – ranging from cells and derelict warehouses, to 'foreign lands' and sparsely populated rural areas[3] – that are separated from the protagonists' everyday experi-ences. Since (a) protagonists face exceptional circumstances (torture), (b) those pressures occur in delimited locations, (c) those spaces and circum-stances are outside of the protagonists' usual spheres of experience, and (d) the spaces are fashioned after the antagonists' cruel impulses, it may appear as if torture porn's action occurs in moral-vacuum situations, where ethical rules no longer apply. However, as Chapter 6 will demon-strate, torture porn narratives habitually support the deontic proposition that because moral agents are authors of their own principles, ethical decisions are not just made in reference to context.

Although deontology is utilised to illuminate these textual mean-ings, it is not the theoretical paradigm that makes the films interesting. Theory is just a means of elucidating the subgenre's already present rich-ness. Moral philosophy highlights the social, powered aspects of torture, rather than torture's political resonances. Numerous academics have placed emphasis on torture as a political issue in their approaches to torture porn, interpreting the subgenre as an allegory for the 'War on Terror'. The allegory defence negates torture porn itself by intimating that the films are validated by contemporaneous political circum-stances. Torture porn's lasting appeal lies in torture's provocative socio-moral aspects, rather than particular instances of torture issuing from the Bush Administration's interventions in the Middle East. This topic will be addressed in detail in the next chapter.

4
'Your Story's Real, and People Feel That':[1] Contextualising Torture

Tallying filmic representations with national events is an established critical mode, one that is particularly popular in horror studies. Scholars have variously deciphered 1950s horror as analogising radiation fears (Skal, 1993: 247–8), and construed *Dracula* as a commentary on the plight of Victorian women (Kline, 1992), for instance. More recently, monographs by Kevin Wetmore (2012), Linnie Blake (2008), Adam Lowenstein (2005), and Kendall Philips (2005) have offered political-allegorical readings of horror cinema. The allegorical trend has been particularly propagated by torture porn's 'directors, experts, and fans' (Riegler, 2010: 27) when defending the subgenre.[2] The consensus is that torture porn comments on the War on Terror: encompassing 21st century terrorism, 9/11, the Abu Ghraib scandal, and the Bush Administration's torture sanctions. Critically invested readings of torture porn's significance have developed from such linkages, and so the allegory interpretation constitutes an important branch of 'torture porn' discourse.

However, although the allegorical reading is not inappropriate per se, its proliferation impedes debate. The cumulative effect of this interpretation's reiteration is that allegory becomes *the* rationalisation for torture porn's significance rather than *an* answer. The allegorical reading has thereby become a stopping point that has inadvertently hindered discussion. The interpretation explains the Anglo-American press's and public's interest in torture porn at a particular moment, but pins torture porn down to that epoch, thereby invalidating the subgenre's lasting relevance. While this chapter begins with a discussion of the allegorical reading and its limitations then, that dissection aims to repudiate the prevailing connotation that torture porn's violent representations primarily refer to concurrent political circumstances, and American politics particularly. Concentrating on immediate political events means overlooking that violence and cruelty are not only contemporary politico-historical concerns. Indeed, as Chapter 1 established, violence and cruelty are among horror's staple themes.

Torture porn films are not just the products of reactionary impulses, as the repeated allegory-reading implies. Political torture itself points towards broader ethical conundrums. Torture porn reflects *those* moral issues, not just the War on Terror. In Chapters 5 and 6, that concept-led understanding will be developed by making a case for torture porn's lasting appeal and inspecting the subgenre's narrative content. As a first step towards such rumination, this chapter's second half will challenge the prevalent allegation that torture porn portrays events primarily from a sadistic point-of-view (see Cumming et al., 2010; Robey, 2007a). As this chapter will verify, the notion that torture porn's viewers are encouraged to identify with torturers is flawed, since the films are more commonly encoded in favour of sufferers' perspectives.

The sadistic gaze argument has been prejudicially applied to torture porn, but derives from established critical narratives used to vilify earlier horror subgenres.[3] However, the sadistic gaze theory also descends from the associations made between torture porn and events at Abu Ghraib since the scandal was rooted in photographs taken by torturers within the prison facility: that is, from a sadistic point-of-view. The sadistic gaze argument intertwines two established discursive narratives. Its proponents apply the resultant amalgam to torture porn films without adequately testing the validity of those propositions. The subgenre's depictions of torture are contextualised by torture porn's fictional mode, formal traits, and narrative structures, all of which should be accounted for. Thus, this chapter founds Part II's overarching contention that torture porn's particularities do not match its objectors' pejorative suppositions.

'[S]omething terribly contemporary':[4] the war on terror alle[-]gory

The War on Terror reading dominates scholarly responses to torture porn. Douglas Kellner's (2010: 6–8) direct comparison between 'violent films of the era' and 'the second Bush-Cheney Administration' – which culminates in Kellner's declaration that *Saw*'s lead antagonist John Kramer/Jigsaw physically resembles Dick Cheney – epitomises how cursory such correlations can be. Other scholars make similarly blunt parallels. Middleton insists that torture porn directly 'aligns with the post-9/11 years' (2010: 3), while Beth Kattelman (2010: 3) proclaims that the subgenre arose as a *'result* of the 11 September 2001 attacks' (emphasis added), for example.[5]

The discursive trend towards allegory is not only cultivated by scholars however. Directors too have made this connection. Roth has been particularly vocal in supporting the allegory-interpretation of *Hostel* (in Hill, 2007; Lockwood, 2008: 42; Murray, 2008: 1), possibly because such readings provide some defence against the scapegoating he has suffered in the press. Directors Joe Lynch and Zombie foster allegorical readings, insofar as they compare their aesthetic approaches to Al Qaeda beheading videos. Berman has also stated that he wanted *Borderland* to evoke US soldiers filming real war-atrocities.[6] In fact, numerous torture porn films – including *Territories, Basement, The Killing Room, Scar, Torture Room,* and *The Torturer* – contain dialogue perspicuously pertaining to the War on Terror.

The allegory reading clearly has some legitimacy in this sense. Specific motifs within the films appear to draw on contemporary, publically contested aspects of torture, thus facilitating the allegorical interpretation. Subjects are tortured based on their personal fears in *Are You Scared?, Dread,* and *The Task,* a method included among Rumsfeld's advocated interrogation techniques (see Paust, 2007: 14–17). Other movies incorporate war motifs that could be construed as making the correspondence plain. These include gasmasks (*Callback; The Final; The Task*), hazmat suits (*Spiderhole; The Unforgiving*), the orange prison jumpsuits that became synonymous with Guantanamo Bay imagery (*Breathing Room; Territories; The Tortured*), and black hoods over abductees heads, which were iconographically associated with the Abu Ghraib photographs (*The Book of Revelation; Nine Dead; Sutures*). However, although those emblems were prominent in imagery related to the War on Terror, none are exclusive to that context. Black hoods, for instance, may be associated with the images of Guantanamo Bay and Abu Ghraib, but they were used in previous CIA and UK torture schemes (McCoy, 2006: 55). Even where such devices openly evoke present politics, their 'obviousness' negates the need for analysis. As such, the allegorical interpretation is one that does not necessarily require elucidation. To read contemporary horror as reflecting the current moment thereby risks corroborating critical accusations that torture porn films are one-dimensional and reactionary.

The allegory reading makes contextual linkages to the immediate present that risk becoming myopic. For example, *Boy Meets Girl* is entirely centred on torture. Its run-time is dominated by depictions of a bound man being physically assaulted by two female abductors. His captors explicitly discuss 'serving [their] nation' and 'terrorism'. Had the film been made in 2004, it would fit torture porn's alleged War on Terror analogy. However, *Boy Meets Girl* was made in 1994. It fits the allegory that has been applied to torture porn because *Boy Meets Girl* deals with the same *concepts*. The film is proto-torture porn inasmuch as it demonstrates that the post-2003 boom in torture-themed horror production organically evolved from existing genre facets. Politically contentious current affairs no doubt spurred public interest in morality and suffering in the early 2000s. That public interest may have fuelled torture porn's box-office performance, leading to increased funding for other torture-themed horror films. Yet when it comes to understanding the narrative content, the *issues* – morality and suffering – should be the focus for interpretation, not the *linkage* between those issues and the historical moment.

As much as references to current affairs are offered in torture porn films, contemporary motifs are related to a network of other elements. For instance, several torture porn narratives that are blatantly about war make reference to current affairs, but situate those discussions against a history of warfare. In *Shadow*, protagonist David finds a bunker decorated with war paraphernalia (gasmasks, medals), alongside film canisters labelled 'Abu Ghraib', 'Pearl Harbour', and 'Saigon'. As such, *Shadow* contextualises contemporary conflicts alongside past skirmishes. No matter how urgent torture may be for *Hostel's* characters (and decriers), the protagonists' visit to the 'Museum Tortury' also verifies that, as David Luban (2006: 37) observes, 'torture is as old as human history'. Moreover, *Territories's* torturers overtly create a neo-Guantanamo. Their actions do not simply mirror human rights violations occurring in Guantanamo Bay. Their deeds indicate that what the facility signified – its conceptual legacy – will live on long after the prison itself has shut down. Underlining that point, footage of Guantanamo Bay's closure is included in *Territories*, and spurs on the torturers. In each of these cases, contemporary events are connected to broader contexts, pointing towards the horrors that humans do to one another. Torture is not a lapse, nor is it exclusive to the early 21st Century. Torture is a sustained feature of human interaction. Torture porn reifies that fact by portraying the world as a place occupied only by torturers and captives, and concretising how distasteful human history is via ugly depictions of cruelty.

The press's resistance to torture porn may be rooted in that unpleasantness, but repudiating these films means failing to address what those representations mean. However limited the political-allegory approach is, those readings at least acknowledge that torture porn films are in some sense significant. In contrast, press-based responses to the allegory paradigm often manifest as outright dismissals of potential meaning. For example, George Romero – who has been critically lauded for his zombie-based metaphoric satires – has been called upon as an authoritative voice to discuss the legitimacy of torture porn's allegorical messages (see Anderson, 2008). In Romero's view (in Onstad, 2008), torture porn films are inadequate because 'they're lacking in metaphor'. This attitude implies that horror *must* have a candid allegorical agenda in order to be considered worthwhile. Other detractors evince torture porn's cultural unfitness by mocking any political commentary they encounter in the subgenre, treating allegory as superficial rather than integral to torture porn's meanings. Anderson (2007b) describes *Frontier(s)*'s political parallels as 'cynical' attempts 'to bring gravitas to the abattoir', for example. The same scepticism is evident in responses to Spasojevic's claim that his *A Serbian Film* is a political allegory (see Maher, 2010b; Kermode, 2010; Phelan, 2010). Elsewhere, the idea that torture porn can be taken seriously is mocked: Michael O'Sullivan (2009) angers Roth during an interview by finding the notion of *Hostel* having a '"subtext"...funny', for instance (see also Hill, 2007; Whittle, 2007).

Torture porn is left in a no-win situation. In this pull between scholars' allegory readings and press derision, the films are lambasted if they lack metaphor, but are frequently dismissed if they do. Any contribution torture porn makes to wider conceptual debates is thereby negated. All of these problems validate Gabriele Murray's (2008) and Lockwood's (2008) proposals that making sharp connections between horror films and current events is a strategy best avoided.

'I can't believe it's fake':[7] fictional versus genuine torture

The allegorical reading draws correlations between narrative and real-world contexts. Such conflation is habitually encouraged in 'torture porn' discourse, as is demonstrated by disparagers' tendency to confuse character motives with audience desires (see Chapter 3). This inclination perhaps arises from the subgenre's occasional evocations of heightened realism. For instance, numerous films – including *Death Tunnel*, *Megan Is Missing*, *An American Crime*, and *Wolf Creek* – impart that they are 'based on actual events' to amplify the horror. Another method – found in *Captivity*, *Dying Breed*, *Gnaw*, and *Madness* – is to open the film with crime statistics, intimating a relationship between the ensuing fiction and real-world abduction. Any visceral violence that follows offers a kind of physiological authenticity that corroborates the credit sequences' claims to heightened realism.

However, while torture porn may be real*istic* in these senses, the subgenre's films rarely obscure their fictionality.[8] Various pundits neglect that distinction, conflating reality with fiction in their discussions of torture porn. For example, multiple reporters mention genuine atrocity footage – such as Al Qaeda beheading videos – alongside discussion of torture porn without discriminating between the two (see Whittle, 2007; Goodwin, 2007). Rosie Dimanno (2011) even refers to genuine beheading videos *as* 'torture porn'. Leaping between fictional and factual suffering in this way misrepresents how different the two forms are. Objections must be raised to such a collapse, which fails to distinguish between four conceptions of torture.

First, torture may be conceived via representations that record actual instances of torture, such as authentic atrocity images. As several scholars including Lilie Chouliaraki (2006: 25–6), Sharon Silwinski (2006: 89), and Sue Tait (2008: 94) have posited, mediating genuine suffering is problematic because agony cannot be conveyed via imagery. Mediation distances the image's viewer from the person captured in the image, whose suffering is rendered as spectacle. Many scholars have raised anxieties over authentic atrocity images' potentially dehumanising effects, particularly in response to pictures stemming from the War on Terror and Abu Ghraib (see Andén-Papadopoulos, 2009: 921–5; MacDougall, 2006: 17). However, choosing to look at atrocity images does not mean that the viewer necessarily lacks empathy for the people depicted qua people. Neither does the image itself prompt such a view, either via its content or its existence.

Second, torture may be conceived as an *idea* without referring directly to particular incidents of torture. The risk of emotional 'deadening' in this case springs from denying what torture involves: that is, forgetting that torture happens to people and causes suffering. For instance, the popular conception that '[a]fter September 2001, a growing public consensus emerged in favour of torture' (McCoy, 2006: 110) is based on a rhetoric of national security and interrogation, but above all on a non-actualised idea of torture. Torture, in this discourse, is hypothetical. It is conceived as being enacted 'somewhere else', out of sight, by and upon 'other people' rather than particularised individuals. This rhetorical strategy elicits a depersonalised view of torture. Unlike the first conception, in which it is acknowledged that torture actually occurs, the idea of torture avoids the realities of suffering, stripping the concept of content.

The opposite is *imagined* torture: conceiving of participating in the act. Unlike the idea of torture where the event itself is bypassed – that is, torture is not envisioned as actually happening to or being enacted by anyone in particular – imagining torture means the imaginer fills at least one of the gaps. Although distance is created between the imaginer and real instances of torture, imagined torture differs from the first two conceptions inasmuch as the imaginer steps into the position of torturer, someone who could intervene, or the tortured. Most common is the latter. 'When most people imagine torture', John Conroy (2000: 88) observes, 'they imagine themselves the victim'. Imagined responses to interpersonal torture result in emotional arousal because imagining involves replacing actual suffering with empathic projection (see Batson et al., 2003: 1192). Although lacking the concrete actuality of atrocity images – proof that someone genuinely suffered – imagined torture intertwines the concept (torture) with the emotive content that was missing in the first two conceptions.

At this stage, the first conception requires revision. Atrocity images are ordinarily met with some kind of imagined response, thereby connecting the first and third conceptions. Scarry (1985: 35), for instance, finds that '[a]lmost anyone looking at the *physical* act of torture would be immediately appalled and repulsed by the torturers'. Detachment from torturers is balanced by empathy for sufferers. That much is validated by consumers' discussions of real war imagery (Andén-Papadopoulos, 2009: 932) and even Abu Ghraib torturer Specialist MP Sabrina Harman's personal correspondence: '[w]hat if it was me in their shoes?' (*Standard Operating Procedure*). Harman's question reworks genuine torture as an empathic narrative.

Fictional representation provides a fourth mode via which torture can be conceived. Drama impels the kind of empathic arousal involved in imagined torture, but hypostatises the event as an instance occurring for someone else (the protagonist). Unlike genuine atrocity images, drama can convey characters' histories, motivations, and various emotional responses to circumstances. Characters can be imbued with agency in order to engross audiences. Fiction permits audiences to interact with violent images while evading the particular political and moral discomforts inherent to engaging with genuine war images, for example, because fiction comes with the assurance that no-one was really harmed. Horror-fiction allows audiences to explore moral dilemmas *because* it is fictional and therefore is partially distanced from the immediacy of politico-historical circumstances.

Although fiction provides a distance from real-world situations, its unreality does not equate to emotional detachment, then. Critics who propose that torture porn narratives are unsympathetic (Derakhshani,

2007) or uncompassionate (McCartney, 2007a) towards sufferers do not account for the differences between the drama mode and other ways of conceiving torture. These complaints replicate anxieties that surround genuine torture images, particularly apprehensions over spectacle and the commodification of suffering. Torture porn films have thus been dubbed exploitative and cynical (Phillips, 2010; Tookey, 2007b), while filmmakers are reproached for using 'irony' as a 'deadening, de-sensitising' tool that legitimates suffering (Cochrane, 2007; see also McGlynn, 2007; Mullen, 2007). These opponents suggest that torture porn filmmakers encourage callous responses to anguish per se. Torture porn's violent depictions are painted as needlessly cruel because they are contextualised as entertainment, and entertainment is interpreted as a process of pleasurable consumption rather than emotional and intellectual stimulation. Torture porn is not a site of cynical indifference, but of complex involvement, and its fictional structures are crucial to fathoming how ethical issues are approached in these films.

'Not All Films Have a Happy Ending':[9] narrative structures

'*Torture* porn' denotes that the subgenre foregrounds depictions of agony. However, some qualification is necessary. First, the observation that torture is one of the subgenre's central facets is a generalisation that bypasses the particular manner in which torture manifests within the subgenre's films. Apprehending how torture is situated within these narratives is pivotal to understanding how torture porn operates, and particularly how the subgenre facilitates engagement with characters. Second, although torture is foregrounded, brutality does not necessarily override emotion in these films. The latter view is held by many of torture porn's detractors, who have asserted that the subgenre's narratives are driven by violent incidents rather than character arcs (see Chapter 2). That belief is inflamed by torture porn filmmakers' tendency to arrange violent incidents as set-pieces, thereby underlining their placement within the overall narrative structure.

Torture porn's set-pieces are often focused more on suffering than on murder. It is important to note then that where a single individual's prolonged torture is presented in torture porn, the set-pieces are encoded to generate empathy with the tortured. *Broken, Senseless, Hunger, Keepsake,* and *99 Pieces* are structured around the number of days the lead protagonist has been imprisoned. On-screen captions tally the duration of their incarceration, dividing their torment into distinct episodes. In each case, set-piecing foregrounds the sufferer's ordeal rather than painting them as expendable. The structure is arranged around their plight. As such, their welfare – that which is jeopardised – is prioritised.

Episodic set-pieces also deliver peaks and troughs of terror across these narratives. Cadence impacts on how effectively these sequences convey the characters' suffering. The unrelenting brutality of Anna's torture in *Martyrs*, for example, is the result of calculated pacing rather than the quantity of violent acts depicted. Anna is only hit 25 times during the entire torture sequence, averaging at roughly one hit per minute of screen-time. Only 22 strikes are seen (three are heard). The impression of gratuitousness is created by the sequence's episodic structure. Prior to Anna being skinned, there are 16 fades to black, five other dissolves, and three flat cuts. There are 24 scene breaks that illustrate time passing: roughly as many as there are physical strikes. Anna's injuries become more severe at each stage, connoting the passage of time in-between each fragment. Anna's suffering feels drawn out because the editing slows the pace. The lack of dialogue accentuates that impedance. 14 minutes pass without a word being spoken, which, by conventional standards, is an unusually long period of speech-free screen-time. Such details demonstrate that torture porn narratives are more carefully constructed than the subgenre's depreciators have suggested.

Narrative structuring thus necessitates detailed attention in order to comprehend how torture porn's violence operates. For instance, Kattelman's (2010: 5–8) reading of '*Saw*'s contained violence' as offering 'reassurance...[and] closure' is inadequate because she ignores how torture episodes contribute to *Saw*'s overarching narrative structure. *Saw*'s set-pieces tend to close with a death, meaning each section is marked by a character's removal from the film. Nevertheless, the episodic quality of its trap-sequences is balanced by *Saw*'s evolving narrative whole. *Saw* employs multiple plot-twists that impact on narrative meaning. Each *Saw* film closes with a revelatory development, and every film contributes to the series' advancement by divulging previously withheld information (see Jones, 2010). While some reviewers have deemed *Saw* 'convoluted' (Friend, 2009; Lee, 2008), this playful structure is entirely in keeping with the plot's gaming motifs. The result is that *Saw*'s events are ever-evolving. Acts are regularly revisited from alternative perspectives and meaning is not fixed, despite each film ending with the refrain 'game over'. *Saw 3D*'s closing sequence, for instance, revises the series' events by unveiling Dr. Gordon – one of the lead protagonists from the first *Saw* – as a co-conspirator in the series' subsequent murders. This last minute revelation entirely shifts the place John's successor (Hoffman) occupied in the series' schema. The twist reveals that Hoffman was always just another participant being 'tested'. *Saw's* revelation sequences might appear to solve puzzles, but each departure opens up new problems for the next film to explore, and that trend even continues in its alleged 'Final Chapter', *Saw 3D*.

Kattelman's conclusion – that news reports about terrorism provide no resolution whereas *Saw* does – is unsound, then. The series' violence is never complete, and the lack of finality is unsettling since it implies that the captives' torment will continue. The vast majority of torture porn films follow suit, eschewing finality.[10] Torture porn filmmakers commonly adopt one of four conventional methods in repudiating narrative closure. The first involves undercutting what looks like a resolved ending. For example, *Madness* closes with two abductees (Tara and Chad) victoriously embracing, having vanquished their captors. Their clinch is coupled with a triumphant score that suggests resolution. However, moments later this tone is usurped by an epilogue in which a surviving clan-member claims a new casualty. This kind of twist ending – also found in *Invitation Only*, *Stash*, *The Hills Have Eyes*, and *Timber Falls*, for instance – gestures towards and then undercuts the possibility of closure. The tonal shift is unnerving, enhancing the horror that preceded it.

The second method is to reject any semblance of moral resolution. Films such as *Deathtube*, *Them*, *Oral Fixation*, *Steel Trap*, and *The Anniversary at Shallow Creek* close once all abductees are killed off. Only the antagonists survive, meaning that they can continue to cause suffering. *The Texas Chainsaw Massacre: The Beginning* and *Vacancy 2: The First Cut* are notable in that respect. Since both are prequels, the lead torturers cannot be brought to justice because they always-already persevere in the series' timeline. Thompson (2007) postulates that this means 'there is never any hope for the victims', insinuating that films should close with villains being punished for their crimes. However, where the status quo is not restored in torture porn narratives, the violence done therein is not necessarily condoned. The very idea that justice prevails, order is restored, and righteousness is preserved is a fantasy that softens violence's disturbing nature. Detractors who refer to torture porn's 'relentlessness' (O'Hagan, 2009; Newman, 2009b) are typically distressed by torture porn's bleak tone, but their responses attest to how emotionally provocative these films are. That disquiet is contingent on establishing 'hope for the victims' so that it can be undercut. Furthermore, although the antagonists survive, these narratives mainly document the protagonists' plights. These films end almost immediately after the sufferers are vanquished because the narratives are concerned with their fates.

Figure 4.1 Kate breaks the fourth wall in the final shot of *Creep* (2004, UK/Germany, dir Christopher Smith)

Films such as *Choose, Pelt, Spiderhole,* and *Tortura* represent a third trait: concluding with one protagonist still at their captor's mercy and with no opportunity to escape. Here, the abductee's plight is underscored, since their terror resonates beyond the narrative cessation. These films defy the prevailing narrative convention of imposing moral resolution to finalise plot arcs. The sufferers' stories remain incomplete, encouraging viewers to consider what will happen next. *House of 9, Gruesome, Senseless, Creep,* and *Straightheads* are among the torture porn films that make this call-to-audience explicit. In these cases, the lead protagonist looks directly into the camera in the final shot, breaking the 'fourth wall'. The horror, it is suggested, is far from over, lingering beyond the narrative's limits.

Thus, the fourth method is to imply that the tortureds' trauma will continue even if they have escaped immediate danger. More than 35 torture porn films – including *The Loved Ones, Shadow, Broken,* and *The Ordeal* – close with the lead protagonist alive, but emotionally and physically deconstructed.[11] In such cases, the sufferer's corporeal and personal decline is again underlined as the narrative's core concern. These four methods imply that once set in motion, the narrative structure cannot contain the horror its tortured protagonists undergo. Each mechanism emphasises how vital the wounded are to creating such meanings, substantiating that sufferers' ordeals are prioritised over sadistic pleasure in torture porn.

'This is a torture show. Where's the emotion?':[12] formal devices

Ide's (2008b) complaint that torture porn does not 'allow the audience a flicker of empathy' overlooks how emotionally provocative torture porn is. Contra to their detractors' assertions, torture porn's filmmakers routinely encode their films in ways that are attuned to sufferers' emotional positions rather than torturers' desires. Structural manipulation is only one narratological device that demonstrates encoded empathy for the tortured. For example, throughout the *Saw* series, abductee panic is expressed formally by speeding-up shots of protagonists struggling against their bonds. Shots that circle around the sufferer are employed to convey their feelings of entrapment. Fragmented injury shots are rapidly intercut with fearful facial expressions, expounding the connection between the sufferer's wounds and their emotional state. Similarly, most chainsaw-based killings in *The Texas Chainsaw Massacre: The Beginning*, including Holden's death, are depicted via rapid intercutting between the wounded, the tormentor, the point-of-injury, and the witness (in this case, Bailey). Shaking camerawork and a noticeable increase in editing pace during such sequences conveys the damage done to the sufferer's body: as it is subject to violent fragmentation, so too is the form. Elsewhere in the film, when lead protagonist Chrissie is captured, the camera swims in and out of focus to match her semi-consciousness. The mise-en-scene reflects the captives' plights during periods of heightened emotion, threat, or significant changes in their mental states. The subgenre's films may display torture, yet the protagonists' subjective reactions are given precedence over the torture itself: emotive impact is accentuated over bloodshed.

The tortureds' emotions 'take over' the mise-en-scene in numerous other ways across the subgenre. When lead protagonist Carole is deafened by an explosion in *Caged*, third-person shots are accompanied by muffled sound and high-pitched tinnitus-ringing to align narrative perspective with her impairment. This deficiency means she cannot locate her pursuer. Foregrounding her internal state heightens tension by providing experiential access to her vulnerability. This type of intimate engagement with sufferers' perspectives is rife in torture porn. *Martyrs*, *Dark Reality*, *Deathbell*, and *Breaking Nikki* are among the torture porn films that exhibit protagonists' psychological delusions within the frame without initially distinguishing their visions from diegetic reality. Memories and flashbacks similarly reify the tortureds' internal vantage points in *Stash* and *Senseless*, foregrounding the protagonists' mental states.

Other torture porn films manifest the tortureds' subjective perspectives while they suffer. During *I Spit on Your Grave*'s traumatic rape sequence, a blue-hued filter is employed to bleach out blurred-edged shots. The incident is portrayed from lead protagonist Jennifer's perspective, the effect mimicking her tear-filled field of vision. Delayed sound is also used to convey her subjective position. The dulled, reverberating sound-scape suggests that she is emotionally drowning, being overwhelmed with horror. These mechanisms provide access to her torment. Those subjective strategies vanish later in the film, denoting a shift in her role and moral position. In torture porn, stress is principally placed on whoever suffers. When Jennifer becomes a torturer in the film's second half, the narrative perspective is no longer aligned with her emotional state. Although Jennifer remains the narrative's lead protagonist insofar as her character arc propels the plot, the rapists' are depicted in greater detail once Jennifer begins her revenge campaign. Storch and Johnny are portrayed in their homes, Matthew's guilt-ridden visions of Jennifer are shown, as are fear-driven arguments among the group as they seek to erase evidence of their wrongdoing.

Thus, although the subgenre predominantly prioritises sufferers' perspectives, torturer point-of-view is not entirely excluded from torture porn's terrain. Both tortureds' and torturers' perspectives are presented in these films, even if the torturers' viewpoints are secondary to the sufferers'. *The Butcher* is an archetypal example. 80 per cent of the film is shot from the vantage point of its lead protagonist, Jae-hyun. In this case, the film is constituted by literal point-of-view shots. *The Butcher*'s conceit is that captives are forced to star in a snuff movie. Abductees are fitted with video-camera helmets. *The Butcher* is constituted by footage taken from Jae-hyun's helmet-cam, and from the captors' handheld video-cameras. So, when Jae-Hyun's fingers are cut off, his suffering is imparted from his perspective. Diametrically, the antago-nists' vantage-point is not offered in a sustained fashion. Killer-cam is reserved primarily for showing bloodshed after-the-fact rather than providing emotional access to the torturers as they inflict torture.

As 'torture porn' discourse has developed, Edelstein's (2006) admission that '[u]nlike the old seventies and eighties hack-'em-ups … the victims [in torture porn] are neither interchangeable nor expendable' has been lost. In a reversal of Edelstein's position, torture porn's detractors have habitually insisted that the films offer sadistic perspectives, and that para-digm does not tally with torture porn's content. Even where torturers' perspectives are available, as in the case of *The Butcher*, it does not follow that the viewer is encouraged to share in any enjoyment those charac-ters gain from causing suffering. Torturers' first-person perspectives are seldom adopted when depicting violence in-progress. For example, both *The Hills Run Red* and *The Hills Have Eyes* reserve antagonist point-of-view for stalking sequences and do not disclose the torturers' viewpoints as suffering is inflicted.

Figure 4.2   Becca feels like she is being watched from afar in *Dying Breed* (2008, Australia, dir Jody Dwyer)

The idea that point-of-view shots encourage the audience to adopt a sadistic perspective is further undermined by another prevailing technique. In numerous cases, shots are staged from what appears to be the antagonist's first-person perspective, creating the impression that protagonists are being stalked. That imperilment and the alleged accompanying sadistic pleasure are then undercut by revealing that the shots are unassigned, third-person perspectives. For instance, in *Dying Breed* repeated shots from high above a local townsperson (Liam) hint that the lead killer Rowan is watching Liam before the kill. Liam even looks up, apparently corroborating Rowan's presence. Rowan then emerges from the opposite direction: on the ground, entering screen right. The same diversion strategy is used early on in the film when one protagonist (Becca) urinates in the woods. The camera is situated at a distance, behind foliage, suggesting that the shot offers a voyeuristic gaze, 'confirming' Becca's fear that she is being watched. On hearing a noise to her left, Becca turns sharply, and the camera switches position to match her eyeline. Again, this second handheld shot implies the presence of a threatening voyeur, but both shots remain unassigned. Her boyfriend Jack's remark that '[i]t's their turf, they're watching' is played out via the camerawork, developing the sense that threat looms from every angle. Rather than offering a sadistic gaze, what seem to be perspectival shots are utilised in *Dying Breed* to foster empathy with stalkees' fearfulness. Moreover, this technique refutes the notion that horror film prioritises sadistic pleasure. By conspicuously undercutting what appears to be an alignment between the narrative perspective and the antagonist's outlook, the former is overtly distanced from the latter.

To deduce that 'these films play with the audience's identification with the torturer – *mainly* because the action is often witnessed through the perspective of the killer' (Riegler, 2010: 27–8, emphasis added) is an oversimplification, then. Indeed, the notion of 'identification' itself is insufficient. Identification suggests that perspectival shots alone trigger empathic engagement, but Riegler's statement is not attuned to the significance of torture porn's other formal techniques. Perspective shots can only validate other encoded messages. Moreover, identification readings insinuate that audiences straightforwardly concur with the seer's desires. Films may be encoded to encourage empathic responses, but that encoding does not guarantee identification.

The term 'sadistic' implies a great deal about the pleasures horror film offers. The gratifications of watching horror have been subject to detailed rumination (see Carroll, 1990; Hills, 2005), and so they will not be dwelt upon here. Of primary interest to the narratological discussion at hand is the assumption that torture porn's torturers are motivated by pleasure, and that their inclinations are validated by textual encoding. Melanie Phillips (2010) declares that torture porn's 'characters take ... pleasure in causing other human beings extreme agony', for instance, yet her conclusion is based on supposition rather than textual evidence. Even on the rare occasion that a torturer's perspective is placed at the narrative centre, their pleasure is not necessarily as palpable as the sadistic gaze interpretation would suggest.

The Human Centipede II is one of the few torture porn narratives to overtly prioritise its sexually violent torturer's view, and so is worth considering in this light. The lead protagonist (Martin) is obsessed with *The Human Centipede*. He abducts twelve individuals and kills three others in his quest to mimic his favourite movie's torturous modus operandi. Martin's home and work-life are portrayed, supplying insight into his existence. That Martin is the film's focus is most evident when one captive (Rachel) escapes. Unlike films such as *P2*, *Vacancy*, and *Turistas* where the camera follows captives who take flight, Rachel vanishes from the film she when drives away. *The Human Centipede II* remains fixed on Martin. Nevertheless, on the few occasions captives are depicted in Martin's absence, his insanity is highlighted. One abductee (Greg) protests, '[y]ou can't do this ... *The Human Centipede*'s a fucking film', for instance. As this is a sequel, *The Human Centipede II*'s audience presumably share Greg's stance on *The Human Centipede* rather than Martin's. In case there was any ambiguity that abducting people and stitching them mouth-to-anus is unacceptable behaviour, Greg's dialogue confirms that Martin's confusion between fiction and reality is a sign that he is deranged. The narrative is underpinned by this essential distance from Martin's mental state. Although Martin is the lead protagonist, the abductees provide the narrative's empathic core. Additionally, what overt pleasure Martin gains from the torture – his joyful tears as he oversees his human centipede, for example – is fleeting and is swiftly undercut. The torture itself is a disaster. Martin eventually kills his revolting captives, sobbing as he surveys their corpses. The reality is far removed from the fantasy he envisaged. When actualised, torture debunks rather than fulfils his desires. The film actively disavows sadistic pleasure then, despite Martin's narrative prominence.

Tony Hicks's (2009) proclamation that torture porn is driven by 'sadists thriving off extreme physical and psychological torture' assumes that the subgenre's torture arises from antagonists' personal, sexual gratification. This is true in some cases – such as *Captivity*, *Keepsake*, and *The Cellar Door* – yet the majority of torture-motives have little to do with sadistic pleasure. Torture porn's torture is variously inspired by moral or spiritual castigation (*Saw*, *Penance*, *Die*); the need to propagate a closed community (*The Hills Have Eyes 2*, *Timber Falls*, *Alive or Dead*); economic profit (*The Truth*, *Vacancy*, *Caged*); political impetuses (*Torture Room*, *Unthinkable*, *Senseless*); sociological research (*House of 9*, *Breathing Room*); hunger (*High Lane*, *Scarce*); and revenge (*The Horseman*, *Panic Button*, *Cherry Tree Lane*). Torture porn's antagonists may immorally inflict suffering for their own gain, but as this range of motives illustrates, they are not foremost pleasure-seeking sadists.

As objectors' assumptions regarding torturers' motives and pleasures evince, the sadistic gaze argument is prejudicial. As a result, moral judgements are imposed onto the texts in spite of narrative content. Some critics even display sadistic attitudes towards sufferers while seeking to denounce torture porn. For example, Terrell (2009) proffers that feelings of 'superiority and laughter' are prompted by watching torture porn's 'unlikeable' protagonists suffer (see also Charity, 2007). Other reviewers refer to protagonists as 'obnoxious...forgettable' (Huddleston, 2010), or 'vapid...[and] stupid' (Longworth, 2010), insinuating that personality flaws are sufficient to mark protagonists as disposable. Theresa Smith (2010) projects her own lack of empathy outwards, proclaiming that while watching torture porn, '*you* don't care what happens to these people, *you* just want it to end' (emphasis added, see also Collum in Piepenburg, 2012). These reporters interpret punishment as an inevitable consequence of protagonists' personal shortcomings, making the case that torture is inherently warranted, and thereby validating the cruelty the characters undergo.

That rhetoric of inevitability closes off moral debate by imposing a simplistic resolution paradigm, which does not fit the open endings so often found in torture porn. Terrell's stance is underpinned by a belief in causal justice: bad things happen to bad people. The same justificatory explanation is well-documented in responses to actual torture situations (Conroy, 2000: 100), and is a trait found more broadly in psychological studies concerning justice and blame (See Correia et al., 2007, 37; Gray and Wegner, 2010: 233; Batson et al., 2003: 1200). The causal justification involves replacing particularities – intricate networks of stimuli, responses and motivations, many of which coincidently converge – with easily digestible generalisations. Disregarding complexities by imposing ill-fitting pre-existent paradigms means bypassing rather than dealing with the core moral issues that drive torture porn.

Saw 3D offers a case by which to trial the proposition that sufferers 'get what they deserve'. Lead protagonist Bobby is abducted because he pretended to have previously survived one of lead antagonist John's torture games, and then profited by selling his contrived story. Bobby's fraud is a claim to have endured and survived John's traps, rather than a claim to have victoriously 'won' the game. Bobby's fraud marks him as callous and 'unlikeable', since he is disrespectful to those who have suffered. When tested, Bobby is subjected to the horrors he previously fabricated. This retributive turn appears to directly balance his wrong-doing. However, numerous complications undermine the idea that his torture is straightforwardly justified. Firstly, Bobby's final game involves having to pierce his pectorals with hooks and lifting himself on a chain–pulley system. He fails only because his pectorals rip out in the final seconds. Since he survives the torture he devised – enduring greater suffering than he claimed to in his lie – he should pass the trial. Instead he is punished further. Secondly, his failure to complete the test leads to his girlfriend (Joyce) being burned alive. Since Joyce is unaware of Bobby's fraudulence, her death denotes how imbalanced the punishment is. Thirdly, Joyce's death is paralleled with Jill (John's wife) being executed by Hoffman (John's successor). Unlike Joyce, Jill chose to enter into the 'game' and provokes her killer. Jill is murdered in retaliation for attempting to kill Hoffman in *Saw VI*'s denouement. *Saw 3D*'s opening trap also features a criminal female (Dina) being killed for her choice to do wrong. Dina, it is revealed, emotionally manipulated and cheated on her lovers (Brad and Ryan), who broke 'the law to fulfil her material needs'. Bookending the film, Dina and Jill are both tortured for their conscious involvement in criminal activity. In both cases, their lovers are implicated in that choice. This theme impacts on Joyce's story. Joyce too dies because of her involvement with a dishonourable lover (Bobby). Bobby's game drives the narrative, and because Joyce is his 'goal', her imperilment is placed at the text's heart. That Joyce does not elicit her maltreatment throws the 'justice' of Hoffman's/John's torture schema – that which results in Dina's and Jill's deaths – into doubt. The film's meanings are not constituted by Bobby's 'game' alone. The narrative's moral dynamic is not explicable by focusing on one characters' actions, or proposing that they are punished because they are 'unlikeable'.

Torture porn's content does not support Terrell's hypothesis that the audience are encouraged to laugh at suffering. The subgenre's films offer scant proof to substantiate the proposition that torturers select their captives based on their personalities. The vast majority of initial abductions – such as those found in *Wolf Creek*, *The Hills Have Eyes*, and *Turistas* – are characterised as unjust because they are unprovoked. Even where sufferers incite their torturers, the distinction between inflictor and sufferer requires delineation. If the protagonists suffer because they are 'unlikeable', the torturers should also suffer causal fates. Yet, as this chapter has already established, reprehensible antagonists often go unpunished in torture porn. Moreover, in the 'karmic' interpretation, if antagonists do suffer, it must be in return for their loathsome behaviour (abducting and torturing). However, this means that wilfully harming others is rendered as equivalent to being 'unlikeable', since both merit the same penalty (suffering). This surely cannot be the case, and torture porn's content does not verify such an explanation. When actions are assessed rather than *people*, it becomes apparent that 'just desserts' readings are insufficient for grasping the moral conflicts represented in torture porn.

Hence, it is vital to assess the material presented on-screen before making judgments about torture porn's meanings. The relationships between torturer, tortured, and their actions – which will be addressed in the next chapter – are much more complex than anti-torture porn rhetoric would suggest. In evaluating a film's moral vision, it is necessary to account for (a) actions, not assumptions about virtue or plain distaste for characters' personalities, (b) the evidence supplied by the film itself, not presuppositions about character motivations, filmmaker intentions, or audience responses, and (c) how those elements are combined into a dynamic in the narrative whole. These three propositions are inter-twined. The particular should be related to the conceptual – in this instance, filmic detail should be related to morality – to give a fuller account of torture porn and its characters.

'Horror Has a Human Heart':[13] conclusion

The sadistic gaze paradigm is founded on a paradox. Torture porn viewers are said to be cynically distanced from and desensitised to violent imagery, and yet simultaneously presumed to enjoy that violence. Engagement is a prerequisite for pleasure, and so the two cannot concurrently hold true. This muddle arises from misreading torture porn's ambiguities as apathetic ambivalences. Morris (2010: 51) concurs that this misinterpretation has stunted critical engagement with torture porn. Morris construes 'being [morally] conflicted' itself as an indication that the viewer has confronted moral issues, since being conflicted is evidence of the 'capacity to feel the pain or the joy of others', be they torturers or tortured. For Morris, 'someone without both of these emotional capabilities does not get torture-horror and is morally deficient' (see also Ochoa, 2011: 206). The confusion between immoral sadistic pleasure and amoral apathy in some pundits' assessments of torture porn certainly confirms that they might not have contemplated ethical issues with enough care, although this insufficiency may stem as much from failing to engage with the films themselves as it does from neglecting ethics.

Torture porn's moral dynamics are not reducible to a dichotomous separation between torturers and tortured. Julie Hilden's (2007) observation that torture porn is antithetical to 'the endless, often bloodless and supposedly well-deserved violence of summer' blockbusters hints that torture porn films eschew clearly defined moral coding. 'Good' does not necessarily or even typically win out over 'evil' in torture porn narratives. As Hilden's comparison to 'acceptable' mainstream representations of violence implies, torture porn offers relatively realistic depictions of physiology and ethics: the two elements are intertwined because morality is played out via physical violence in these films.

Moral binarism ('good' versus 'evil') is refuted by torture porn narratives' ethical complexities. Consequently, torture porn's violent interactions are seldom simple affairs. As this chapter has illustrated, sufferers' stances are habitually prioritised in torture porn narratives. However, torture porn's protagonists typically move from apparent innocence to rather murkier, morally dubious positions as the narratives progress. The moral tensions that result from those shifting character positions will be explored in the next chapter.

5
'Some are Victims. Some are Predators. Some are Both':[1] Torturous Positions

The notion that torture porn fosters 'sadistic' responses results from a failure to probe how torture porn's filmmakers use form – narrative structure, sound cues, camera position, and so forth – to convey sufferers' emotions and perspectives. The sadistic gaze argument is also flawed because it implies that torture is an interaction between two dichotomous parties – torturer and victim – whereby torturers are entirely 'evil', and victims are wholly innocent. For instance, Hicks (2009) describes torture porn as being constituted by 'graphic depictions of innocents imprisoned by sadists'. Alex Williams (2006) also separates 'sadist' and 'victims' when synopsising *Saw II*: Williams brushes over the violence protagonists do to each other in the film by attributing 'sadism' to John, *Saw*'s lead antagonist. The adjective 'sadistic' is often used to describe torture porn's antagonists (see Williamson, 2007c; Wigley, 2007), the violence depicted (see Beckford, 2008), the subgenre's audience (see Kenny in Johnson, 2007), filmmakers (Molitorisz, 2012), and the films themselves (see Gordon, 2006). Protagonists-turned-torturers, on the other hand, are not directly accused of sadism in any of the press articles consulted while compiling this book.

The assumption that torture is a dichotomous binary relationship is not exclusive to torture porn discourse. The same supposition is made in theoretical responses to torture itself. For example, in Scarry's influential work on torture, she surmises that 'torture happens between *two people*' (1985: 139, Scarry's emphasis). In this view, the 'victim' is subordinated to the torturer's dominance, which is expressed as violence. Torture porn's objectors have typically adopted a similarly dichotomous stance, responding to torture porn narratives as if characters represent either 'good' or 'evil'. Torture porn narratives rarely depict morality in such stark terms, and their failure to fit the 'good versus evil' moral dichotomy imposed upon them has resulted in the subgenre being dismissed as amoral or even immoral (see Whedon in Utichi, 2012; Wise, 2011; Driscoll, 2007).

Oversimplifying torture in this way entails moral typecasting: the 'general perceptual tendency to view others as either victims of pain (moral patients) or perpetrators of misdeeds (moral agents), but not both' (Gray and Wegner, 2010: 233). Moral typecasting involves assessing whether individuals appear to deserve their fates rather than judging deeds. That is, roles are assigned by making estimations about virtue, and vice versa. Evaluations of fictional drama are often skewed in the same way. Protagonists may be morally typecast as innocent, heroic, or plainly 'good' based on narrative position alone. Thus, narrative conventions frequently prejudice how characters' actions are interpreted. If lead protagonists' intentions are presumed to be inherently 'good', one may overstate how unjustly a protagonist has been treated if they suffer, or overlook the immoral acts a protagonist perpetrates, for instance. Another consequence of this supposition is that even where protagonists commit exactly the same wrongs as antagonists, those deeds may be deciphered differently. Adopting a deontic stance – focusing on the morality of acts rather than virtue – throws such partialities into relief.

Torture porn's character interactions mostly involve blunt cruelty, but that does not mean they are simple. Scarry (1985: 36) contends that the gulf between torturer and tortured is unassailable because pain means 'the distance between their physical realities is colossal'. In torture porn, however, violence does not just occur between parties who occupy unwavering positions: torturers may be tortured, and those tortured often consequently become torturers. Although Morris (2010: 45) recognises that in 'most torture-horror, one or more of the victims acquires at some point the intentions of a torturer', he describes the shift as binary role-reversal. Characters are either torturers or victims in this view, which does not adequately address the moral complexities that arise from such transformations. Morris's assertion, for example, risks advocating torture if it is brought about in return for suffering previously endured. The ethical implications resulting from characters' moral inconsistencies need accounting for. Torture affects character relations, causing them to be reimagined. That transference underlines violence's traumatic, disruptive effects. Protagonists move between tortured and torturer positions, demonstrating that these are not dichotomous poles, and rendering the lines between those roles indistinct.

The notion that torture is a binary interaction is further debunked by a third prevailing character position. Torture porn's torture is typically played out via torturer, tortured, and *witness*. These witnesses are harmed by the torture they observe, and/or augment the tortureds' suffering by witnessing it. Scarry does not account for witnesses, despite drawing on torture in order to dissect agony's incommunicability. In Scarry's bilateral interpretation, the only witness to the tortureds' suffering is the torturer (1985: 53). Pain then is stripped of emotional resonance because it only signifies the torturer's success. Torture porn's witnesses undercut that dichotomy, and torture's significations require reconsideration on those grounds.

The aim of this chapter is to unpick the intersections between these character positions. The conceptual framework – morality – elucidates that these seemingly fixed positions are actually relational. The chapter begins by illustrating that torture porn's protagonists are not innocent victims per se. This is clearly exemplified when tortured protagonists become torturers, and in films where the lead protagonist is also the narrative's lead torturer. These latter cases raise doubts over the moral righteousness of retaliation. The chapter's final stages will be devoted to examining how torture porn's diegetic witnesses expose moral complications. Contra to detractors' complaints that torture is foregrounded to provide one-dimensional, sadistic pleasures in torture porn, the violence depicted in these films complicates characterisation and stimulates ethical questioning.

'Do you think I chose this?':[2] problems with victims and virtue

Since torture is commonly envisaged as a dichotomous binary interaction, 'torturer' and 'tortured' carry opposing connotations in 'torture porn' discourse. Torture porn's torturers are typically described as sadists and so, in contrast, torture porn's sufferers are implied to be 'victims'. Although possibly intended as shorthand for 'person on whom the torture is inflicted', 'victim' also intimates that the tortured party is a righteous, innocent sufferer. That divergence between 'victim' and 'sadist' creates an impression that the two positions are stable, balanced and fixed. Even when antagonists are tortured in retaliation for their immoral actions then, they are rarely described as victims. It is insufficient to presume that a character's actions are morally homogeneous, since doing so implies that the character is inherently 'good' or 'evil'. Protagonists should not be perceived as morally righteous throughout a given narrative merely because they are initially or predominantly limned

Figure 5.1   Playing the innocent: Tonya in the opening of *Breathing Room* (2008, USA, dirs John Suits and Gabriel Cowan)

as sufferers. Rather than using the overtly value-laden terms 'victim' and 'sadist' then, 'protagonist' and 'antagonist' will be utilised to refer to the role a character chiefly occupies in the narrative arc. 'Tortured' and 'torturer', along with 'captive'/'abductee' and 'captor'/'abductor', will be used to denote character positions in the moment being described, with the proviso that those positions may shift across the narrative.

The subgenre's films themselves customarily undermine attempts to impose virtue – reading characters as inherently 'good' or 'bad' – based on their inceptive positions. Indeed, numerous torture porn films adopt narrative twists that redefine apparently stable roles. In *Breathing Room*, for instance, lead torturer Tonya is cast as the film's lead protagonist. When Tonya is introduced, she seems to be one of the captives held in a laboratory. The film opens with Tonya's fearful breathing in pitch blackness. As she falls into the laboratory setting, naked and cowering, the narrative assumes her perspective, sharing her (apparent) attempt to comprehend her surroundings. Tonya is thereby established as the film's vulnerable, sympathetic centre from the first scene. This alignment continues until the climax. Once her final cellmate (Lee) is mortally wounded, Tonya's expression switches from trepidation to angered disgust, then to a wry smile as she leaves him bleeding to death. In parallel to Tonya's fraught, vulnerable entrance in the film's opening shots, here she looks at Lee coldly, calmly turning out the lights as she leaves the laboratory. She washes the blood from her hands and starts the process again with an alternative group in another room. The revelation that Tonya was a lead abductor entirely inverts her character position and the moral meanings of her actions.[3] The switch reframes her 'innocent' attempts to escape as facilitating other captives' torment. Furthermore, the next room Tonya enters contains prisoners who resemble the previous cell's occupants. The abductees fall into types – the alpha-male hero, the aloof outsider, and so forth – accentuating that *Breathing Room*'s twist was contingent on Tonya herself being misinterpreted as a standard type: the helpless victim. As *Breathing Room* illustrates, performing and *being* a victim are entirely separate.

Narratives supply limited information from biased perspectives. These restrictions are clear where characters preliminarily presented as cruel torturers are revealed to have been previously wronged by tortured captives. Twist denouements again challenge the notion that 'right' and 'wrong' can be straightforwardly assigned to acts based on character positions and narrative perspective. *Nine Dead*'s abductor, known only as Shooter, is obscured at the film's outset. He is portrayed from a distance, in silhouette, or by concentrating only on his hands. Shooter spends the majority of the film's duration masked. Both his identity and motives are uncovered only in *Nine Dead*'s closing minutes. In contrast to their faceless captor, the captives are visible throughout, and their outrage is discernible from the outset. A binary is established, connoting that the captives have been unjustly wronged by their captor. By the climax however, Shooter is unveiled as a grieving father. Each captive played some role in the events leading to the death of his son (Wade). Lead protagonist and District Attorney Kelly, for instance, planted evidence that ensured Wade's wrongful prison conviction. Shooter's explanation for their abduction is accompanied by a sentimental string score, encoding his tale sympathetically despite his crimes and his introduction as a torturer. The opposite is true of Kelly, who is unremorseful for her part in Wade's death. Once freed and no longer in danger, she cold-bloodedly kills Shooter and the two remaining captives – including her child's father – in order to obscure her part in Wade's death. This reversal exposes Kelly's criminality, which is concretised in the final shot of Kelly fleeing from the police. Shooter may have been literally masked, but Kelly was also disguised. The twist exposes the extent to which inaugural semblances can impact on moral judgments. Conventional, empathetic protagonist-positions are established only to be undermined as the tortureds' immorality unfurls.

These mechanisms demonstrate that torture porn's morality cannot be grasped based on suppositions about character roles, since (a) narratives offer partial perspectives on events, (b) characters' motives are often contingent on events that occur prior to the diegetic present, and (c) characters may shift away from the roles they preliminarily appear to occupy. Virtue-based judgements do not offer a full-enough picture of torture porn's ethical meanings. If virtue is to be assessed, it must be so by the complete sum of a character's actions and intentions. Narrative drama's snapshots do not permit this kind of adjudication. The positional and perspectival progressions found in torture porn resist such role-demarcation. For both reasons, it is more prudent to evaluate deeds rather than virtue.

'Survival Can Be Murder':[4] from tortured to torturer

Unlike *Breathing Room*, which withholds then reveals information about the lead character's role, films such as *Captivity* and *Hostel* depict protagonists who become torturers after undergoing torture themselves. Such position shifts raise different questions about how narrative effects moral judgment. *Captivity* is aligned with lead protagonist Jennifer's confusion and suffering for the majority of the film. Seven torture sequences close with Jennifer losing consciousness, and these lapses are reified formally by fading to black.[5] Her torturers remain faceless for the first 56 minutes of the film, while Jennifer occupies virtually every shot until that moment, underlining that she is the focal point. In contrast, the torturers' blankness renders their pleasure hard to comprehend. The narrative clearly invests in Jennifer then, positioning her in the archetypal righteous hero-protagonist role. Yet, those connotations are problematised by the film's epilogue. After escaping her confinement, Jennifer becomes a torturer. In order to achieve 'redemption', she hunts untried criminals such as a 'triple woman killer' who 'slip[ped] though [a] legal loophole'. Although she only targets allegedly 'guilty' parties, her vigilantism is nevertheless immoral. Justice is measured by Jennifer alone, and her willingness to torture and kill connotes that Jennifer is too unstable to make rational assessments. The ending is less assured than Jennifer's final voice-over assertion – 'they got what they deserved' – proposes. Narratological allegiance with Jennifer's perspective continues in the epilogue, but that sustained loyalty conflicts with the narrative's predominant mode: fostering distrust for and distance from Jennifer's torturers. That is, Jennifer's slippage into the torturer position is particularly disquieting because a torturer/tortured dichotomy was so clearly established and maintained during her captivity. The disparity between Jennifer's narrative position and her subsequent actions underscores how morally questionable her final deeds are.

Characters' transpositions from sufferers to inflictors are more ethically problematic than has been accounted for in 'torture porn' discourse. For example, in Middleton's (2010: 22) reading of *Hostel*, Paxton is the hero, whom 'the viewer can identify [with] and cheer on'. Middleton states that Paxton's violent actions in *Hostel*'s climax are 'cathartic' and 'justified by the brutality of his enemies' (see also Thompson, 2007). Middleton validates Paxton's violence by creating a moral dichotomy between 'hero/protagonist' and 'enemy/antagonist', assuming that Paxton's murders are justified by his role. Yet Paxton's 'hero' status is not as clearly established as Middleton's interpretation suggests. Paxton's fellow traveller Josh is painted as the lead protagonist in the film's early stages. Only when Josh dies is the focus displaced onto Paxton. Josh's demise undermines the notion that character roles are fixed in *Hostel*. Indeed, Paxton's violence evinces his motion *away* from heroism.

Paxton's slippage from tortured to torturer undercuts the supposition that morality can be assessed by role. The impression that Paxton is 'good' stems from his apparently selfless actions in *Hostel*'s climax; Paxton risks his own safety by returning to save another captive (Kana), and seemingly avenges his friend Josh's death by killing Josh's torturer (the Dutch Businessman). However, Paxton is initially characterised as obnoxious, making odious statements such as 'I hope bestiality is legal in Amsterdam because that girl is a fucking hog!', and using derogatory terms such as 'fag', 'pussy', and 'bitch' in earlier scenes. Readings that employ Paxton's virtue to explain his actions must also account for his detestable attitudes. Moreover, Paxton's moral outlook is established before he becomes a 'hero', and the thematic strands introduced earlier in the text impact on what Paxton's later actions mean. Midway through the narrative, Paxton recounts that when he was eight, he watched a girl drown rather than risking his life to save her; '[she] was yelling for me to help her...I could have done more'. Paxton's inaction evidences his willingness to prioritise his own safety above others'. Although Paxton returns to save Kana when he hears her cries for help, his action is not necessarily motivated by concern for Kana's well-being as much as it is by assuaging his past guilt. The rescue could be interpreted as signalling Paxton's transformation into a 'hero', but the form instead suggests that Paxton's egoistic characterisation remains unchanged, despite his role-shift. In the context established, Kana is a symbol for Paxton. His self-orientation is echoed in the mise-en-scene, which is driven by Paxton's emotions. Musical cues alter with Paxton's fear and threats to his well-being. When Kana jumps before a speeding train after being rescued, Paxton's horrified eyes are shown, since *his* horror is central rather than *her* death.

This context underlines how unethical Paxton's decision to torture the Dutch Businessman is. Paxton is not in any immediate danger when he becomes a torturer, so he does not act in self-defence.[6] Middleton reads the torture-murder as evidencing Paxton's heroism, presumably since it avenges Josh's death. Even if that were an ethically sound justification, the act is self-motivated rather than selfless. Paxton's choice to torture the Businessman by removing his fingers mirrors the torture *Paxton* underwent, not Josh. Paxton is interested in avenging the wrongs done to *himself*. This action cannot be retributive, since it does not provide moral balance, it only assuages Paxton's personal anger.[7]

Paxton's revenge is far more significant than Morris (2010: 48) accounts for in terming it 'a retributivist back door'. Morris views Paxton as a correlative retributivist, who takes 'a finger for a finger'. Yet Paxton's anger is not aimed at Paxton's torturer. He takes the *wrong* fingers. Deciphering Paxton's actions as heroic means reading the same violent deeds – finger removal and murder – differently depending on who inflicts pain on whom. Reading Paxton as a heroic avenger means that when the Businessman suffers, his pain is construed relative to his blameworthiness. When Josh and Paxton suffer, it is explicated according to their presumed innocence. Attributing justice divergently in this case demonstrates the sway character typology and narrative devices have on moral judgment. This dissonance entails bypassing the unnecessary suffering caused via revenge. The Businessman's prior wrongdoing cannot make Paxton's decision to torture morally acceptable.

Hostel's content verifies how ethically problematic Paxton's deeds are. As Paxton murders the Businessman, the extra-diegetic score is horror-themed rather than triumphant, and is reminiscent of the music that accompanied Paxton's torment in the torture-chamber. By linking the two incidents, the score denotes that Paxton becomes akin to his own torturer in choosing to hunt the Businessman. Various parallels are established between Paxton and the film's other nameless torturers, connoting Paxton's role-slippage. Paxton dresses in his torturer's business-wear in order to escape the torture-space, meaning he steps into his assailant's shoes both literally and figuratively. Once he does, he kills at least six people. He also cuts off Kana's dangling eye with torture-chamber implements: despite his intent to help Kana, in deed he replaces and continues her torturer's efforts. A torturer Paxton meets in the torture-chamber's dressing room proclaims 'pussy is pussy', mirroring Paxton's own derogatory comments early in the film. The gap between Paxton's early verbal violence and the physical torture he inflicts in the closing scenes is bridged via the unnamed torturer's misogynistic proclamations.

These positional elements crucially affect *Hostel*'s moral meanings. The narrative closure that follows the Businessman's death only superficially justifies Paxton's choices. The solemn music accompanying Paxton's departure in the final shot casts doubt over murder's potential to resolve. The minor score is particularly striking since it contrasts with the major key music accompanying Paxton's earlier attempt to escape by rail. The earlier scene's uplifting melody conveys that Paxton's getaway would be a victory, but the music sharply falls away when Paxton hears the

Businessman's voice. The exultant score is aborted along with Paxton's retreat, connoting that Paxton forsakes any chance of either triumph or escape by choosing to kill. Hence, when major strains enter the closing soundscape, they are intersected by bass notes that move from major to minor key. The tone is fitful, not conclusive. *Hostel: Part II*'s opening – in which Paxton is bluntly decapitated – confirms that Paxton's violence provides no justificatory closure.

'Justice is Blind. So is Vengeance':[8] avenging torturers

Morris's and Middleton's interpretations of *Hostel* rely on Paxton – understood as the lead protagonist – providing a stable moral index. The suffering Paxton inflicts is evaluated according to the supposition that his actions offer narrative resolution. The emotional satisfaction that may stem from seeing antagonists castigated conflicts with the basic deontological principle that killing is wrong. Since it bridges between the twin intuitions that violence is 'wrong' and yet revenge is acceptable, revenge fiction is founded on moral conflict. As Jeffrie Murphy (1990: 210) theorises, despite principled opposition to revenge, 'most typical, decent, mentally healthy people' approve of 'righteous' retaliation in a 'common sense' way. Rather than justifying immoral behaviour, however, revenge creates dialectics in which the supposed connection between justice and morality is problematised (see Rosebury, 2009: 20).

Tortured-torturer position shifts are only one means of highlighting such conflicts. Numerous torture porn narratives probe the relationship between ethics and protagonist positions by prioritising revenge from the outset. In revenge-based torture porn, the central torturer is often also the narrative's lead protagonist and empathic core. Many such films – including *The Tortured*, *The Horseman*, and *Law Abiding Citizen* – centre on parents whose children are abducted and killed, and who exact revenge by kidnapping and torturing. The wrong done to the protagonists is established as a point-of-entry, and the narrative perspective remains aligned with the protagonists as inaugural sufferers. This allows the filmmakers to explore moral dilemmas that ensue from protagonists' engagement in immoral acts.

To illustrate, revenge is never vindicated outright in *7 Days*, despite opening with an emotionally-loaded stimulus. Lead protagonist Bruno abducts and tortures Anthony for raping and killing Jasmine, Bruno's eight year-old daughter. After torturing Anthony for a week, Bruno relinquishes himself to the police. When asked '[d]o you still think vengeance is the right answer? ... [do] you regret what you've done?', Bruno flatly answers 'no'. His ambivalence does not indicate moral indifference, but rather Bruno's inability to balance his unethical behaviour with his desire to commit those acts. That is, his conflicted state does not mean *7 Days* itself is amoral, but rather that it is morally provocative.

That ethical provocation stems from narrative construction. Bruno is established as the wronged party, but the narrative arc gradually reveals how questionable his revenge impetus is. Other characters preliminarily support Bruno's campaign, suggesting that he is right to seek revenge. A gas station attendant and other parents congratulate Bruno, and even police officers ask why they should prevent Bruno from harming Anthony. That initial empathy is misleading. When the mother of another of Anthony's targets (Diane) publically decries Bruno's revenge, Bruno kidnaps and assaults her. These actions are clearly unjustifiable, yet abducting and brutalising is precisely what Bruno did to Anthony. Bruno's retaliation is not justified because Anthony has committed crimes, then. Bruno's unprovoked attack on Diane elucidates that imprisoning and hurting other people is immoral per se, despite the prevailing intuition that Anthony deserves his fate.

The narrative exemplifies how tenuous the line between guilt and innocence is. Bruno's anger is understandable. However, the torture is laid bare, and Bruno's revenge is evacuated of emotive satisfaction. The narrative tone remains cold. The film's soundscape is crucial in establishing that distance between Bruno's anger and the instance of revenge. The film has no extra-diegetic score, lacking music that would conventionally cue shifts in Bruno's journey from sufferer to torturer. Also, Bruno never utters a word to Anthony. Bruno's silent stoniness casts doubt over his motivation. Anthony's protest – 'you're worse than me … you don't even seem to be enjoying yourself' – draws attention to the disparity between Bruno's emotionally removed manner and his supposed anger. These gaps highlight how questionable Bruno's actions are. Bruno's deeds gradually erode the apparently clear moral dichotomy established in the film's opening scenes. The narrative does not elicit salacious, emotionally fuelled responses to violence then. Instead, the narrative leads to a pivotal moral question: at what point do Bruno's acts cease to be heroic?

'Deep Down … We're All Killers':[9] who is capable of and responsible for torture?

Films such as *7 Days* refute the notion that suffering equates to victimhood per se by collapsing the expected torturer/tortured dichotomy. These narratives do not just exhibit violence's physical impacts, but also torture's emotional and moral effects, both on torturer and tortured. As Conroy (2000: 88) observes of genuine torture, 'most torturers are normal people...most of us could be the barbarian of our dreams as easily as we could be the victim' (see also Otterman, 2007: 58). Conroy's second clause magnifies the terror of the first: under the right circumstances anyone could be tortured or could become a torturer. This horror pervades torture porn, since the subgenre's narratives primarily pertain to the human capacity for inflicting and enduring suffering.

Protagonists' propensity for exacting and undergoing violence is disturbing, and raises torture porn's most uncomfortable moral challenges. As is befitting of the horror idiom, discomfort does not alienate, but rather involves audiences in those moral quandaries. Often audiences are directly prompted to consider how they would react to having their capacity for violence tested. Nine torture porn films, including *The Last House on the Left*, *Exam*, and *Unthinkable*, pose such questions to the audience in their taglines. For example, *Hunger*'s tagline asks '[h]ow far would *you* go to survive?', while *Saw*'s asks '[h]ow much blood will *you* shed?' Even if it remains unclear whether agony results from enduring injury, or whether anguish results from doling out torture – the *Saw* tagline does not specify *whose* blood 'you' will shed – these questions are most commonly positioned from the perspective of one who suffers.

That onus is concretised where protagonists self-torture in order to escape. Numerous films including *Hush*, *The Devil's Rejects*, and *Meat Grinder* feature abductees harming themselves; cutting off or breaking their fingers in order to escape handcuffs, or tearing nailed-down limbs free in order to escape confinement. Self-torture blurs the torturer/ tortured distinction. Torture is not an infliction from without in these instances: torture is exposed as a collaborative process whereby captives become their own torturer. The self-torture motif draws on genuine torture principles. Since the 1950s, torture techniques such as stress-positioning have been designed to turn the captive's own body against them. In these forms of torment, the tortured 'does battle with his or her own body. The prisoner can come to see the pain as self-inflicted; it continues when no oppressor is present' (Conroy, 2000: 169). Self-imposed suffering is widespread in torture porn because its double-injury is so horrific. For instance, Riegler (2010: 27) notes that *Saw*'s most 'excruciating pain is self-inflicted'. '[E]xcruciating' indicates that events such as Lawrence sawing through his foot to escape in *Saw* provoke visceral responses, engaging the audience. Such reactions are empathic, involving an instinctive form of self-appraisal about one's own capacity to engage in violence under duress.

These queries are intertwined with more complex conundrums regarding who is responsible for the suffering in such cases: the captor who coerces, or the captive who enacts violence on themselves. If the torturer is deemed culpable, the limit of their liability requires delineation. For example, if the tortured individual inflicts violence on others subsequent to their suffering, the torturer may also be held accountable in some way for the ensuing violence. Narrative cause–effect structures may impact on how characters' positional changes and their moral responsibilities are understood. For example, one interpretation of Jennifer's arc from tortured to torturer in *Captivity* is that she is transformed by the narrative's events. In this construal, the causal structure partially absolves Jennifer of the torture she inflicts in *Captivity*'s epilogue: it is her abductors' fault that she becomes a torturer. This reading is disturbing for two reasons. First, it divests Jennifer of responsibility for her conscious choice to inflict pain once freed and no longer in danger. Second, the impact narrative development – typically from complication to resolution – and emotive engagement with lead protagonists have on assumptions about morality must be accounted for. As with revenge-themed torture porn, to comprehend Jennifer's acts of torture as morally acceptable is to mistake narrative resolution or emotional satisfaction for justice.

The Torturer combines these concerns, encompassing tortured-torturer slippage, self-torture, and shifting narrative perspective. The film follows Rick, a military interrogator who is ordered to torture suspected terrorist Ayesha. In order to probe Rick's capacity for violence and accountability for his deeds, torture is depicted in two conflicting ways. The diegetic present is set in Rick's debriefing session with his commanding officer (Doc), and is intersected by flashbacks to the torture itself, seemingly relayed from Rick's perspective. However, contrary to this point-of-entry and the film's title, *The Torturer*'s opening half facilitates emotive connection with Ayesha. The flashbacks are not strictly mediated via Rick's memory. Every sequence begins and closes with Ayesha in the torture-room. Rick is an interrupting, antagonistic presence. Although Ayesha is masked and gagged, her discomfort is evinced, for instance, via her struggle against a mosquito that bites her hand. Empathy is fostered for her position despite her inability to verbally express her suffering. In contrast, Rick's jargonistic, contradictory responses to Doc's enquiries and his aggressive manner when dealing with Ayesha encode him as an ambiguous and potentially unsympathetic character.

Irrespective of Rick's initial proposition – that he 'felt nothing during the interrogation' – in due course he confesses that interrogation involved 'mindgames so complex' that he became 'trapped in them' himself. At first, he states that he was 'just doing [his] job'. Eventually he undertakes liability for devising the torture method and 'fail[ing] to stop the interrogation'. Vitally, he confirms that he was not wholly coerced into conducting torture. He is torn between professional 'duty' and his compassion for Ayesha. He concludes that 'torture is wrong' and that 'there are two victims' – tortured and torturer – in each instance of torture. The breakdown between tortured and torturer reaches its fullest expression as Rick binds and gags his superior (Doc) to her office chair, physicalising that positional collapse. Doc's punishment literally parallels Ayesha's torture, since both are bound to chairs and tormented by Rick. Doc's castigation also figuratively parallels Rick's inner-torment and his sense of feeling duty 'bound'. Rick may have tortured Ayesha, but Doc is also culpable for setting the order and ratifying every deed Rick claims to have engaged in, including Rick's false confession that he 'brutally' raped and murdered Ayesha.

The Torturer affirms that the divergence between versions of 'right' and 'wrong' is dependent on presumed roles, such as 'government-authorised torturer' or 'narrative hero'. Yet, the denouement – in which Rick is revealed to have rescued rather than killed Ayesha – underlines that positions are always in flux. Rick's preliminary characterisation as arrogant torturer is reversed via the revelation that he rescued rather than killed Ayesha. It is also intimated that while the state would permit murdering a torture suspect, Rick would be condemned for abetting Ayesha's escape. *The Torturer* is founded on thematic conflicts between subjective, immediate involvement and distanced rationalisations, between emotive, personal responses and rule- or role-based duties. *The Torturer* illustrates the effect shifting character positions and narrative perspectives have on what initially appear to be clearly defined moral quandaries.

'The Audience Isn't the Only One Watching':[10] witnesses

Despite their hands-off approach to torture, leaders such as Doc share some responsibility for the violence they sanction. In the same regard, those who witness rather than physically participate in torture are drawn into and significantly complicate the moral flux. This is particularly the case when lead protagonists are witnesses rather than captives or abductors per se. Witnesses are situated in three ways that designate further role slippages and amplify the ethical issues raised so far.

First, as *Saw III* exemplifies, witnessing is active involvement. The first casualty in lead protagonist Jeff's test is Danica. Prior to the diegetic

present, Danica witnessed Jeff's son (Dylan) die in a hit-and-run accident but did not testify at the driver's trial. Danica thereby sought to
distance herself from the death she witnessed. Resultantly, the driver was
not punished adequately in Jeff's view. John, Danica's abductor, force-
fully iterates her involvement by imprisoning her in a freezer, placing
her under Jeff's judgement. For Jeff, witnessing and subsequent inaction
renders Danica as culpable for Dylan's death as the hit-and-run driver
was. Where Danica could not have saved Dylan, Jeff has the chance to
take hands-on action to 'grant her the gift of life'. Jeff refuses, sentencing
her to death. Jeff's judgment is impugned via Danica's and Jeff's parallel
roles as passive witnesses. If Danica is accountable for Dylan's demise,
Jeff is even more condemnable for witnessing Danica's death despite his
ability to rescue her. Danica's torture only intensifies Jeff's grief, adding
to his suffering (not least since her death is part of his torture test). Jeff's
hypocrisy creates tensions that flag the moral problems at hand.

Second, witnessing is torturous. Jeff's torment is augmented by his exposure to Danica's torture. In *The Girl Next Door*, witnessing is more directly
equated with punishment. *The Girl Next Door*'s narrative is constituted
by lead protagonist David's memories. As an adolescent, he witnessed his
adult neighbour (Ruth) torturing her orphaned niece (Meg). The events
are chronicled from David's childhood perspective, intertwining the
story of Meg's imprisonment with David's disempowerment. Being only
a juvenile, David feels helpless to hinder Meg's suffering. The parallel
between David's powerlessness and Meg's subjugation is elucidated when
David is held captive while Meg is branded. Witnessing is spotlighted
as a source of horror: David declares 'I don't want to see this', to which
Ruth replies, '[t]hen close your fucking eyes'. Ruth's conspirators – other
neighbourhood adolescents – stop David from leaving, and his thwarted
desire to escape is reflected by cutting to a peaceful exterior shot as the
branding begins. The lasting impact the events have on David's life verifies that witnessing is torturous. As an adult narrator, he confesses that he
is 'plagued with the torment of failing somebody again'. This distress is
reified in his actions. In the opening, the adult David resuscitates a home-
less man injured in a hit-and-run incident. Unlike the inactive onlookers
around him, David understands that seeing is a verb: witnessing is active,
regardless of whether the witness chooses to participate.

It is not only his inability to save Meg that haunts David, but also
his complicity in her suffering. Since to see is to participate, witnessing
contributes to the tortureds' suffering. This theme is established early on
in the narrative when Ruth punishes Meg's sister (Susan) for Meg's 'bad
behaviour': Meg hits Ruth's son because he touches Meg's breast. Ruth

asserts that Susan is 'in connivance with' Meg because she did not intervene in Meg's actions. As Ruth puts it to Susan, 'you're guilty too, even though maybe you didn't do anything in particular'. Ruth's assessment haunts the narrative, highlighting why David is tormented by his inaction during Meg's torture. Ruth decrees that Susan should be spanked for not halting wrongdoing. In tandem, David chastises himself for his 'connivance' in Meg's torture.

Third, as *The Girl Next Door* illustrates, witnesses are positioned as conspirators in the tortureds' suffering. *Untraceable* exploits that conceit, featuring a website ('killwithme.com') that broadcasts torture. The intensity of the torture is directly proportionate to the quantity of online viewers. Witnessing is active participation here, as FBI chief Brooks professes in a press conference: '[a]ny American who visits the site is an accomplice…We are the murder weapon'. This direct accusation notwithstanding, lead protagonist Jennifer notes that 'nobody [who visits the site] thinks they [are doing] anything wrong'. *Untraceable*'s cyber-witnesses undertake a 'transactional mind-set' which, according to Ya-Ru Chen et al. (2009: 25), is commonplace when people are involved in 'exchanges with distant others'.

This mind-set is crucial to the film's thematic concerns, and is underlined by the fact that *Untraceable*'s witnesses are never portrayed. The witnesses are only represented via their on-site comments, and their support for torture is fickle, suggesting that they perceive their role in torture as superficial.[11] Their anonymity in the text is apposite, signalling why these witnesses may deny liability. First, their anonymity means they cannot be singled out, and therefore they evade being directly labelled as immoral. Being *seen* to do wrong, it is implied, means being held accountable and having to atone for wrongdoing. Second, the witnesses share responsibility as a grouping, meaning no individual is compelled to feel solely responsible.[12] Third, because witnesses view remotely, they cannot disrupt the torture first-hand. Being present on-scene would unambiguously involve them, provoking a moral duty to intervene. Their distance offers these witnesses a means of denying their involvement.

The witnesses' anonymity is contrasted by antagonist-abductor Owen's presence. Since their anonymity, collectivity and distance from the torture-space appear to offer the witnesses a shield against blameworthiness, Owen's identifiable, individual presence marks him as directly involved in the torture. On its surface, *Untraceable* is driven by an overt moral conflict between criminal (Owen) and police (Jennifer). That plain 'protagonist versus antagonist' plot arc is balanced by the semi-present

cyber-witnesses' more ambiguous moral positions. Because their contribution to the tortureds' suffering is actualised, *Untraceable*'s witnesses
are implicated in the suffering they watch, even if the extent of their
culpability is uncertain. Owen highlights that without the witnesses, the
torture situations he contrives would remain inert. For instance, when
Owen films Jennifer's daughter, the site users presume that Owen will
harm the girl, commenting that he is a 'SICK FUCK!!!!!' Owen responds
by asking '[d]id you really think I would let you people hurt that little
girl?' His projection ('you people') confirms that Owen considers the
witnesses to be torturers, not just 'accomplices' as the FBI terms them.
That ambiguity remains unresolved. The conventional 'police versus
criminal' plot-line cannot offer simple moral resolution, because the
'criminal' position is not fixed.

Accordingly, *Untraceable*'s principally punitive narrative does not
create a simplistic moral dichotomy where the police are faultless.
Parallels are made between the site users and the FBI, debunking any
implication that the police are self-evidently righteous simply because
they are law enforcers. The only people shown using Owen's website
are the police themselves. Investigating the crime means logging onto
killwithme.com, and so the FBI also contribute to the torture therein,
despite their castigatory aims. Furthermore, because law enforcers
denounce killwithme.com in a press conference, the site gains broader
notoriety. The FBI are partially culpable when the next target's death is
expedited as a result.

Moreover, the final sequence involves lead FBI investigator Jennifer
escaping a killwithme.com trap and shooting Owen. Jennifer holds up
her badge to the webcam after firing, incriminating the site viewers and
also validating the homicide she commits. Her use of the FBI shield
implies that the killing is rationalised not because she acts in self-defence,
but because the FBI are righteous per se. In the film's final webcam
shot, Jennifer is obscured by her FBI identification. She hides behind
the shield, becoming as anonymous as the site users. Jennifer's group
affiliation is exposed as a justificatory structure, akin to the witnesses'
collective diffusion of blame. Prior shots of FBI agents cheering 'get
him, Jennifer!' as they witness the killing via web-stream undercut the
apparent moral closure offered by this climactic sequence. Although
celebrating Jennifer's survival is ethically sound in itself, the proclamation 'get him' is morally dubious: the agents are exposed as wanting to
see Owen pay (die) for endangering their colleague. The FBI agents glee-
fully consume his streamed death. In earlier scenes, those same officers
express disgust at live-torture broadcasts. Neither their legal status nor

Figure 5.2   Jennifer hides behind her FBI badge in the final shot of *Untraceable* (2008, USA, dir Gregory Hoblit)

Owen's criminality make cheering on Owen's demise significantly better than pleasurably consuming the other deaths streamed on killwithme. com. Morality must be assigned according to more than just positional roles then. The FBI agents assume the line between right and wrong is still firmly intact, whereas *Untraceable*'s viewer may be less assured, particularly when the final killwithme.com user comment is imparted on-screen: 'how cn I dwnld this video?' [*sic*]. For this user, murder-spectacle is divorced from role: it does not matter who perishes on-screen, just that death occurs. For the FBI, *all* that matters in this incident is who dies. *Untraceable* closes without resolving that dialectic, punctuating the moral problems that result.

The film's trajectory typifies the tendency to disturb sharp divisions between 'right' and 'wrong' in torture porn films. *Untraceable* begins with what appears to be a clear moral dichotomy. Annie (Jennifer's daughter) asks her mother 'did you catch any bad guys?', implying complete separation between police and criminal. Yet that distance collapses as the film progresses: Jennifer's partner Griffin is abducted and tortured; a live-feed of Jennifer's home is broadcast on killwithme. com; and finally Owen attempts to torture Jennifer in her own basement using her lawnmower. That escalating personalisation is mirrored by Jennifer's declining professionalism. She begins by referring to Owen as 'the subject', and later adopts her colleague's suggestion that they instead refer to Owen as a 'piece of shit'. That faltering means righteousness – dressed as professional intent – is impugned alongside Owen's actions and the witnesses' motives.

Various shifting vantage points are presented in the film, displaying a range of moral positions. Many reviewers find such ambiguity problematic, complaining that *Untraceable* is hypocritical because the film 'revels in graphic violence' while also 'trying to make a statement about the public's fascination with tragedy' (Puig, 2008; see also Hornaday, 2008a; Schneller, 2008).[13] These objections presume that *Untraceable*'s creators and viewers are incapable of negotiating the narrative's moral balances. Ironically, such complaints disclose much more about their authors' unwillingness to negotiate the text's moral dynamic than they do about *Untraceable* or its audience. Opponents' grievances fail to differentiate between in-text witnesses – killwithme.com's users – and *Untraceable*'s viewers, who engage with fictional narrative structures.

'She was torturing herself when nobody was looking':[14] conclusion

Witnesses are directly involved in torture porn's action, supplying a viewpoint from which violence is reflected on and morality is questioned within the diegesis. *A Serbian Film*'s slippages between witness, torturer, and tortured epitomise how naturalistically such evaluation is integrated into torture porn films. Waking from a three-day blackout, lead protagonist Milos has flashbacks to events that occurred during his lapse. A snuff-porn director (Marko) drugged Milos, coercing him into performing heinous sexual violence on camera. *A Serbian Film*'s third act is constituted by Milos's memories and Milos watching back that footage: that is, Milos is witness to his own wrongdoing. The combination of Milos's memory-flashbacks and the camcorder footage mean that he simultaneously witnesses both from an experiential perspective – substantiated, for example, by point-of-view shots deployed throughout his flashbacks – and also from the diegetic camcorder's external position. Moreover, Milos witnesses not just his wrongdoing, but also his own slippage between torturer and tortured positions. Recalling that he raped and decapitated a woman during his fugue state, Milos vomits and bites his own hand in self-disgust, establishing that his actions violated his moral principles. Having acted beyond his conscious will, he too was being tortured. Video-footage of Marko's henchman raping Milos verifies that Milos did not just inflict suffering: he also suffered. Recalling that he raped his own wife and son finally tips Milos over the edge, leading to his family's group-suicide. Despite being unaware of what he was doing, the recording underscores that he cannot evade taking responsibility for the blood on his hands. By deconstructing Milos's role at the centre of a moral continuum – whereby he slips between tortured, torturer, and witness positions – *A Serbian Film* delineates how devastating torture can be. These complex balances are seamlessly integrated into the film and are essential to its ethical dynamic. *A Serbian Film* epitomises the way in which torture porn's violence and character positions create moral fissures that defy straightforward resolution.

In this subgenre, torture opens up ethical queries that disrupt rather than fix character-positions. Acknowledging this trait is crucial to understanding torture porn's cultural value. Some scholars have reasoned that horror 'is constructive' because it 'makes us recognise evils that must...be wrong' (Tallon, 2010: 40). However, this view underplays what horror can reveal about morality. Beliefs that murder is abhorrent, that rape is unacceptable, that torture is ethically problematic, are ubiquitous. It is not necessary to reiterate those principles via horror. Much more palatable is Philip Tallon's (2010: 40) view that 'horror pushes us to take seriously our deepest moral convictions...cast[ing] doubt on our highest moral *intentions*'. The emphases placed on human interactions and confined situations in torture porn films mean that those frictions are foregrounded and are integral to the subgenre's meanings. Edelstein's (2006) proposal that torture porn's 'only point seems to be to force you to suspend moral judgments altogether' is profoundly unsatisfying, then. Torture porn narratives are founded on moral conflicts. Contra to Edelstein's view, this chapter has evinced that torture porn filmmakers naturalistically integrate moral questions, stimulating ethical rumination. Rejecting torture porn indicates that Edelstein is unwilling to contemplate the subgenre's shifting character positions at length.

Contentions regarding position are integral to torture itself. Torture is only perceived as righteous from the perspective of those who sanction it. As Michael Otterman (2007: 21–2) recounts, in the 1950s the CIA were terrified by the possibility that torture experiment data might fall into 'unscrupulous hands'. The distinction 'unscrupulous hands' has less to do with violent acts than it does pre-determined moral judgments about who those hands belong to and what their intentions might be. Torture porn narratives dramatise those assumptions, elucidating that there are no 'bad' people, only contexts, actors, choices, and actions. Torture porn's role-slippages offer a continuum of positions, which are validated or challenged as characters interact. The subgenre's horror is contingent on these conflicts. As the next chapter will demonstrate, such clashes result in power struggle. Those mêlées do not only manifest via torture and positional negotiations, however. They equally entail characters grappling for control over torture porn's diegetic spaces.

6
'In the Land of the Pig, the Butcher Is King':[1] Torture, Spaces, and Power

Torture porn does not simply entail 'luxuriating in the sight of another human being's suffering' (Fern, 2008), as numerous detractors have claimed. The characters' struggles advance torture porn's narratives. Such battling involves physical violence (torture), but it also shifts the characters' positions relative to one another. Physical brutality reifies the characters' symbolic grappling for control. The characters' initial relationships are unmoored by violence, resulting in role-slippages. Contra to Scarry's (1985: 36) interpretation of torture then, torture porn's violence does not fix power. Rather, torture porn films depict the contestation of power.

Because abduction/confinement themes are foregrounded in torture porn, its character clashes predominantly occur in delimited diegetic areas – dedicated torture-spaces – such as cellars, warehouses, or even rural villages. Consequently, supremacy is equated to spatial control in torture porn. Spatial control tends to be severely skewed in the antagonists' favour in the subgenre's narratives, meaning protagonists must resist that power in order to survive. Pertinent questions regarding moral duty elicit from those power-struggles. Frequently, torture porn's captives have to choose whether to torture others in order to facilitate their own escape from the torture-space, or whether to risk their lives to save others. The protagonists' duty to moral principles and to others is thereby tested by pushing those responsibilities to their breaking point.

Since the torture-spaces are (a) extraordinary situations, distant from protagonists' daily experience, and (b) skewed towards antagonist control (being designed for their immoral purposes), torture-spaces appear to be moral vacuums, which are defined by violence. However, these circumstances do not necessarily vindicate any immoral acts protagonists commit. Torture porn dramatises the personal costs incurred by protagonists who fail to maintain moral principles. Control-seizing antagonists are characterised as cruel. Equally destructive are protagonists who consciously choose to commit immoral acts. The ethical choices faced by torture porn's protagonists could not be any more serious or difficult. As this chapter will illustrate, protagonists who make such decisions also suffer as a result of their choices. In torture porn, ethical decisions are rendered as life-and-death matters, accentuating why taking ownership over moral principles is both so necessary and so demanding.

'Once You're In, There's No Way Out':[2] space, torture, and character arcs

Spatial control is among the most pernicious of torture techniques. As *Martyrs*'s antagonist Madame proposes, spatial control is torture's only necessity: 'it is so easy to create a victim...lock someone in a dark room. They begin to suffer'. Donald O. Hebb's highly influential 1950s isolation-based torture experiments confirm Madame's proclamation. Hebb (in Otterman, 2007: 42) concluded that 'without physical pain...the personality can be badly deformed simply by modifying the perceptual environment'. Similarly, the CIA's Kubark Manual (1963) suggests that torturers should 'create an environment that elevates the interrogator', so they ostensibly control 'all aspects of the interrogation' (McCoy, 2006: 136). The same logic is utilised in torture porn narratives. The action is often set in artificially constructed torture chambers, such as the experimentation areas of *Breathing Room*, *The Killing Room*, *Torture Room*, and *Basement*. These titles distil the narratological emphasis placed on constructed torture-spaces across the subgenre.

In fact, characters' motions through space commonly drive torture porn's plot arcs. Torture porn narratives typically open with what appear to be torturer/tortured dichotomies. As the narratives progress, however, the dichotomy collapses. That failure manifests spatially: the physical distances between torturer and tortured also fold. For example, in *Untraceable*, torturer and tortured positions intertwine as those parties are brought into closer proximity. The physical distances seemingly provided by cyber-interaction diminish. As killwithme.com's users 'enter' the site and precipitate some stranger's demise, they also cross a moral line. Similar movements are pivotal in other torture porn films. *Roadkill*'s protagonists use a CB radio to play a humiliating prank on a trucker. The trucker then bridges the physical distance radio-mediation offered the pranksters by physically hunting them. *The Hills Run Red* revolves around protagonist

Tyler's infatuation with a lost horror feature. Seeking its maker, Tyler is eventually abducted by the film's director and becomes part of the movie which, it transpires, is constituted by genuine murder. These narratives each begin with mediated interactions that separate torturer and tortured: cyberspace, radio, and film. As the narratives progress, distanced interfaces are replaced by physical engagements: abduction and suffering. The initial 'safe' distances between torturer and tortured are closed.

The spatial language used to describe these events – entering, crossing, bridging – conveys how vital torture porn's spaces are to fathoming the subgenre's moral exchanges and the transpositions characters undergo in these narratives. For instance, Paxton's decision to kill the Dutch Businessman in *Hostel* is the culmination of a broader narrative arc in which the characters move from 'seeing' to 'feeling'. *Hostel*'s opening is constructed around its protagonists' sexual voyeurism. Travellers Josh, Paxton, and Oli simply want to 'check out' naked women. When they become physically involved with the hostel's Sirens (Natalya and Svetlana), the narrative becomes more broadly fixated on touching rather than just watching. Subsequently, the travellers are each abducted and tortured. The protagonists begin as observers, and increasingly become involved in intimate physical interactions.

The same is true for the Dutch Businessman who tortures Josh. The torturer first encounters the travellers on their train journey to the hostel and meets Josh again outside a club prior to Josh's imprisonment. What appear to Josh and to *Hostel*'s viewer to be chance meetings are reframed by the abduction. The Businessman was aware that he would be Josh's torturer and was stalking his prey. The Businessman too moves from seeing to touching. His encounters with Josh become increasingly physically intimate. Josh's first interaction with the Businessman culminates in the Businessman briefly touching Josh's knee. Josh's over-reaction to this gesture signals from the outset that touching equates to infringement, foreshadowing the travellers' shifts from voyeurs to participants – consumers to consumed – and Paxton's eventual positional slippage from tortured (touched) to torturer (toucher).

This correlation again stresses that witnessing is active involvement, since witnessing is intertwined with torture. In Josh's death sequence, Josh and the Businessman are reflected in a mirror just before Josh's throat is cut. A matching shot is offered in the climax: on the threshold of homicide, the Businessman catches his reflection of himself and Paxton before Paxton slits the man's throat. These parallel shots verify the characters' relative positions. During the act, the torturers are reflected to themselves as torturers, and the tortured witness their own torture. The two incidents are connected by these shots, evidencing

Figure 6.1 and 6.2   Parallel shots, analogous acts: Josh's throat is slit by the businessman, and the businessman's throat is cut by Paxton in *Hostel* (2005, USA, dir Eli Roth)

that Paxton's role has altered by *Hostel*'s denouement. Additionally, Paxton's mid-narrative recollection regarding his failure to rescue a drowning girl he made 'eye contact' with is evoked when he saves Kana. Cutting off Kana's dangling eye indicates Paxton's transference from inaction to interaction, from watching a girl drown at a distance to physical involvement in a woman's suffering. Closing that distance entails messy visceral engagement, just as *Hostel*'s other developments from watching to touching do. Reprising his earlier recollection with a visceral, literal form of 'eye-contact' may be a rather dark joke, but it evinces how important proximal collapse is to *Hostel*'s character arcs. The positional slippages found in torture porn are power-shifts, which manifest via characters' engagements with space.

'How Can You Escape...If They Can See Everything?':[3] power as spatial control

Scarry (1985: 18) theorises that torture is power-based, inasmuch as pain is an 'obsessive display of agency' that validates the torturer's control over the tortured. However, that control does not begin with suffering. Power derives from consent violation and imprisonment, which infringe on the tortured's autonomy. Torture-spaces are terrifying before any violence occurs, because they are isolating and alienating. During incarceration, captives are severely disadvantaged because they are separated from their usual support-networks – their kin, community, friends – and their familiar surroundings. The torture-space itself represents an initial power-bias that captives must overcome.

That partiality is usually inflated in torture porn films. One method of stressing the captives' disadvantage is to exaggerate their confinement, thereby expounding their impotence. For example, *Trunk* creates a claustrophobic atmosphere by depicting lead protagonist Megan trapped in a car-boot for the film's duration. *Breaking Nikki* too utilises an excessively small prison-space – a locker converted into a cell – to intensify the captive's horrific isolation. In contrast to these highly restrictive spaces, distanced long-shots are employed in *Wolf Creek, Storm Warning*, and *Naked Fear* to convey entrapment without confinement. The protagonists are dwarfed by the environment that surrounds them, attesting to their profound remoteness. They are alone and vulnerable, lost in spaces that they are unfamiliar with, and are unsure how to escape. The abductees are just as disempowered as they are in confined areas, despite being able to move through space.

In parallel to the tortureds' disempowerment, the torturers' power is expressed as spatial control. Torture porn's abductors fashion torture-spaces to allow continuous monitoring of their abductees. CCTV features in over

Figure 6.3 Trapped in the expansive outback: Kristie cannot evade her killer in *Wolf Creek* (2005, Australia, dir Greg McLean)

Figure 6.4   Martin is attacked after discovering the CCTV monitors in *Detour* (2009, Norway, dir Severin Eskeland)

40 torture porn films, including *Deathbell, Are You Scared?*, and *Vacancy*. This prevalent leitmotif expresses the torturer's power. In *Captivity, The Killing Room*, and *Hunger*, for instance, CCTV is used to monitor a single confined room. The abductors are able to study their captives in intimate detail in these cases, making prisoners fully aware that they are watched incessantly. Such monitoring is not limited to small spaces, however. In *Detour*, for example, CCTV grants visual access to an entire woodland area, meaning antagonists can stalk their targets from afar. The captors' ability to oversee such a large area creates the impression that they are everywhere, meaning the protagonists face all-consuming peril. In *Detour*, that feeling is amplified by alerting the audience to the antagonists' use of CCTV before the protagonists are aware that they are under threat. Dramatic irony underscores the protagonists' vulnerability and the antagonists' power. A musical sting accompanies *Detour*'s first CCTV-shot, confirming surveillance's sinister function. When protagonist Martin discovers the captors' CCTV system, live-feed footage of his girlfriend (Lina) is juxtaposed with past recordings of their journey on adjacent monitors. The CCTV motif establishes that Martin and Lina were disempowered from the outset, meaning their capture feels inevitable. Martin's terror at this realisation is underlined by the score – atonal low drones and high pitched violins – as well as physical threat. One screen exhibits a gagged woman sobbing, elucidating the imminent peril that Martin and Lina face. As soon as he sees the footage, Martin is physically attacked. Their abductors' control is embellished via the CCTV motif, building tension and demonstrating the odds Martin and Lina eventually overcome in thwarting their captors.

In these ways, the subgenre's torture-spaces are akin to a form of prison architecture – the panopticon – designed to facilitate inmates' 'permanent visibility'. The panopticon, as Michel Foucault (1995: 201) has it, is constructed to assure 'the automatic functioning of power'. *Exam*, *Saw*, and *Breathing Room*'s locked-box gameplay arenas epitomise that logic. As with other post-*Saw* challenge-based narratives – such as *The Task*, *Steel Trap*, *Panic Button*, and *Die* – the captors' control is estab- lished via concrete rules coupled with the threat of physical violence. Yet the space functions as an 'architectural apparatus...for creating and sustaining...power' (Foucault, 1995: 201), meaning only minimal enforcing of physical threat is required. The captors establish cues in advance, but leave the captives to torture themselves and each other. These abductors utilise torture-spaces to foster the idea that they have absolute control over the abductees.

99 Pieces embodies these panoptical traits. The protagonist (Joshua) obeys the nameless antagonist's instructions, evacuating his house of food and light bulbs, turning off his water supply and boarding up his windows. The torturer takes complete environmental control only because Joshua agrees to imprison himself. Joshua conforms to his tormentor's 'points system', whereby Joshua elects whether to sacrifice food, water, or electricity on a daily basis. In one instance, Joshua decides to sacrifice his food ration, and then covertly eats. The torturer immedi- ately punishes Joshua. Via minimal enforcement early in the narrative, the torturer creates the impression that he is omnipotent and omnis- cient, evincing his overarching threat. Such spatial control is the most devastating tool at the torturers' disposal, since it coerces the captive into self-submission.

99 Pieces is representative of home-invasion themed torture porn,[4] in which spatial incursion carries additional symbolic weight: the antagonist colonises the protagonist's immediate, familiar spaces, rendering them unfamiliar. As *99 Pieces*'s tagline has it, '[y]our home is now your nightmare'. The home's connotations as the owner's terri- tory – which they control, and which provides them with security – are inverted, suggesting the captor has complete control over the captive. In contrast, the vast majority of the subgenre's torture-spaces – such as *Creep*'s underground rail network, *Matchdead*'s desert trailer, or *Hunger*'s dungeon-bunker – are outside the abductees' usual experiential spheres.[5] Estrangement is also highlighted in cases where captives are 'outsiders' who interlope into foreign territories; for example, where city-dwellers infringe on rural areas (*Wolf Creek*, *Storm Warning*, *The Hills Have Eyes*), or where holiday-makers enter other countries (*Turistas*, *Donkey Punch*, *Borderland*). In such cases, the captives' isolation is augmented for the audience because their homes are never depicted. Tonally, the captives' chances of escape are disparaged because it is difficult to grasp where they can escape *to*. Their distance from home – their sanctuary – is implied to be insurmountable, accentuating their disadvantage.

In contrast to captive protagonists – who are alienated in all circumstances – even where antagonist torturers are transient and incur on normative spaces (*Roadkill*, *Switchblade Romance*, *Rest Stop*), their power is undiminished. They violently shape the environment to befit their immoral deeds. The protagonists are disempowered, fettered, and shrink in number. Antithetically, antagonist torturers seem invulnerable, even when apparently defeated. In *Hoboken Hollow* for instance, Trevor evades his captors, reporting them to the police. However, the narrative cessation reveals that his captors' slave-ring business is unhindered. The same is true of *Wrong Turn*, *The Hills Have Eyes*, and *Hostel*: escaped captives manage to kill key torturers, yet sequel movies elucidate that the torture regimes established in these films are not impeded by such losses.

'Dying is Easy … Staying Alive is Torture':[6] disempowerment, passivity, and renormalisation

Thus, the role-labels 'torturer' and 'tortured' convey that the former is active and latter is passive. That difference is reified via their respective relationships with space. The tortured qua tortured lack control and are acted upon. In contradistinction, torture-spaces are artificially constructed to meet antagonist torturers' needs. The large-scale machinery that characterises *Saw*'s torture-spaces is prototypical of such architecture. The antagonists' spatial-constructions permit them to engage in immoral pursuits such as torture and murder. In other cases – particularly in rural torture porn – these activities include other prohibited behaviours such as cannibalism (*Scarce*, *The Texas Chainsaw Massacre*), incest (*2001 Maniacs*, *Wrong Turn 2*), and bestiality (*Storm Warning*, *The Ordeal*), which are facilitated by the locale's lawlessness and remoteness. However, despite these constructions, neither the abductors' immoral behaviours nor their power are naturalised in these films. Captors' imperative-violating behaviours are narratologically antagonistic and are portrayed as horrific, tonally.

Captors attain their power by *seizing* control over space and people. Therefore, their power is neither natural nor incontestable. Initial abductions are able to occur for the same reasons that captives may later overthrow their abductors: in torture porn narratives, power is not fixed. That fluidity is actualised via a noticeable dearth of official authority figures in torture porn's environments. Much like in the slasher film

(Rockoff, 2002: 11–12), torture porn's diegetic spaces are rarely governed by apparatuses that effectively curb immoral action.[7] Where police are present, they are corrupt (*Saw*, *The Unforgiving*, and *Header*), or are quickly slaughtered (*Captivity*, *Gag*, and *Inside*). In *The Texas Chainsaw Massacre: The Beginning* for example, lead executioner Tommy Hewitt is made redundant from the town abattoir, and kills his manager when he is told to leave. The town sheriff's feeble attempt to apprehend Tommy is thwarted by lead antagonist Hoyt Hewitt, who murders the lawman and adopts his uniform. Hence, the Hewitt family take over the township by violently usurping its two main authority figures (manager and sheriff). The Hewitts then express their authority spatially, turning their home into a microcosm of the town. Their abode becomes both a slaughter-house and the sheriff's station, reifying their control over the territory.

In parallel to captors' aggressive seizing of space, captives are frequently subsumed into the antagonists' immoral way of life. This sometimes entails attempting to diminish the captives' ties to their established world-views. For instance, in *Broken*, 'The Man' requires his prisoners to relinquish their previous lives and submit to his control, stating 'I'm your family now…you have no name…forget your past'. He literalises his rhetorical control by manacling the abductees. Similarly, in *Timber Falls*, *The Ordeal*, and *Wrong Turn 2*, captives are forced into conformity with the captors' daily life, a system of control that is literalised by strapping the protagonist to a chair at the antagonists' family dinner-table. In *Scarce*, *Razor's Ring*, and *Frontier(s)*, abductees are similarly imprisoned in their captors' homes. In each case, captives are made to join abductors in committing acts that infringe on the prisoners' beliefs. *Scarce*, *Razor's Ring*, and *Frontier(s)* depict captives being served meals of human flesh, for example. Although the protagonists are not immediately aware that they have participated in distasteful acts, the narratives expose those problematic deeds. For instance, as protagonist Ricky eats his meal in *2001 Maniacs*, the camera dwells on the distinctive tattoo adorning the meat on Ricky's fork. A fleeting flashback insert-shot confirms that the tattoo belonged to Ricky's fellow traveller Kat. Dramatic irony under-scores both the protagonists' vulnerability and their unawareness regarding the antagonists' intentions.

Captives' immersion into the torture-space further verifies captors' apparently all-encompassing control. To escape, captives must tip that power imbalance. It may seem that the tortured must use violence to seize control, since (a) the torturers' power is enforced by (threat of) violence, (b) the torturers have constructed the space to partake in immoral, usually violent acts, and (c) confinement inhibits the prisoners' options. Nevertheless, renormalisation – imprisoned captives aligning their morality to fit their circumstances[8] – does not excuse captives if they choose to commit actions that contravene their moral principles.

The 'renormalisation' justification for immoral action is repudiated within the films themselves. Customarily, protagonists' moral stances are explicitly established early on in torture porn narratives, flagging the moral tensions that ensue when they slip from being tortured to inflicting torture. In *Razor's Ring*, for example, lead protagonist Scott is abducted by Razor and Julie, who kill for fun; they intentionally drive over a dog and shoot a police officer. Scott decries their 'sick game', exhibiting his moral stance. On crashing the car, the trio are abducted by a cannibalistic family, and imprisoned on their farmland. Julie and Razor are killed, yet Scott is allowed to live because he obeys his captors. Having internalised their control, he is released from his physical shackles, and freely partakes in meals with his abductors. On discovering that his captors are cannibals and that he too has been consuming Razor's body, Scott is horrified. He immediately vomits, substantiating that his original values remain intact irrespective of his adaptation to their control. However, after escaping his abductors and destroying the farm, Scott complains that he cannot eat because 'nothing tastes the same anymore'. After cutting his thumb and tasting his own blood, he elects to abduct his girlfriend (Vanessa). Scott buys the farmland that belonged to his ex-captors, starting a new life modelled after the anthropophagic incarceration he suffered. The film ends with this indication that he has renormalised to his captors' tenets.

Scott's modification propagates the film's horror. Scott's final deeds contravene the moral principles he previously endorsed. Although he overthrows his captors, Scott does not seize back control. He remains passive. His imprisonment continues regardless of his captors' deaths. Erasing his past – planning to kill and eat Vanessa – corroborates that he wilfully forces his life into alignment with their immorality. Scott's trajectory also debunks the notion that immoral behaviours are acceptable when committed in the torture-space, since his unethical acts are directly linked to his life outside of that space, and preceding his abduction. The torture-space is not moral vacuum.

Captives who renormalise are reactive, responding to stimuli rather than making decisions according to steadfast principles. They become beholden to their immediate circumstances. That slippage demonstrates the vital counterpoint deontic principles offer to the notion of renormalisation. Absolutists deem immoral acts to be outright impermissible. The weakness of non-absolutist stances is that they accept that under the right circumstances, immoral acts might be sanctioned. Once one immoral action is permitted, it is unclear why other immoral acts remain prohibited. Absolutists counter such slippages by defining morality in relation to integrity, insofar as moral agents must not relinquish their principles when faced with immediate, emotional pressures.

If captives forsake their moral principles, they relinquish their autonomy. Renormalisation therefore validates the captors' complete control over the captives. This is what is especially horrific about tortured protagonists becoming torturers once they are no longer directly coerced. *Razor's Ring*'s Scott, *Hostel*'s Paxton, and *Captivity*'s Jennifer, for instance, become torturers despite (a) having experienced the horrors of torture, (b) having every opportunity not to torture once they have escaped, and (c) having made it evident that they believe their ex-captors' actions to be immoral. Characters' positions may change across narratives as power balances shift, but the righteousness of specific behaviours does not. Only by relating specific acts to the concepts those acts represent – in this case, their violation of moral principle – can the significance of such deeds be apprehended.

Captives who relinquish to captors typically do so because they are initially unprepared to defend themselves. That passivity is discernible in films such as *The Texas Chainsaw Massacre: The Beginning* and *Spiderhole*, where captives cite unspecific theoretical 'rights' as an immediate response to their imprisonment. In *Torture Room*, lead protagonist Anush also protests 'I have rights, you know. Don't I get a phone call or something?' Her comment reveals that she has mistaken her situation. Even accepting that her right to liberty is inalienable,[9] the particular rule Anush refers to – relating to police procedure – is circumstantial. It does not apply in Anush's case because she has not been legally imprisoned. Her 'rights' statement itself is intended to evince that Anush has suffered a moral violation, yet it fails to articulate which principles have been infringed. In turn, it is established that Anush does not have a firm grasp on her own claim to rights.

These assertions are expressions of moral passivity. These captives expect *someone else* to uphold the principles that support their rights. No effective official authority is usually available to defend torture porn's protagonists, meaning that as autonomous authors of moral principles relating to these rights, captives themselves must take ownership of and uphold those entitlements: as Hoyt retorts to Dean in *The Texas Chainsaw Massacre: The Beginning*, 'freedom ain't free'. Captives' claims to morality and autonomy are challenged by their entrapment. Imprisonment infringes on their freedom, but that circumstance may only create a gap between morality and autonomy if the captives never truly had a grip on either. Captives commonly die in these films when they fail to react to, or because they adopt and thus confirm their abductors' violent tenets. Both responses signal moral passivity, suggesting that the captives have failed to defend their rights in a way that is consistent with their principles.

'Better her than me...That's the way it is':[10] selfishness, self-preservation, and morality

Characters who expect someone else to uphold their rights on their behalf radically underestimate how valuable other people's assistance is, particularly when those who might help are faced with mortal danger. One's choices are not simply made on the basis of survival instinct, or with one's own welfare in mind, however. The moral actor must take responsibility for their choices. Deontologists convey that onus by underscoring that one's moral principles are relational – formulated with other people in mind – even though principles only require one to govern her/his own behaviour. Interdependency is central to ethics itself because morality is a social construct. All social interactions are ethical engagements. That prevalence does not suggest that behaving morally is easy, especially in exceptional circumstances. Doing what is right commonly means acting against one's own interests. Torture porn narratives are routinely founded on scenarios which explore that clash between instinct and principle. In such situations, characters are presented with options, and are ethically culpable for the actions they choose to commit.

Recurrently, torture porn's protagonists face ethical tests that are quite literal. In *Kill Theory*, *Hunger*, and *wΔz*, for example, antagonists demand that captives choose whether to condemn others in order to preserve their own lives. The antagonists previously failed such a moral test themselves. In *Kill Theory*, for example, lead torturer Walter decided to cut a support rope during a mountain climbing accident, killing 'his own friends...to save himself'. Walter states that 'anyone would have made the same choice'. To substantiate his theory and attain 'closure', he creates a torture-space in which he torments a group of teens – including the son of a psychologist who refutes Walter's theory – giving them the choice to 'kill [their] friends, or die'.

By using captives' responses to justify their own past failure, these antagonists contravene the imperative that people should not be treated as a means to an end. The torture they inflict exacerbates their prior wrongdoing by inducing further harm. The antagonists are not particularly interesting in an ethical sense then: they make unambiguously immoral choices. Emphasis is instead placed on protagonists' moral decisions in the moment of threat. In each of these cases, the lead torturer's motives are exhibited via backstory exposition or flashbacks. The antagonist's prior immoral deeds pre-exist the diegetic present, and are distant compared with the abducted protagonists' immediate peril. The captives remain the narrative's empathic core, and their suffering spotlights that the protagonists are being used as mere instruments. In these films, horror is contingent on the sufferers' plights. The antagonists are presented as ethical foils by which the protagonists' actions can be assessed, then. The protagonists in *Kill Theory*, *Hunger*, and *wΔz* are not excused from committing immoral deeds because they face immediate pressure in the artificially constructed torture-space. Regardless of whether the decision is made by an antagonist or a protagonist, the willingness to use others for one's own ends is immoral because preventable suffering is caused.

Self-preservation, while a comprehensible drive, is frequently depicted as self-investment in torture porn. The subgenre's narratives embody the stance that behaving morally entails overcoming one's 'bent toward selfishness and self-serving motives' (Pauley, 2011: 97). Ethics is a framework that encourages the individual to think beyond reactionary impulses. Moral agents perceive themselves and their actions relationally: every individual is social, and so one's choices should be made in reference to others. *Saw V* reifies that ethos, requiring five captives to abandon their 'singular way of thinking' to solve deadly puzzles.[11] Their 'lifelong instincts' towards selfishness lead them to condemn one another. Charles is killed in an explosion after Luba hits him with a pole, for instance, and Luba is stabbed in the neck by Brit. It is only on reaching the final trap – which requires the remaining captives to collect ten pints of blood – that Brit realises they 'were supposed to work together' and 'all survive'. The five could have contributed two pints of blood each, but instead the two survivors have to shed five pints apiece. This final game highlights that the protagonists violated their moral obligation to one another at each stage of the trial. The cost of those decisions manifests via the captives' deaths and the physical damage done to the two remaining survivors. The same ethos is supported outside of *Saw V*'s torture-space. The FBI agents trying to stop John – Strahm, Matthews, Rigg, and Erickson – are equally doomed, each failing because they act alone. Solipsistic mind-sets are broadly associated with death in *Saw V*. The series' antagonists take advantage

Figure 6.5   Chrissie dwells on the threshold of escape in *The Texas Chainsaw Massacre: The Beginning* (2006, USA, dir Jonathan Liebesman)

of disunity, succeeding only because the protagonists act alone and in their own favour. Moral interdependence and social integration, it is implied, would reduce communal suffering.

Questions regarding moral obligation are also raised when captives have to choose whether to rescue a fellow captive or flee, preserving their own life. In *The Texas Chainsaw Massacre: The Beginning*, lead protagonist Chrissie has the opportunity to escape the torture-space – the Hewitt residence – after seeing her boyfriend (Eric) murdered. The film form accentuates the gravity of this dilemma, emblematising her choices. The camera follows behind Chrissie as she runs towards the exit. On hearing fellow captive Bailey screaming, Chrissie pauses, looking back over her shoulder. The angle reverses to outside the house, and swiftly zooms out. In contrast to the imprisonment occurring within, the pull-back illuminates how vast the outside space is. Movement away from the house is thereby equated with freedom. This shot also underlines the danger Chrissie faces. The doorway frames her cowering figure, connoting that she is entrapped by the house structure. The pull-back magnifies her vulnerability, dwarfing her against the ominous building.

Chrissie's anguished expression attests to both her fear and also her inner torment as she weighs up her options. Self-preservation instinct is likely to conflict with moral thought in such circumstances since it seems counter-instinctual to remain duty-bound in the face of self-endanger-ment.[12] Kant's appeal to universal rationality in moral decision-making seeks to circumvent purely self-interested motivation. Kant (1979: 152) thus recognises the powerful emotional sway of self-preservation instinct, even if he concludes that 'it is better to sacrifice one's life than one's morality'. Chrissie's case dramatises the dilemma in a way that feels less counter-instinctual than Kant's proposal. Chrissie is clearly torn between two conflicting emotional states. Chrissie fully understands the danger involved in returning into the house, having witnessed Eric die immediately beforehand. Nevertheless, she decides to return to the fray. *Pace* Kant's appeal to rationality to quash instinct, Chrissie's moral righteousness is unambiguously irrational. Closing her eyes to the world beyond the doorway, Chrissie cries as she re-enters the house and her body slumps, physicalising the self-negating nature of her act. *The Texas Chainsaw Massacre: The Beginning* thus illustrates how difficult it is to behave honourably.

Chrissie's capture and ultimately her demise result from her choice. However, Chrissie's death does not signal her failure. Behaving righteously is not inspired by nor does it lead to causal rewards. She does not return to save Bailey to boost her own esteem in others' eyes, or even out of direct pressure from Bailey, since Bailey is not aware of Chrissie's presence. If Chrissie left, only Chrissie would know what she had done. The pressure Chrissie faces is internal[13] since one's behaviour is assessed against the standards that one holds true. From a deontic stance, it would not be immoral for Chrissie to leave Bailey. Chrissie does not endanger Bailey or use her as a means to facilitate her own escape. Chrissie's supererogatory act demonstrates her devotion to others, and to ethical principle. Chrissie is a fully autonomous agent, the author of principles she upholds.

The same dilemma faces those abductees who are forced to choose whether to inflict pain on others to save themselves. In these cases, the protagonists are placed under direct external pressure, having to make their decision in the presence of the captive who would be harmed. Although antagonists typically promise freedom to the captives who hurt their peers, neither party's survival is ensured because torture porn's antagonists seldom keep their word. In *Choose*, *99 Pieces*, and *Grotesque*, a captive elects to undertake pain to protect their fellow abductee, but then both are killed. Their fates do not devalue the choice to self-sacrifice, however. The process of choosing itself is spotlighted, rather than the consequences. The antagonist's ignoble volte-face contrasts with the martyr's staid morality. To read self-sacrifice as futile is to undermine the moral significance of the sufferer's devotion to others, which starkly contrasts with the antagonist's willingness to abuse others.

Not all of torture porn's protagonists are so noble. In *The Anniversary at Shallow Creek*, *The Final*, *Rest Stop: Don't Look Back*, and *Tortura*, for example, captives decide to save themselves by sacrificing another captive. Here, the burden of moral responsibility is literalised by the blood on their hands. Horror emanates from the captive-turned-torturer's willingness to (a) act immorally, (b) place their own safety above their kinship with the sufferer, and (c) relinquish to the captors' immoral commands, which means forsaking their autonomy as a moral agent. None of the captive-turned-torturers in these films are granted freedom. Again, their continued suffering is not karmic payback for their deeds, since the same is regularly true for those captives who choose to undergo suffering to save another. The antagonists' untrustworthiness does not impact on the moral significance of the captive-turned-torturer's self-invested choice. Accordingly, when protagonists decide to forsake another to survive, they are tormented by guilt: their recognition that they did wrong by the standards they hold true. By torturing or acceding to a peer's torture as a means of facilitating their own survival, the chooser forsakes their principles and contributes to their own subjugation.

Scar exemplifies how that toll manifests in torture porn. *Scar*'s torturer divests his criminal responsibility onto the tortured parties, torturing them until one agrees to sacrifice another. *Scar*'s plot is focused on Joan, who survived torture by consenting to her friend's death. Joan's choice haunts her, exhibiting the emotional cost of her survival. The film opens with Joan jogging in the diegetic present. The sprinting scene conveys that Joan is unable to 'outrun' her memories, which are hypostatised via on-screen blood splatters, newspaper headlines – such as '[y]oung heroine Joan Burrows grateful to be alive; sorrowful' – and flashbacks of Joan and her friend screaming, which are interpolated throughout the sequence. Joan's inescapable past is the narrative's point-of-entry. Even the title *Scar* refers to the injury Joan attained during the torture. Although Joan hides the scar with make-up, it is a palimpsest: a past she cannot erase.

That theme pervades the film. Joan's guilt is echoed across the narrative's events. Joan's brother (Jeff) cannot relinquish his dead wife's jewellery, for example. In another case, Joan is distressed to find that her torturer's home has been turned into a museum 'to remember him' via a collection of 'artefacts'. Past trauma perpetually haunts. Ultimately, those anxieties erupt: Joan is abducted by a copycat torturer. This time, Joan manages to defeat her captor by inflicting self-damage – cutting off her thumb – of her own volition, rather than assenting to another's harm. Even this climactic choice cannot resolve the original trauma. The film's final line is Joan's assertion that 'it never stops'. Captives are inexorably tormented by their immoral choice to sacrifice another, regardless of the duress they face. In *Scar*, that perpetual internal disturbance is externalised as cyclic violence.

Rather than being 'sadistically nihilistic' (McCartney, 2007a), torture porn's horror is contingent on sociality. Morality is a means of elucidating how torture porn centralises interdependency rather than nihilism. In *Hunger* and *Saw* the first line of dialogue is a cry for help, foregrounding the protagonist's belief in compassion and their hope that 'someone' will try to assist irrespective of the evident risks. When protagonists have their throats bleached (*Hard Candy*, *Mum and Dad*, *The Loved Ones*) or tongue mutilated (*Senseless*, *The Human Centipede II*), their distance from help is underlined. Although assistance rarely comes, gagging – one of torture porn's predominant motifs – implies both that captives will cry for support, and also that their calls are likely to be responded to.

Antagonists usually do their utmost to deter captives from working together. The narratives thereby code collaboration as empowering. Turning captives against one another or coercing them into becoming torturers is particularly abhorrent in that sense. The subgenre's most obvious driving force is the human propensity for cruelty, and the ethical dilemmas offered in torture porn films amplify how horrific that capacity is. However, less attention is paid to callous human-monsters in torture porn narratives than to normal people who are pushed to make ghastly choices. The horrors that ensue in torture-spaces – where captives are isolated and attempts to help are usually thwarted – are undergirded by the cumulative message that being stripped of social support is utterly terrifying. In parallel, self-interest is characterised as abhorrent auto-abnegation since it reinforces those fears.

'When the time comes, I'll do my best':[14] conclusion

Those protagonists who choose to commit immoral deeds cannot escape the knowledge that, by their own standards, they have done wrong. Moral violation carries a self-imposed emotional penalty that is illuminated in torture porn via the subgenre's alignment with sufferers. Where protagonists act immorally, that empathic alignment becomes disquieting. This mechanism thereby implicitly critiques the extent to which emotion colours moral judgements.

Torture porn narratives are not 'morally duplicitous' (Holden, 2008) or 'morally degraded' (Heal, 2007) as numerous reviewers have professed, but neither are they one-dimensional moral propaganda. Torture porn dramatises difficult ethical questions: is it ever necessary to take another person's life? To what extent does self-preservation outweigh one's obligation to others? What pressure could lead one to knowingly commit immoral acts? Playing out particular responses does not necessarily entail unanimously vilifying some choices and valorising others. Doing so would preclude the need for engagement with the underlying principles. The difficulties, ambiguities, and morally dubious choices found in torture porn narratives offer various contentious scenarios for ethical scrutiny. The exaggeratedly dangerous circumstances characters face reflect how gravely important ethics is as a social bedrock. For captives who are depicted as initially agreeing with standard moral imperatives but who face life-and-death choices, the cost of forsaking their principles could not be higher.

As Scarry (1985: 18) notes, torture is an exceptional event that leads to the suspension of 'ordinary assumptions [about] culture'. Torture porn films illustrate that morality should not be taken for granted: ethical agents must take ownership of their principles, since those beliefs are rooted in the individual. That is, principles are meaningless as external, universal edicts. Principles only become meaningful when they are internalised by the moral agent: when the gap between the universal ideal and the subject's particular circumstance is bridged. That spanning manifests in various ways in torture porn, as demonstrated throughout this chapter. The panopticon paradigm, for instance, appears to be an external source of pressure, incarnated in the CCTV cameras that haunt many of torture porn's terrains. However, coercive power is located in the subjects themselves, since they submit to the control connoted by those symbols. In *Razor's Ring*, it is not simply the captors' pressure that drives Scott to cannibalism, but his internalisation of their control and his choice to replicate those behaviours. The stimulus is located within Scott himself. Indeed, Scott's turn to murder is triggered by the taste of his own blood, which he re-internalises. Another internalisation model is found in *Scar*. Joan is haunted by her choice to self-preserve. However, she only provided verbal assent to another captive's torture. The captor confers responsibility onto Joan, yet her internalisation of that responsibility is her own doing. Morality itself is a system of self-governance. Although external forces trigger moral decision-making in these films, the ensuing internal conflict is pivotal.

By seizing power, antagonists establish control, and that violence is hypostatised in the external environment, or on their captives' flesh. However, it is the internal – the tortureds' suffering, their on-going emotional trauma – that propels the narratives. In this way, torture porn films redress Scarry's concern that torture only conveys power because suffering is invisible. As Chapters 4–6 have evinced, power, pain, personal perspectives, and emotive responses are intimately entangled in torture porn narratives. This is the contribution torture porn's empathic drama makes to understanding those philosophical issues. Without examining the relations between external forces that exert moral pressure and moral agents' contribution to authoring those principles, or between principles and their applicability, ethics remains abstract and inert. Even if audiences do not think of these films as philosophical thought-experiments, torture porn filmmakers routinely prompt moral reflection by placing protagonists under extraordinary pressures and offering means for audiences to emotively involve themselves in characters' dilemmas.

Part III

'Porn' (Extremity)

Introduction

'Torture' only represents one half of 'torture porn'. In Part III, 'porn' and its overtones will be examined. 'Torture porn' discourse's bedrock – the comparison between horror film and pornography – is nothing new in itself (see Bor, 2007: 35). Sex and death habitually coincide in horror films, manifesting in *Dracula*'s (1931) vampirific seductions as much as the undead sex-work of *Zombie Strippers!* (2008). Insofar as porn and horror are both visceral, physically affecting genres, the dual elements of 'torture porn' seem to fit together. However, the label's implied hybridity raises numerous problems that require dissection. As J. M. Bernstein (2004: 10) affirms, critics who use porn as a metaphor typically fail 'to distinguish what in the pornographic requires acknowledgement and what [requires] denunciation'. Torture porn's detractors have frequently fallen foul of this fault, offering little account of the 'porn plus horror' context 'torture porn' is predicated on, or what that combination reveals about visual representation and its limits. Rather than addressing what 'porn' means, the subgenre's decriers commonly veer towards vague generalisation. The result is that 'torture porn' is imbued with a host of conflicting connotations, and that dialectic provides the focus for Part III.

In order to assess what is at stake in using 'porn' to describe a horror subgenre, it is necessary to inspect the political meanings of 'porn', which have been swept over in existing discussions about 'torture porn'. Anti-pornography feminism is referred to throughout Part III as a way of accessing those political meanings. Having epitomised and concretised misogyny for several of feminism's most vociferous proponents since the 1970s, 'porn' remains discursively associated with misogyny. In her influential text *Pornography: Men Possessing Women* (1989), Andrea Dworkin proposes that mainstream pornography is constituted by sexual violence aimed towards women. Those allegations are largely unsubstantiated since the depictions she describes belong to porn's niche sub-categories rather than being normative conventions as Dworkin characterises them. However, her concerns are becoming increasingly relevant to recent feminist debates regarding sexual representations. As Stacy Gillis, Gillian Howie, and Rebecca Munford (2004) have observed, since the mid-1990s feminist scholars have paid less attention to pornography as an embodiment of sexual politics. In tandem, Robert Jensen (2007) has posited that cruelty and humiliation aimed at women have increased in mainstream pornography since the mid-1990s.

Together, these scholars' concerns might suggest that violent pornography has bloomed because feminists have become less vigilant in objecting to such representations. These arguments are related to torture porn discourse in two ways. First, Jensen adopts anti-porn feminists' tendency to refer to pornography as horrific. As Chapter 7 will demonstrate, numerous anti-pornography feminists forged very explicit linkages between porn and horror. That sense of genre hybridity is equally reflected in 'torture porn'. Second, torture porn's disparagers characterise the subgenre as unconstrained, sexually violent material. Those detractors are mostly preoccupied with misogyny,[1] accusing torture porn of 'featur[ing] astounding amounts of sex and violence ... mainly directed against women' (Hunt, 2007), for example. Examining the relationship between 'torture porn' and anti-porn debates elucidates those political connotations, which contribute to the prevailing sense that torture porn is culturally problematic. Although torture porn has been accused of containing titillating misogyny, those indictments are prejudicial, stemming from the connotations of 'porn' rather than from torture porn's content. In Chapter 7, it will be contended that torture porn films are not plainly misogynistic, either in the quantitative or qualitative senses. Instances of sexual violence occur less frequently in multiplex torture porn than its depreciators have alleged, but when they do occur, those depictions are more complex than has been postulated.

The 'porn' in 'torture porn' connotes that the subgenre's films are sexually driven, and that they gratuitously flout taboos. Resultantly, torture porn is gauged to be 'extreme' (see Cochrane, 2007; Tookey, 2009; Zinoman, 2007), yet the relationship between 'porn', 'violence', and 'extremity' requires explication. Since sex and sexual torture are less common than non-sexual forms of violence in torture porn, if the subgenre is pornographic – as the label suggests – it is so because of the non-sexual bloodshed contained therein. If violence is pornographic, it is unclear what label should be used to categorise non-violent forbidden images. It is also unclear what position sexual depictions occupy on the 'extremity' scale, or whether sexual images *are* still 'pornographic'. The meanings of 'porn' have become indistinct because the term is used to refer both to a conventionalised genre/industry, and also to that which is taboo by contemporaneous standards. This conflation is not problematic as long as the porn genre's content *is* taboo. Since mainstream pornography does not carry the same social stigma it has in previous decades according to those involved in the industry (see *Frontline*; *9to5*) and its critics (see Sarracino and Scott, 2008; Dines, 2010), various forms of explicit sexual imagery are not currently prohibited. The gap between the two definitions of 'porn' has therefore widened, resulting in ambiguity. Critics' utilisation of 'porn' as a metaphor attests to the term's haziness in contemporary discourse. 'Torture porn' is the product of an era in which 'porn' became applicable to all manner of visual imagery, including portrayals of poverty, food, and architecture, for instance (see Lovece, 2010; Yong, 2010). This overuse of 'porn' is symptomatic of a discursive struggle to impose meaning, which constantly eludes. Subsequently, in order to distinguish what imagery is unacceptable within the porn genre, a qualifying term has been employed: 'extreme porn'.

Textual detail provides a way into grasping what exactly 'extremity' means in this context. This dissection is not limited to torture porn alone: extreme porn and hardcore horror will also be drawn upon in Part III. Those three forms will be approached in Chapters 7–9, respectively. Unlike torture porn, both extreme pornography and hardcore horror films offer graphic combinations of sex and violence. Although they have been largely ignored by the press, these peripheral subgenres fit the term 'torture porn' more aptly than films such as *Martyrs* and *The Human Centipede* do. Thus, 'torture porn' discourse can usefully inform non-horror filmic analysis. Referring to Jensen's submission that pornography has become increasingly cruel, Chapter 8 will illustrate the forms of 'torture' offered within extreme porn. This discussion will be exemplified with reference to Tusion's sado-degradation porn series, *Meatholes*. As the analysis of camerawork, dialogue, and diegetic contextualisation will confirm, Tusion celebrates humiliation and sexual 'torture' in ways that torture porn filmmakers do not. Tusion seeks to 'expose' female performers, both sexually and psychologically. Tusion is both camera-operator and anti-counsellor in these films, probing female porn-stars about their personal lives during the sex act. The result for performer Nikki Hunter is that she halts her scene in *Meatholes 2*, breaking down in tears while Tusion continues to film. This incident epitomises the kind of 'torture pornography' *Meatholes* offers.

By comparing Tusion's mode of obscene unveiling to Chapter 7's horror-based discussion, the differences between extreme porn and torture porn's aesthetic practices will become apparent. Many of extreme porn's conventionalised facets – point-of-view shooting, graphic realism, bodily exposure, titillating misogyny – precisely match accusations that have been inappropriately levelled at torture porn. Comparing torture porn to extreme porn therefore underscores how hyperbolic 'torture porn' rhetoric is. Chapter 8's latter segments will be devoted to further unpicking the relationship between porn and horror by briefly engaging with horror-themed pornography. In contrast to torture porn, which has been publically scapegoated as the nadir of sexual horror, horror-porn's unambiguous union of intercourse and violence has received virtually no attention from journalists or scholars. As Jay McRoy (2010: 191) notes, many film scholars have compared hardcore pornographic cinema to the splatter subgenre's 'goriest offerings', yet literal porn-horror amalga-mations remain under-theorised. The flawed combination 'torture *porn*' has flourished because of that very under-theorisation.

The conventions that signal porn's 'extremity' according to contem-porary standards – particularly extreme porn's 'authenticity' and its overt merging of sex and violence – are also found in hardcore horror. Hardcore horror, as it is termed herein, refers to a branch of independent horror films that differ from torture porn in significant ways. First, geni-tally explicit depictions of sexual violence are prioritised in hardcore horror. Second, little context is provided for that violence since narra-tive storytelling is usually downplayed in these films. Third, many hard-core horror filmmakers employ a realist aesthetic, connoting that the violent content is spontaneous and genuine rather than performed and contrived. These three attributes are shared by both hardcore horror and contemporaneous extreme pornography: that is, both differ from torture porn for the same reasons. The language of porn ('hardcore') is adopted to connote those similarities, and to underscore the differences between hardcore horror and torture porn.

However, extreme porn and hardcore horror also differ. Hardcore horror's violent displays are achieved via special-effects, whereas extreme porn's spectacles chiefly derive from bodily interactions. Also, hardcore horror is not illegitimated in the same way extreme pornog-raphy is. The industry standard for distributing hardcore pornography is via age-restricted websites and licensed 'adult' stores, for example, and hardcore horror is not necessarily impeded in this manner. Such industrial factors also highlight further differences between hard-core horror and torture porn. Hardcore horror is mostly produced on micro-budgets. Even modestly budgeted torture porn films are mainstream by comparison. The 'extreme' content that marks hardcore horror as hardcore also precludes hardcore horror filmmakers from utilising the supply chains that are open to torture porn's distributors. Hardcore horror's routes to market are limited to self-publication and independent distribution. Such exclusion may be intentionally self-imposed. Hardcore horror filmmakers may deliberately eschew theatrical success by choosing to include taboo imagery, opting instead for infamy and moderate commercial accomplishment relative to their micro-budget productions.

The difference between torture porn's and hardcore horror's distributional paths is markedly clear in the UK context. All DVD content sold in the UK must be certificated by the BBFC. In contrast, the MPAA's submission process is voluntary, and filmmakers have the opportunity to release unrated DVD versions of their movies in America. Even if the unrated DVD system is economically coercive inasmuch as non-certification hampers exhibition opportunities (see Sandler, 2002: 208), hardcore horror may be legally sold alongside unrated torture porn films in America. Hardcore horror filmmakers utilise the unrated DVD system to their advantage since it provides freedom to explore taboo subject matter. The same is not true in the UK. Although fictional, hardcore horror films' sexual violence violates the BBFC's criteria for classifying even hardcore pornographic DVDs. Hardcore horror is akin to extreme pornography in this regard.

Together, Chapters 8 and 9 will delineate the relationships between 'extremity' and 'porn' in order to better elucidate the function of 'torture porn'. Comparing these three forms verifies how inapposite it is to describe torture porn as 'extreme'. This appraisal also illustrates that 'extremity' is a relative assessment. Particular acts and images are deemed 'extreme' if they violate contemporaneous standards of acceptability. In that sense, the standards themselves matter less than the violation. 'Extreme' images today are no less extreme than 'extreme' images were a hundred years ago, since those images were taboo according to their contemporaneous standards. It makes little sense to compare past and present pornographic or horrific images and then proclaim that contemporary images are more extreme or 'worse', as torture porn's opponents frequently put it. The specific traits that signal 'extremity' have changed over time, but what those attributes conceptually signify in comparison to their contemporaneous context does not. Analysis should not simply aim to demarcate which images or acts violate current standards, but to consider what these texts signify *by* violating standards.

Following the same method utilised when discussing morality in Part II, 'extremity' is a conceptual framework that will drive Part III's analyses. Textual particularity will be used as a route into grasping conceptual concerns. The examples drawn upon here are limited to commercially made films that are aligned with the porn or horror genres since these are relevant to torture porn's generic context. This is not to imply that extreme porn or hardcore horror offer the most 'extreme' material available. Extreme porn is excessive by the standards of mainstream feature pornography. Even so, compared with genuine child-rape images ('paedophilic porn'), for instance, the commercial availability of extreme porn renders it mainstream. This comparison further demonstrates how relative 'extremity' is. Contemporary debates regarding a 'turn to the extreme' in visual media are, like 'torture porn' discourse, primarily directed towards commercial material (see Horeck and Kendall (2011), for example). 'Extreme' and 'peripheral' will hereinafter only be used in reference to commercial films. 'Extreme' designates that acceptability standards have been breached within the commercial context. Torture porn's detractors have regularly employed the term 'extreme' to establish where the threshold of acceptability lies. However, without a synchronic account of porn and horror's 'extreme' materials, it is unclear what torture porn's 'extremity' is being measured against. Addressing relative points on the 'extremity' spectrum is vital in order to test how valid 'porn' is as a descriptor for torture porn.

7
'Ladies First'?:[1] Torture Porn, Sex, and Misogyny

Although Edelstein (2006) uses the 'porn' metaphor to portray contemporary horror as 'extreme', he remains vague about what constitutes gratuity, and why he employs 'porn' to convey excessiveness. His incendiary article dwells on moral ambivalence more than gore, and he barely mentions sex. That foundational imprecision is evident in subsequent conflicting interpretations of the 'porn' in 'torture porn'. First, torture porn has been characterised as horror in which images of nudity and/ or sexual violence are given precedence (Dipaolo, 2011: 208; Bor, 2007; Cochrane, 2007). Second, torture porn is indicted for showing non-sexual violence in such gory, close-up detail that its aesthetic is akin to pornography. Torture porn filmmakers are thus accused of emphasising 'lush, saturated close-ups of oozing, gaping wounds' (Schiesel, 2009; see also Terrell, 2009). Edelstein's (2006) comment that director Gaspar Noe 'rub[s] your nose' in *Irreversible*'s violence may have influenced this line of thought. These proposals corroborate the insinuation that torture porn's violent spectacles are excessive, being unnecessary to convey narrative meaning. Graham (2009a) refers to violence as replacing narrative meaning, citing 'home-made YouTube montages simply comprising torture scenes from the *Saw* films' as evidence that torture porn fans regard gore sequences as the equivalent of feature-pornography's sex scenes. In Graham's estimation, 'context is just an irritation' for fans. Ergo, a third interpretation is that torture is 'porn' because the subgenre's violence is presented 'for titillation' (Kirkland, 2008b; see also Hayes, 2010). It is averred that the audience find torture sexually stimulating. For example, Sarracino and Scott (2008: 162) report that 'men' respond to *Hostel: Part II* with 'orgasmic ... erotic joy'. The authors thereby decry torture porn, claiming that the subgenre is misogynistic and encourages sexual violence against women (2008: 164; see also Platell, 2008).

In sum, what constitutes torture's 'pornographication' is subject to disagreement. The three-pronged attack on torture porn outlined above entails 'porn' being utilised as unspecific, pejorative shorthand for all three accusations. Objectors' failure to define what is meant by 'porn' or to distinguish between the three complaints leads to inconsistencies. These assumptions will be scrutinized in this chapter by examining torture porn films themselves, leading to the conclusion that torture porn is not pornographic in any of the three aforementioned senses. Quantitative analysis of torture porn's content will be employed to evince that sexual violence is nowhere near as widespread in torture porn as the subgenre's detractors have propounded. In the remainder of the chapter, torture porn's content will be analysed qualitatively. Dialogic references to sexual violence and sex–violence juxtapositions have been misconstrued as sexually violent content by many critics, for instance, and this may explain why torture porn's pornographic reputation persists despite its non-pornographic content.

The second aim of this chapter is to challenge the assumption that torture porn is a misogynistic subgenre per se. Here it is argued that accusations of misogyny stem more from the label 'porn' and its discursive history than from torture porn's content. The majority of torture porn's sexual violence is perpetrated by men against women. However, qualitative evaluation of filmic content will demonstrate that misogynistic attitudes are contextualised as sources of horror in torture porn. Moreover, misogyny is inadequate to encompass how varied sexual horror is. Since torture porn has been painted as both misogynistic and pornographic, scrutinising torture porn's most horrifying instances of sexual violence is a necessary intervention, despite the relative scarcity of such depictions in the subgenre.

'Jane Doe: The Object':[2] 'porn' and misogyny

Torture is illicit, always-already requiring justification. For example, the 1984 Geneva Convention against torture declares that '[n]o exceptional circumstances whatsoever...may be invoked as a justification of torture' (Upadhyay, 1999: 34), pre-empting efforts to rationalise torture. Following the Military Commissions Act in 2006, the Bush Administration was called upon to retrospectively justify sanctioning CIA torture programs. The need to validate torture has also infected the term itself: as Chapter 3 illustrated, even filmmakers who evoke torture in fictional contexts are required to vindicate that choice. 'Torture porn' is situated by the prohibition written into the concept of torture.

The term 'torture' itself implies that the subgenre's violence is morally problematic, excessive, and perhaps indefensible.

The combination 'torture porn' is both powerfully provocative and punitive in tone because, like 'torture', 'porn' is typically met with calls for rationalisation. For instance, Maher (2009a) demands 'cultural justification' for *Embodiment of Evil*'s 'misogyny'. Such attacks have compelled directors to defend their films' sexual content, especially when it is violent. Some such vindications are production-based. Shankland, for example, notes that the two female actors playing sufferers in *wΔz*'s rape sequence (Selma Blair and Sheila Kerr) fully consented to performing in the scene. According to his DVD commentary, Kerr even thanked Shankland, saying it was 'the best night of her life'. Antithetically, Shankland reports he 'felt ill' and the crew were 'weeping'. These dual statements underline that actor safety was a priority, that *wΔz* is fictional, and that the crew were sensitive to the rape scene's emotional affect. In his DVD commentary accompanying *The Collector*,[3] Patrick Melton takes a different line, referring to the narrative's sexually violent connotations as thematically necessary.

These apologias indicate that filmmakers expect to be censured for evoking sex, attesting to the prevalence of such disdain. However, much like the critical accusations they face, filmmakers' justifications commonly lack specificity. Several filmmakers undermine their own defences by using the lexicon of pornography to describe violence. Shankland refers to *wΔz*'s torture set-pieces as 'money shots', for instance, and Roth refers to *Hostel*'s pus-laden eye-removal as an 'eyegasm'.[4] These directors acknowledge the 'porn' problem, but assimilate and replicate those discursive associations rather than unpicking and overturning them.

Additionally, these directors' flippant remarks fail to acknowledge how politically provocative the label 'porn' is. The term's history is vital, as it reveals why their explanations are required in the first instance. The politically epithetical connotations that surround 'porn' today were predominantly founded in feminist anti-porn discourse. Those highly impactful debates linked pornography with 'woman hating' (Dworkin, 1974), the main consensus among anti-porn feminists of the period being that pornography manifests misogyny. More recent critical accusations regarding torture porn's alleged misogyny and pornographic violence proliferate these established discursive narratives. The porn-horror connection propounded via 'torture porn' is reminiscent of numerous anti-pornography campaigners' conflations of pornography with popular horror film. For example, horror movies such as *The Texas*

Chainsaw Massacre (1974) and *I Spit on Your Grave* (1978) have been explicitly referred to as 'porn' (Everywoman, 1988: 19). Fourteen years before Edelstein coined 'torture porn', Jane Caputi (1992) similarly used the term 'gorenography'[5] to denigrate popular horror film. According to these anti-porn campaigners, popular horror film is akin to porn because both genres privilege male pleasure to the detriment of female liberty.

Following the same logic, torture porn filmmakers are routinely charged with misogyny. Reviewers recurrently assert that the subgenre's violence is 'directed primarily against women' (Riegler, 2010: 27), many singling-out Roth's films in this regard (Scott, 2010; Sandhu, 2007). Torture porn is not the first horror subgenre to fall privy to such grievances. Slasher films, for instance, have also been unjustly dubbed misogynistic.[6] Both subgenres, it is often postulated, specifically centre on men victimising women. Many of torture porn's detractors replicate these complaints rather than engaging with filmic content, taking this well-established discursive correlation between porn, horror, and misogyny for granted.

Torture porn's objectors have principally drawn on two high-profile examples to demonstrate that the subgenre is misogynistic. The first is *Hostel*'s depictions of nudity in its opening third and murder in its latter sequences. It is rare for torture porn films to be as sexually oriented as *Hostel*, but as one of the subgenre's most financially successful films, and one that Edelstein discussed when coining 'torture porn', *Hostel* became a touchstone in the torture porn/misogyny debate. The second example is *Captivity*'s original poster campaign, which was publically decried for depicting a woman undergoing a four-stage execution ritual, labelled 'Abduction. Confinement. Torture. Termination' (see Brodesser-Anker, 2007; Kermode, 2007). The poster is clearly of greater concern than the film itself, since *Captivity*'s tame content is seldom mentioned in such articles. For instance, Sarracino and Scott (2008: 164) cite the poster to illustrate *Captivity*'s vileness, but disregard the narrative entirely (see also Leydon, 2007; Williamson, 2007c).

Since these high-profile examples have been perceived as corroborating existing critical paradigms regarding horror and misogyny, the majority of critics have arrived at the consensus that *all* torture porn films are misogynistic. Consequently, misogyny has become an attribute of 'torture porn'. This same logic is in operation where reviewers extract single unrepresentative elements such as Danica's full-frontal nakedness in *Saw III* – the only instance of nudity in a series that contains no sex or sexual violence – as proof that the whole franchise is misogynistic (see Kinsella, 2007). Subsequent detractors have propagated that presumption, erroneously concluding that *Saw* is fixated on 'starlets being strung up' (Orange, 2009) and 'taboo-breaking sex and violence' (Graham, 2009a).

'You must excite me sexually...with your will to survive':[7] a closer look at content

The contention that torture porn is pornographic/misogynistic is undermined by press pundits' tendency to misrepresent the subgenre's content. In the 45 films that have been referred to by three or more major International English language publications as 'torture porn' (at the time of writing),[8] 244 males and 108 females are killed. 293 male characters and 144 female characters are severely injured. More than twice the number of males than females die or are injured in these films. 206 incidents of males harming females are nearly equalled by 155 occasions of females harming males. Furthermore, these figures are dwarfed by 351 instances of males harming other males. Patently, torture porn is not as skewed towards men harming women as disparagers have suggested.

These 45 torture porn films contain 67 acts of sexual violence, but also feature 42 consensual sex acts, so it would be misrepresentative to suggest that torture porn filmmakers are fixated on sexual violence. Torture porn is certainly not as sexually graphic as claimed: only half the consensual sex acts are shown on-screen. More sexual violence occurs off-screen (37 incidents) than is presented on-screen (30 occurrences). Torture porn narratives are clearly not dominated by sexual imagery since these quantities are overshadowed by the 579 severe injuries and 311 deaths displayed on-screen. Quantitatively, torture porn's content is neither as misogynistic nor pornographic as its depreciators have assumed.

Qualitative assessment of torture porn's sex and violence requires greater detail, examining character motivation and narrative contextualisation. Qualitative assessment also helps to expound why torture porn is believed to be sexually oriented despite the quantitative evidence failing to support those assumptions. The quantitative statistics above do not account for symbolic violence arising from misogynistic language, for instance, or the effect such dialogue has on tone. In *Storm Warning*, patriarch Pop informs his sons that 'women are only good for getting fucked', and that attitude is replicated in Jimmy's verbal threats to lead protagonist Pia ('I'm gonna tear your eyes out and fucking skull fuck ya, bitch'). Regardless of what acts actually ensue then, *Storm Warning*'s dialogue connotes gender-biased sexual violence.

Similarly, *I Spit on Your Grave*'s physical violence is significantly augmented by the degradation lead protagonist Jennifer endures. Jennifer is made to perform a strip-dance after Johnny threatens to cut her from 'chin to cunt', for example. This is a form of sexual violence that is hard to quantify because it is demeaning and coercive rather than physically injurious. The film's emblematic violence is embodied via Sheriff Storch. Storch is introduced as Jennifer's saviour because he represents the law, yet it transpires that he is the lead rapist. His betrayal destroys Jennifer's hope and intensifies her crisis. Storch's role-shift thus significantly impacts on the tone of the rape sequence. Storch's cruel dialogue – whispering 'you can thank me later' to Jennifer after the first rape, for instance – exemplifies how verbal exchanges and role shifts embellish the material acts of sexual violence that occur. Jennifer's terrorisation is prolonged and hard to stomach. The degradation she suffers is certainly a form of symbolic sexual violence, yet relatively little physical violence is exhibited on-screen prior to the revenge sequences. Only two rapes are portrayed, three more being conveyed by dialogue. The film's figurative violence may cultivate the impression that more material violence has occurred on-screen than is actually the case because Jennifer's ordeal is so harrowing.

In other instances, sex and violence are juxtaposed, which may also lead critics to misassess the quantity of sexual violence depicted. Torture porn's diegetic environments are often imbued with sex, even if sexual violence is not actualised. The presence of strippers in *Live Feed*, *Hostel: Part III*, and *I Know Who Killed Me*, or prostitutes in *Breaking Nikki*, *Borderland*, and *Death Factory: Bloodletting* might foster the impression that violence is somehow connected to sex in these narrative contexts. In other cases, sex acts or nudity are directly apposed with gore. 21 of the 42 consensual sex acts in these 45 films are situated alongside violence. There are 19 occasions of non-genital male nudity, 13 of which are adjacent to images of bloodshed. Fourteen out of 20 incidents of full-frontal male nudity are paired with violence. Of the 65 occurrences of non-genitally explicit female nudity, 17 are depicted in conjunction with bloodshed. 32 of the 41 occurrences of full-frontal female nudity are contiguous with violence. Female nudity is more widespread than male. Torture porn features over double the amount of female full-frontal nudity and nearly five times the quantity of female non-genital nudity compared with male nakedness. Commonplace nudity-bloodshed collocations may have contributed to the belief that torture porn's violence is sexualised. The bias towards coupling full-frontal female nudity with bloodshed in torture porn may have also concretised the impression that torture porn is misogynistic. Moreover, when compared with

Brian Sapolsky, Fred Molitor, and Sarah Luque's (2003) study of 1980s and 1990s popular horror movies, these findings suggest that torture porn films juxtapose nudity and bloodshed more frequently than their generic predecessors. This increase alone may explain why torture porn has been accused of pornographication, even if sexual violence is not as ubiquitous as has been contended by torture porn's detractors.

When violence *is* gendered – especially where men commit violence and women are subjected to violence – it is necessary to scrutinise the impact narrative has on interpretation. For example, *Penance*'s characters display alarming attitudes towards female sexual agency. *Penance*'s protagonist (single-mother Amelia) struggles to pay for her daughter's medication. In desperation, and under the advice of her friend (exotic dancer Suzie), Amelia tries stripping. Amelia discovers that she is 'a natural'. Once sexual commodification has been naturalised in this way, it is consequently associated with gendered subordination: Suzie refers to her black eye as 'an occupational hazard'; a male threatens to rape Amelia at Suzie's strip-show; Amelia is then abducted by a psychotic male ex-gynaecologist (Geeves) *because* she is a stripper. Amelia is portrayed as having no choice other than to use her body to make money, and then sexual commodification is equated with persecution. Only women are imprisoned against their will in *Penance*, and Geeves's agency ('my work') takes precedence over their agony.

However, that is not to say that *Penance* is plainly misogynistic. 'Misogyny' denotes hatred for women, but also implies a bias: that men are not also represented negatively (otherwise the representations would be 'misanthropic' rather than 'misogynistic'). Men have power in *Penance*, but they are also painted as psychotic. Suzie's jeering clients are would-be-rapists. Geeves imprisons and attempts to 'cleanse' strippers by genitally mutilating them. Geeves correlates corporeal modification with spiritual purification. Because he sees women only as bodies, his outlook is paralleled to the male strip-show audience's. Women are objectified in both viewpoints, and those attitudes are ultimately reified as monstrous violence (genital mutilation). Additionally, since Geeves's torture-experiments are fuelled by his sexual perversity, and are placed in a continuum with the strip-show audience's attitudes, any voyeuristic pleasure *Penance*'s audience derive from seeing Amelia and Suzie strip is undercut by the subsequent genital violence. By paralleling Geeves and the strip-show audience, *Penance* underscores that misogyny – whether physically enacted or symbolic – is inherently violent.

These representations do not code male dominance as appealing.[9] Lead antagonist Geeves is the text's most powerful male, yet he is also

Figure 7.1   Geeves castrates himself in *Penance* (2009, USA, dir Jake Kennedy)

clearly deranged. He castrates himself as well as mutilating Amelia's genitals. His agency is not only destructive: it is also self-destructive. Because Geeves's occasional control of the camera occurs at the text's most horrific stages – namely its dual genital mutilation sequences – his perspective is coded as alienating. Geeves's stance is not cultivated as a point of empathy. In contrast, Amelia is the focal point of the film. Amelia presents her ordeal in the first-person, and so the form validates her narratological power. Talking directly to camera, she positions the spectator as witness to her ordeal, referring to the camcorder footage as 'proof'. This repeated term unambiguously characterises the violence she suffers as an immoral crime.

Even when Amelia is being filmed rather than controlling the camera, her character arc drives the story. The *narrative* perspective primarily attends to Amelia's emotive responses. Amelia's backstory is the narrative's point-of-entry, fostering empathy for her plight. Her motivation – to help her daughter – is understandable, being rooted in compassion. Geeves's motives, in opposition, are vicious and incoherent. His backstory – that he 'mutilated the genitals of over three hundred women' while working as a gynaecologist – is only imparted via a caption at the film's cessation, and further substantiates his villainy. *Penance*'s plot-synopsis sounds irredeemably misogynistic. In practice, the film is unpleasant, yet the narrative is directed towards vilifying Geeves's sexual violence rather than ogling Amelia's terror.

Female protagonists' perspectives are customarily foregrounded in torture porn narratives. *Manhunt*, *The Strangers*, and *Caged* reserve first-person shots exclusively for central heroines (Camilla, Kristen, and Carole, respectively). Similarly, *Wolf Creek* follows its female protagonists (Liz and Kristy), never its male torturer (Mick). The narrative's only male protagonist (Ben) is missing throughout their torture, spotlighting that the narrative is female-driven. These cases illustrate how the subgenre's lead female protagonists are typically demarcated as significant. Like *Penance*, these films encode their plight as the narrative's empathic core.

Nevertheless, that engagement may also explain pundits' pejorative responses to torture porn. Sapolsky and Molitor (1996: 46) aver that grievances regarding the prevalence of sex–violence juxtapositions in horror commonly stem from misperception. According to their study, when sex and violence do collude, that combination offends audience sensibilities. The result is that audiences remember those instances more vividly than other forms of violence, and so imagine that a greater proportion of the film was devoted to exhibiting sexual violence than was actually the case. Given that 'porn' is discursively linked with gender inequality, this same memorability is exacerbated by the prevailing tendency to narratologically privilege threatened female protagonists' perspectives in torture porn. When those characters are harmed, empathic allegiance with their suffering may lead audiences to surmise that greater harm was done. Narrative mechanisms that centralise female protagonists' emotional states may lead critics to believe that violence against women is more frequent, prolonged, or intense than violence aimed at male characters.

Concentrating on isolated violent moments and failing to address structure's impact on meaning can lead to flawed assessments of filmic content, then. A case in point is Linnie Blake's analysis of *Creep*'s sexual violence, specifically antagonist Craig stabbing a female protagonist (Mandy) in the vagina. Blake's (2008: 179–80) complaint that not enough detail is given to rationalise Craig's actions is unsound. Were his backstory revealed as motivation, Craig would become more understandable. Since Craig's motives are unidentifiable, the narrative discourages viewers from tolerating his cruel actions. Blake's conclusion that excluding Craig's backstory evinces 'the director's intention' to frame Craig as 'the real victim' is illogical.

That Blake is offended by the incident is clear in the language she uses. Blake (2008: 180) proclaims that 'it is hard to know precisely what the film thinks it is doing, if indeed it thinks at all'. Her argument hinges on the same supposition that pervades popular journalistic responses to torture porn: that such violence requires justification. The flaws in her reasoning underscore that no matter how affronting the content may be, in order to adequately account for torture porn's sexual violence, factors such as symbolic violence, narrative contextualisation, and discursive contexts must be addressed.

'There's a lot of things not right down here':[10] rape, narrative, and horror

Where it occurs in torture porn, sexual violence mainly manifests as rape. This can be both attempted (*Breathing Room*, *Grindhouse*, *Wilderness*), or committed (*Stash*, *Deadgirl*, *The Devil's Rejects*, *The Hills Have Eyes*). Where rape does occur, its portrayal can affect how the film is perceived as a whole. For instance, *Irreversible*'s rape sequence lasts eleven minutes in total, and is filmed in a single unbroken shot. The camera's stasis during the scene is accentuated by its contrast to the nauseating, kinetic camerawork employed in the film's earlier sequences. Although these formal devices are unusual in torture porn,[11] *Irreversible* has been dubbed (proto-)torture porn by numerous reviewers, insinuating that the film is 'extreme' (Zoc, 2008; Newman, 2009a). For these critics, the protracted rape sequence dominates the film, eclipsing the rest of the narrative.

It is not just the duration of *Irreversible*'s rape sequence that is affecting. The lack of cut-aways or angle switches during the scene aligns the narrative with lead protagonist Alex's plight. Since she is pinned down, the single shot that captures her rape offers no escape from her suffering. To highlight her entrapment, a background figure briefly appears in the distance during the rape. The figure pauses before hastily walking away. To notice this minor detail, the viewer has to have been searching the screen, actively avoiding the rape that

Figure 7.2   A background figure walks away from the rape in *Irreversible* (2002, France, dir Gaspar Noe)

dominates the frame. Looking away equates to evading Alex's ordeal, as the background figure does. This mechanism inculpates *Irreversible*'s viewer as witness to the rape. One's compassionate instinct to help Alex is also frustrated by the same device. Intervention is impossible. Edelstein's (2006) recollection of *Irreversible* is imbued with that sensibility: 'I stared at the EXIT sign, then closed my eyes...I didn't understand why I had to be tortured, too'. His response attests to how emotionally affecting the sequence is, and how effective the structural devices are in conveying Alex's distress. Rape is depicted in *Irreversible*, yet that does mean the film is misogynistic or titillating as Edelstein's evocation of 'porn' proposes.

Although Edelstein acknowledges that *Irreversible*'s rape sequence is designed to be emotionally provocative, what he 'didn't understand' is the purpose of empathic manipulation. In this case, Alex's boyfriend (Marcus) responds to the rape by exacting violent revenge. Depicting the rape in its full horror encourages the viewer to share in Marcus's outrage, but the gap between the comprehendible, emotionally-loaded impetus (rape), and Marcus's response (revenge) raises queries over morality, revenge, and emotive sway. Marcus perceives Alex's rape as a slight on his manhood: proof that he failed to protect her. He discusses the rape as if he was injured rather than Alex, stating 'it's my problem. [Revenge is] my right'. Displaying Alex's ordeal so unambiguously is a means of underscoring that Marcus's outdated machismo is inappropriate. Far from marking *Irreversible* as misogynistic then, the rape sequence (a) is encoded in empathic alignment with Alex's suffering, (b) underlines Marcus's chauvinism, and (c) undermines that chauvinism. Indeed, Marcus's behaviour is far from heroic as he slaps and insults a prostitute (Guillermo) to obtain information. Marcus's actions – pulling Guillermo's hair and pressing a glass shard against her face – directly parallel Tenia's attack on Alex. Marcus's revenge is presented as futile since it is analogous to his impetus (the violence Alex undergoes).

Marcus's friend Pierre exposes Marcus's hypocrisy, declaring '[i]t won't make Alex any better...Even animals don't seek revenge'. The dialogue signposts gaps between outraged emotional responses and rational thought, casting doubt over the righteousness of revenge.[12] Most importantly, the plot's incidents are imparted in reverse chronological order. As the narrative portrays the events, Marcus's retaliation precedes his impetus (the rape), elucidating that it cannot resolve Alex's suffering. Pierre's objection ('you don't know what happened...What's your anger all about?') is thereby supported by the narrative structure in which Marcus's violent response is not contextualised until after the fact.

Although few rape-revenge torture porn films share *Irreversible*'s distinctive formal manipulations, most evoke the same thematic concerns. Brutality is predominantly emphasised over sex in torture porn. Accordingly, the subgenre's depictions of rape are unambiguously presented as unprovoked, horrific violence. Torture porn's rape-violence is not straightforwardly about misogyny, and attending to narrative contextualisation is necessary to ascertain these meanings. As with other forms of violence in the subgenre, rape-revenge stimulates moral problems, rather than sexual arousal.

Missing is a case in point. The film's depictions of rape and revenge generate moral challenges that are akin to those found in *Irreversible* and other torture porn films that eschew narrative resolution. Ms. Kang, *Missing*'s lead protagonist, escapes from and murders antagonist-abductor Pan-gon, who raped and murdered Kang's sister (Hyun-ah). Kang's revenge is not celebrated in *Missing*, even though Pan-gon has been prevented from committing future harm. Kang admits 'I wasn't myself when I shot [Pan-gon]', but is adamant that she lucidly and intentionally mutilated his body. As she recounts the event to her defence attorney her expression is hateful, and wholly unlike her demeanour elsewhere in the film. Her trauma cannot be resolved by eradicating Pan-gon. Kang refuses to plead temporary insanity, and faces a jail sentence for her actions. The end result is that Hyun-ah is dead, and Kang is incarcerated. Kang is irrevocably changed by her experience, and nothing can compensate for her loss. In cases where rapists go unpunished – including *Irreversible*, *Dying Breed*, and *The Great Ecstasy of Robert Carmichael* – the same horror resonates just as clearly. The narratives remain unresolved because nothing can compensate for the suffering rape causes.

Another means of raising moral tensions is to imbalance the two types of violence – rape and revenge – thereby problematising the narrative's retributive aspect. For example, revenge dominates *Callback*'s duration, and only in the climactic moments is it disclosed that the lead protagonist-avenger (Meadow) has been raped. The rape that impels Meadow barely features in the narrative. The prominence of revenge reflects how all-consuming Meadow's anger and suffering are. Simultaneously, her vengeful violence cannot be contextualised until after the rapist (Levi) has been tortured. Since it is unclear why Levi is being harmed until the film's finale, two questions are continually raised: what triggered the torture, and is the torment justified? Once revealed, one may conclude that Levi does indeed deserve to be punished, yet characterising Levi as a sufferer for the film's duration distances the viewer from

Meadow's outrage. Revenge is divorced from retributive satisfaction, casting doubt over revenge's ability to provide emotional resolution. The gap created between cause (rape) and response (revenge) raises doubts over how morally sound retaliation is, in spite of Meadow's understandable motivation.

Imbalances between rape and revenge are not only contingent on the proportion of the narrative devoted to each. One reason *I Spit on Your Grave*'s rape is more horrific than its revenge is because the torturer-to-tortured ratio is so skewed. Jennifer is raped by five men, but is alone in taking revenge. In both rape *and* revenge, she is severely disadvantaged by their group power. No matter how brutal the torture she inflicts, that disproportion means her revenge can never match the rape: each rapist is only tortured and murdered once, whereas Jennifer is raped five times. For some anti-porn feminists, representations of rape are politically significant because rape is always-already imbalanced. Prominent anti-porn campaigner Catharine MacKinnon (2007: 129) postulates that rape symbolises gender inequality. In this view, rape hypostatises centuries of patriarchal dominance and misogyny. Revenge does not carry the same symbolic weight. In *I Spit on Your Grave*, that gender disparity is literalised via Jennifer's proportional power-disadvantage. Acquiescing with facets established in earlier rape-revenge films such as *Ms. 45*, a few torture porn rape-revenge films such as *Naked Fear* literalise MacKinnon's ethos that rape is a crime that impacts on an entire gender. *Naked Fear* depicts a female who is raped and subsequently takes revenge not on her male attacker specifically but on *men* in general.

Several problems arise from this assessment of rape as emblematic, misogynistic violence. Principally, personal suffering is overshadowed by the act's symbolic nature. Torture porn narratives conflict with that assessment, since the subgenre's films chiefly hinge on the woundeds' emotive responses. Furthermore, interpreting rape as a signifier of gender inequality insinuates that only women are affected by rape, and that only men commit rape. Related positions – such as Teresa de Lauretis's (1987: 152) argument that '[w]hen a man is raped, he too is raped as a woman', and Susan Brownmiller's (1976) vision of men as penetrators[13] – conform to this logic. The notion that a woman cannot rape because she does not have a penis spotlights specific physiological differences between men and women. Rape is equated with an exclusively male body part to explain the logic that only men rape.[14] Moreover, if rape embodies gender conflict as the figurative reading suggests, rape also epitomises an unassailable gender difference. As such, the emblematic appraisal risks positing that rape results from that difference. This interpretation both essentialises gender and supports a dichotomous vision of gendered power.[15] Such argumentation intimates that gender conflict is natural and unavoidable, which is one reason that these paradigms have been rejected by numerous third-wave feminists. However, these somewhat outmoded ideas are sustained via common critical presumptions about torture porn, particularly the twin assumptions that torture porn must be misogynistic and biased towards heterosexual male pleasure.

'I don't want to fuck you, but I'd like to kill you very much':[16] beyond misogynistic sexual violence

In framing torture porn as a subgenre invested in sexual violence enacted by men on women, torture porn's detractors propagate the notion that only women are targets of sexual violence. It is not surprising that rape is positioned at the forefront of discussion about torture porn's sexual violence since, as Sarah Projansky (2001: 20) has submitted, 'rape is central to cinema itself'. However, misogynistic rape does not constitute a complete account of sexual violence. Ergo, when it *is* depicted, sexual horror manifests in numerous ways in torture porn. These other forms of violation have been overlooked in 'torture porn' discourse, perhaps because there are fewer established critical paradigms available to explain such depictions. Indeed, these alternative forms of sexual violence not only evince that torture porn is not simply a misogynistic subgenre, but also offer multiple challenges to the prevailing notion that sexual violence equates to male-on-female rape.

First, women are not the only casualties of rape in torture porn. Male-on-male rape, for instance, is both attempted (*Resurrection County*) and occurs (*Madness* and *Header*). In *The Butcher*, it is implied that one female captive is raped, but only a male abductee (lead protagonist, Jae-Hyun) is shown being raped. That attack is presented from Jae-Hyun's point-of-view. The contrast between dialogic references to female rape and the perspectival rendering of male rape is particularly striking, and emphasises the latter.

Second, films such as *The Book of Revelation* openly challenge the notion that men cannot be raped by women. Lead protagonist Daniel is abducted by three women who perform oral sex on him against his will, sodomise him using a dildo, and force him to masturbate. After escaping, Daniel reports the crime to the police. He opens by testifying that 'a friend of mine – a male friend – was abducted by three women'. One of the male officers taking Daniel's statement responds 'poor bastard', and laughs. Statistics about rape's prevalence are considered to be unreliable due to connotations of disgrace that surround the crime, particularly for male sufferers (Weiss, 2010). Daniel's unwillingness to identify himself as the injured party articulates that sense of shame. The scene also exposes a key preconception: the officers treat the idea of women raping men as a joke. Daniel's story, in contrast, attests that rape is traumatic, regardless of the perpetrators' or sufferers' genders. Rape destroys Daniel's life, impacting on his ability to maintain interpersonal relationships.

The Book of Revelation debunks the myth that men are not sexually vulnerable, then. The narrative also repudiates the parallel claim that rape is only perpetrated by men because only men have penises. *The Book of Revelation* is one of several films in which rape is not restricted to penile penetration.[17] In some cases, men use objects rather than their penises to rape women (*The Great Ecstasy of Robert Carmichael*) and other men (*Deaden*). In other cases, women use objects to rape men (*Callback, I Spit on Your Grave, Straightheads*) and other women (*Deaden, wΔz*). None of these ghastly violations are contingent on the rapist having a penis, and so do not characterise rape as exclusively male power inflicted solely on women. Each of these incidents verifies that sexual violence is not primarily abhorrent because it reifies misogyny, but rather because sexual harm is horrific per se.

Genital injury is utilised to illustrate that the male body is sexually pervious in *Neighbor*. The film's nameless female torturer rapes lead protagonist Don by inserting a rod into his penis. Her declaration 'I'll show you what it's like to be violated' overtly characterises genital injury as sexual violence. In this instance, the presumed connotations of 'penile penetration' are reversed: the penis is treated as an orifice rather than an impermeable object. As Geraldine Terry (2007: xiv–xv) observes, 'gender-based violence' is commonly misused as a synonym for 'violence against women' because of the perception that 'the vast majority of [gender-based violence] victims' are female. Attitudes towards genital mutilation highlight that disparity. Claudia Forster-Towne (2011: 33) lists genital mutilation as a form of sexual violence aimed at women for example, whereas Victor Cheney's *Brief History of Castration* (2006) only paints male genital mutilation as a response to sexual assault rather than a type of sexual violence (see also Taylor, 2002). That skew proliferates the notion that women are sexually vulnerable in ways that men are not. Characterising male genital injury as sexual violence, as *Neighbor* does, is an important step in countering such biases.

Castration is rare even in horror, a genre that dwells on bodily deconstruction.[18] Horror's most notorious castration sequences are found in exploitation films such as *Cannibal Ferox* and *I Spit on Your Grave* (1978) rather than in high-profile theatrical offerings. These two films became infamous for their castration scenes precisely because male genital injury is seldom depicted in cinema. Compared with that scarcity, castration is relatively common in torture porn, occurring in *Carver*, *Torture Me No More*, *The Cellar Door*, and *Storm Warning*, for example, and being threatened in *Hard Candy*, *The Loved Ones*, and *Matchdead* amongst others. Torture porn's objectors rarely mention castration, however. That oversight is both symptomatic of and cultivates the prevailing discourse, in which 'porn', sexual violence and misogyny are intertwined. That discourse is also nurtured via censorial decisions. The BBFC ruled that *Neighbor*'s penile penetration shots must be excised for its UK release, for instance, and *Madness*'s male rape sequence was removed for its American unrated DVD release. Since *Madness*'s rape sequence is not especially graphic – it is certainly no more explicit than depictions of women being raped found in some other uncensored torture porn films – one may surmise that the decision to remove the scene was based primarily on the injured party's gender. Literally excising portrayals of male-oriented sexual violence propagates the scarcity of such representations. Moreover, the disparity between rape's prominence and castration's rarity in cinema implies that male-centred sexual violation is unmentionably horrific, whereas female-focused sexual violence is culturally acceptable. By ignoring or removing torture porn's male-focused sexual violence, critics and censors elide the subgenre's oppositional representations.

That is not to suggest that torture porn's depictions of castration simply gainsay hegemonic suppositions about gendered violence. For instance, like many other torture porn films, *Hostel: Part II* includes castration in response to rape-threat. That correlation could be interpreted as proposing that castration is apt punishment for rape because castration emblematically disarms the rapist. Such a reading equates the penis with potency, since its removal is disempowering. This interpretation maintains the discursive narrative that only women are subjected to sexual violence, and that sexual power is an exclusively male privilege. However, *Hostel: Part II*'s contextualisation of rape and castration challenges those biases. Rape and castration are framed differently. The rape-threat is constituted by a single shot of antagonist Stuart looming over lead protagonist Beth, and the sound of Stuart unzipping his fly. Conversely, the castration is displayed via two distanced shots, two close-up crotch/injury shots, one mid-close up and two mid-distance shots of Stuart screaming, and two reaction shots of guards wincing. *Hostel: Part*

II thus displays castration graphically, and only implies rape-as-threat. Male-focused genital injury is accentuated over female-focused sexual violence.

Troublingly, it might appear as if castration is the film's horrific pinnacle. As Roth has it, 'once we cut the dick off, that's the end of the movie'.[19] Although the male antagonist is portrayed as sexually vulnerable then, by reserving that violence for the gory climax Roth presents castration as the film's most horrific incident. *Hostel: Part II* thereby risks feeding the same bias that underpins the BBFC's decision to expunge *Neighbor*'s penile penetration sequence: both suggest that male genital mutilation is the worst imaginable terror. However, the penis is not tallied with gendered power in *Hostel: Part II*. Stuart performs supremacy by threatening to rape Beth and pretending that Beth is his domineering wife. The castration unveils the falsity of that performance. Money buys life or death in *Hostel*'s torture-space: gendered power is a defunct currency within its cells. Beth is revealed to be extraordinarily rich, and consequently vastly more powerful than Stuart. Stuart's castration does not signal a reversal in sovereignty (Beth taking over), because his dominance was an illusion. Stuart's fantasy involves seizing control over Beth via rape, thus envisaging a connection between his penis and power. However, his delusion is swiftly deflated. Once castrated, a dog eats Stuart's severed member, substantiating the appendage's symbolic emptiness: it is just meat, not an instrument of potency.

Sarracino and Scott (2008: 166) decipher Beth resisting rape and castrating Stuart as a power-inversion in which Beth becomes '*the* man'. Their reading supports the idea that manhood denotes power. However, the castration is more accurately Stuart's punishment for trying to reduce Beth to a 'cunt'. Stuart's fantasy entails perceiving all women as interchangeable, irrespective of Beth's repeated protests ('I'm not your wife'). For Stuart, genital difference and gender are inseparable and define power relations. Hence, it is apposite that Beth leaves Stuart to 'bleed to death': *he* is defined by his genitals, since without them, he dies. This does not mean Beth becomes '*the* man', but rather than she overturns the logic that Sarracino and Scott's '*the* man' is founded on. Orchestral music accompanies the sequence from the moment Beth grabs the severed penis until Stuart's cell door is closed. Rather than swelling in the lead up to castration, the score elucidates that Beth's control – not genital mutilation or Stuart's suffering – is *Hostel Part II*'s climax.

Finally, it is notable that torture porn's castration sequences are not exclusively limited to punishing guilty rapists. In *I Saw the Devil*, a genital attack is conducted on an innocent man who is mistaken for a murderer, for example. Castration is not reserved only for textually justified retaliation, or specifically for balancing gender conflict. In *Carver, Inside, 2001 Maniacs,* and *The Book of Revelation*, male genitals are mutilated without any provocation at all. In these cases, assaults on male genitalia are forms of violence in their own right rather than being contingent on or related to rape. Such instances confirm that male bodies are pervious to sexual and genital attacks. Torture porn's various forms of sexual and genital violence are mainly driven by the subgenre's emphases on bodily vulnerability, harm, and human cruelty, rather than misogyny.

'It's going to be upsetting':[20] conclusion

Although torture porn's sexual imagery has clearly upset numerous critics, the subgenre is less sexually graphic or violent than its detractors have typically proposed. Depreciators' umbrage exposes more about critical discourses that situate sex and violence than it does about torture porn's content. Torture porn's opponents almost unanimously agree that sexual representations and female subjugation are contentious subjects, yet 'porn' is used to dismiss the subgenre and close-off debate, subsuming the subgenre's most provocative material into pre-existing discursive narratives regarding gender discrimination and representation. Little attention has been paid to how sexual violence and inequality are contextualised as horrific in the subgenre's films. 'Torture porn' discourse is plagued by this failure to contemplate (a) the terms on which gender stereotypes are corroborated or contested in the subgenre's narratives, (b) the facets that define males or females as weak or powerful figures in these films, and (c) how narrative context shapes meaning. Torture porn's objectors have predominantly failed to account for how varied sexual violence is and how sexual violence intersects with torture porn's moral themes. Instead, 'porn' has been used to validate the erroneous notions that torture porn narratives are invested in sadistic pleasure and that fans concur with antagonists' outlooks.

None of the torture porn films surveyed are simply encoded to encourage viewers to adopt misogynistic characters' viewpoints. The discourse used to rebuke torture porn on these grounds stems from flawed reasoning. Symptomatic of such a mistake is Blake's (2008: 180) disdain for *Creep* because it is unclear 'what the film thinks it is doing'. Films are incapable of intent and thought. What Blake means is that it is unclear what *writer/director Chris Smith* thinks he is doing. Yet, to assume that filmmakers are misogynistic based only on antagonists' actions is an extraordinary leap. Characters must be interpreted as fictional constructs within a narrative context. This entails dealing with filmic detail and adjacent characterisation in order to decode meanings. Narratives about sexual violence depict sexual violence. It does not follow that the creators advocate, or urge viewers to support sexual violence, as Blake infers. Once creator intent is removed from the equation, what remains is tautology: a claim that misogynistic dialogue or action is misogynistic.

The same inadequacies surround pejorative responses to *The Woman*. *The Woman*'s antagonistic patriarch (Chris) is amongst torture porn's most reprehensible characters. Chris abducts the eponymous and anonymous Woman, rapes her, excuses his son for sexually torturing her, beats his timid wife (Belle), and murders his daughter's female teacher. The film is excruciating to watch because Chris is so well performed as a villain. His abusive power is especially frustrating because it remains unchallenged until the film's finale. The power-bias is emotionally loaded. The film's effectiveness is evidenced by one upset viewer's public proclamation that *The Woman* 'ought to be confiscated [and] burned' for its 'degradation of women' (Miska, 2011). The narrative's power dynamic is unambiguously skewed towards male privilege, but that is not to suggest that *The Woman* endorses misogyny. The film's title intimates that the narrative represents a gendered dynamic, yet men who abuse women are unambiguously vilified. Chris's misogynistic attitude is reified as physical and sexual torture, elucidating how monstrous his attitudes are. Furthermore, the Woman kills Belle once freed, propounding that women who remain passive when faced with misogyny are complicit in its mechanics.

Complaints regarding filmmaker intent stem from the twin suppositions that torture porn filmmakers are not politically mindful and that the subgenre is misogynistic per se. In fact, *The Woman*'s illustration of gender inequity shares commonalities with Dworkin's anti-porn diatribes inasmuch as both evoke gendered-power imbalance in an emotionally inflammatory fashion. Indeed, women are also frequently portrayed as imprisoned, sexually abused victims in Dworkin's writing. For example, in *Pornography: Men Possessing Women* (1989: xxiii), Dworkin describes an abusive relationship thus: '[h]e tied her up when he raped her; he broke bones; he forced anal intercourse; he beat her mercilessly; he penetrated her vagina with objects'. This extract epitomises Dworkin's incendiary rhetorical style, which serves as a call-to-action against misogyny. *The Woman*'s intense gendered power-bias is provocative on the same grounds. Regardless of these similarities, critics have presumed that torture porn is antithetical to feminist politics per se. Although Dworkin's polemical style has since been criticised (Williams, 1989: 20–2; Strossen, 2000: 275), and despite the discernible formal differences between narrative drama and political campaigning, being more attentive to similarities may stimulate productive future debate about torture porn's sexual representations.

One final trend requires explication. On the whole, the body of direct-to-DVD, independent torture porn movies released after 2008 contains more sexual violence than is found in the press's 45-film 'torture porn' canon. In *A Darker Reality*, *Megan is Missing*, *The Hike*, *Keepsake*, *Slave*, and *Break*, for instance, abductees are selected by male torturers because they are female, and abductions are overtly sexually motivated. The antagonists in these films are also more vocally misogynistic than in earlier torture porn movies. For example, while raping a female captive, one of *The Hike*'s male antagonists poses the question 'you came this far out with no one to protect you: what did you think was going to happen?' Again, this dialogue alone does not evince that *The Hike*'s creators are misogynists, or that these later torture porn films elicit sympathy for misogynistic attitudes. What is of interest is how an increase in sexual violence in later direct-to-DVD torture porn sits alongside torture porn detractors' responses to earlier multiplex torture porn. Hyperbolic press responses to multiplex torture porn concretised the idea that sexual violence made the subgenre popular. Ironically then, characterising torture porn in this way may have led producers and distributors to believe that sexual violence is a key trigger in appealing to torture porn fans, resulting in increased sexual violence in later direct-to-DVD torture porn. By vilifying torture porn, press critics may have inadvertently expedited production of the very representations they sought to suppress. Simultaneously, if torture porn's popularity has waned as pundits have averred, that may be *because* sexual violence has increased in direct-to-DVD torture porn. Torture porn fans were not likely to have been originally attracted to the subgenre for its sexual violence since theatrically released torture porn films contained far less sexual violence than derogators asserted.

An alternative explanation for the increase in sexual violence in direct-to-DVD torture porn is that these films have largely evaded the press's scrutiny because they are not high-profile releases. That is, the DVD context provides a space in which controversial ideas might be explored more openly than they can be in the multiplex since DVD releases attract less attention from press reviewers. The various depictions of sex and violence torture porn offers notwithstanding, commercial and industrial contexts impact upon filmmakers' freedom to amalgamate those motifs. As the next two chapters will demonstrate, away from the multiplex context and critics' punitive responses, filmmakers can blend sex and violence in much more explicit ways than torture porn filmmakers can.

8
'Why Are You Crying? Aren't You Having Fun?':[1] Extreme Porn

'Torture porn' misrepresents the subgenre's sexual content, and torture porn's decriers have failed to adequately explain the label's implied porn-horror confluence. Where direct comparisons between torture porn and pornography have been made, they fall short. Some critics have pointed out that 'torture porn' is inapposite for describing horror film, and would be better suited to defining, for instance, a 'video of a professional dominatrix beating someone up' (Thompson, 2007). Thompson's evocation of BDSM (bondage/degradation/sadomasochism) porn lacks detail because he dismisses 'torture porn' rather than considering what can be learnt from the label's amalgamation of genres. Equally disparaging is Lacey's (2009) contention that 'the term ["torture porn"] seems a little hard on something as innocuous as pornography'. Although he queries how valid the comparison between pornography and popular horror is, Lacey presumes that porn is inherently depraved, and admonishes torture porn for being 'worse'. Lacey does not explain why 'porn' is synonymous with 'badness'. One aim of this chapter is to unpick the problems Thompson and Lacey gesture towards. In order to better expound the connotations of 'torture porn', the discourse that situates 'porn' must be scrutinised. Examples of pornography will be utilised to flesh out those significations.

Pace Lacey's comment, sex and violence have comingled in less candid ways in torture porn than they have in concomitantly produced pornographic films. Numerous reviewers and scholars have responded anxiously to a perceived increase in degradation-themed hardcore pornography since the late 1990s. Such porn has been commonly termed 'extreme', intimating that it is excessive even by porn's illicit standards (see Tyler, 2010: 56). Since violence is the 'new element' that distinguishes extreme porn from other forms of pornography (Amis, 2001; see also Jensen, 2007: 16), 'extremity' results when porn strays towards the realm of the horrific. Like 'torture porn', 'extreme porn' connotes that sex–violence synthesis is problematic and requires prohibition.

The similarities between porn and horror have received much more attention in 'torture porn' discourse than the differences between these genres have. That emphasis on similarity is perhaps rooted in a generalising discursive narrative that unifies 'extreme porn' and 'torture porn': both subgenres are deemed to epitomise an ostensible turn towards 'extremity' in visual media. Understanding how 'extremity' operates as a discursive framework is vital in order to decipher why 'porn' and therefore 'torture porn' are pejorative terms, then. Despite how similar the rhetorical mechanisms underpinning 'torture porn' and 'extreme porn' are, the two subgenres are not equally 'extreme'. Rather than treating 'extremity' as a means of sweeping over differences, the tensions that arise from conflating porn and horror will be examined in order to better understand 'extremity' itself. For example, bringing together 'torture porn' and 'extreme porn' elucidates that 'porn' has two divergent meanings. 'Porn' designates a genre, but it also refers to a concept. 'Torture porn' is indicative of the conceptual use, whereby 'porn' denotes that acceptability standards have been breached. The repercussions of that dual usage will be unpicked in this chapter's conclusion. Pornographic films will be used to illustrate ways in which porn's conventions are sustained and challenged by extreme porn's sex–violence convergences and by horror-porn filmmakers' adoption of horror tropes. As a foundation for that discussion, it is first necessary to establish what is allegedly wrong with porn and how the discourses surrounding 'torture porn' and 'extreme porn' fit together.

'This is what they make those Federal laws for':[2] [torture] porn is 'bad'

The chief purpose of the porn genre seems to be to show sexual acts at length and in explicit detail. On the whole, conservative critics have maintained that copulating bodies epitomise indecency, and have characterised porn as simply filmed licentiousness. However, the prohibition of sexual imagery has not been entirely uniform. Indeed, at various points in history, sexual imagery has become somewhat acceptable in mass culture. *Deep Throat*'s box-office performance is one such occurrence (see Bronstein, 2011: 63). More recently, and in concurrence with torture porn's cinematic boom-period, sexually graphic portrayals have been tolerated in mainstream cinema. *9 Songs* and *Shortbus* are notable examples of films featuring genitally explicit images that were theatrically released during the era of torture porn's incursion on the multiplex.

This increased forbearance for sexual imagery was paralleled by an upsurge in 'extreme porn'. The label 'extreme porn' was coined to encapsulate the idea that porn was becoming unduly excessive, perhaps as a result of relative cultural tolerance for sexual imagery in this period. Extreme porn's ostensible exorbitance derives not just from porn's conventional genital displays, but from numerous additional traits. A number of featured sex acts – particularly those related to bodily excretions (urine, faeces, vomit, blood) or violent behaviours (choking, slapping) – have been deemed 'extreme' because they contravene censorial edicts. Extreme porn filmmakers have been charged with fixating on such acts, privileging 'cruel and brutal sex' which is 'designed to dehumanise and debase' (Dines, 2011: 3; see also Kammeyer, 2008: 186). 'Extremity' thus arises from the impression that performers are being humiliated. Additionally, extreme porn is associated with a reality-based style known as 'gonzo'. Gonzo is typically filmed from a performer point-of-view, or involves performers interacting with behind-the-camera crew. Despite being staged, it is implied that gonzo is authentic because the production process is apparently rendered transparent. In contrast to mainstream, sexually-explicit, narrative-based films such as *Shortbus*, gonzo films are usually constituted by unconnected vignettes. Although each episode is typically based around a stock routine – interview, strip, sex, orgasm – very little time is devoted to anything other than sex in gonzo, meaning the films are essentially plotless. The gonzo form suggests that these films are solely designed to exhibit sex. The style is 'extreme' inasmuch as gonzo directly flouts obscenity law, because it lacks 'any serious literary, artistic...or scientific value', appealing directly 'to prurient interests'.[3] Gonzo porn again contrasts with its cinematic sexually-explicit counterparts such as *9 Songs* in this regard, since the latter are usually deemed acceptable because of their authors' (presumed) artistic intentions.

Although these complaints bear little relevance to torture porn's content, the comparison to 'extreme porn' illuminates much about what the 'porn' of 'torture porn' connotes. As Alan Sinfield (2004: 64) proposes, 'labelling a practice pornographic reflects a decision to regard it as bad', designating what cultural products or practices 'are worthwhile and which are not'. 'Torture porn' discourse follows this logic, being based on the presupposition that 'porn' is a pejorative label. Indeed, torture porn's alleged extremity is couched in terms that are commensurate to those surrounding 'extreme porn'. Torture porn films too are accused of being obscene, overly graphic, and lacking artistry, or of being constituted by detached set-pieces, spectacle, bodily exposure, and degradation rather than intellectual substance. 'Torture porn' discourse echoes earlier anti-pornography protests in which pornographic representation is perceived as violence (see Caputi, 1992: 203–19).[4] Moreover, anti-porn and anti-horror discourses are both underpinned by fears that images will trigger real violence.[5] That discursive crossover surfaced in 2011 when Vincent Tabak was convicted for murdering Joanna Yeates. It was claimed that Tabak had viewed extreme asphyxiation porn prior to the murder. In the subsequent commentary, critics such as Tookey (2011) declared that Yeates's murder was an inevitable 'social and criminal consequenc[e] of' torture porn. Other reporters misused the phrase 'torture porn' to describe the asphyxiation pornography that Tabak reportedly consumed (see Dawar, 2011).

This coverage typifies a prevailing error in such criticism: 'porn' is evoked to rebuff in an unspecific manner. Although many journalists referred to porn-use to exemplify murderer Derrick Bird's abnormality (see N.a. 2011), for example, none have evinced how murder and pornography tally in any specific sense. Equally imprecise are Maurice Chittenden and Matthew Holehouse's (2010) discussion of youth addiction to porn, and Annie Brown's (2009) 'Battle to Ban Extreme Porn': neither article scrutinises particular pornographic representations. Brown, for instance, concentrates on unnamed rape-porn websites' salacious taglines rather than the content of those sites. In each of these cases, critics link porn with events such as Yeates's death or proposed outcomes such as banning, yet the porn in question remains conspicuously anonymous. Detail is substituted by the catch-all term 'porn'. Consequently, an entire industry is maligned without adequately stipulating the grounds for such condemnation.

These established associations between porn and 'effects' have leaked into 'torture porn' discourse, resulting in similarly vague attempts to blame films for wrongdoing. Craig Jackson (2012) decrees that Daniel Bartlam murdered his mother because he was 'inspired by' torture porn's 'sick imagery', for example, yet does not detail any evidence to support the connection. David Wilson's (2012) explanation that Benjamin Scott stabbed his neighbour and also 'owned the box-set of the *Saw* films' illustrates how spurious such arguments typically are. Nevertheless, these assertions befit the tendency to privilege off-screen factors over on-screen content in anti-torture porn discourses. McCartney's (2007b) proclamation that torture porn 'encourag[es] the fusing of extreme violence with sexual excitement; casually eroding social taboos on attacking women, children and defenceless victims' is symptomatic of that rhetorical strategy. Such reasoning is undermined by McCartney's failure to examine particular objects or the alleged effects, which results in confusion between what happens on- and off-screen.

The genre-amalgam implied by 'torture porn' further contributes to that confusion. Since content remains unexamined in such argumentation, the differences between porn and horror are not established. Much like Beverly Labelle's (1992: 189) discussion of the fictional horror film *Snuff* (1976) – which she supposes aimed to entice 'the curiosity of the regular [pornographic] market' – torture porn's detractors ubiquitously fail to distinguish between these genres' audiences, conventions, or tones. At the most basic level, sexual depictions dominate the run-time of porn films. Pornography's bodily displays foreground at least one participant's sexual pleasure, and the camerawork is geared towards capturing sexual interactions. In contrast, violence, suffering, fear, and/or physical harm are spotlighted in horror. The label 'torture porn' sweeps over such distinctions, and has been used to emphasise commonalities between porn and horror. Their shared status as body-genres is one such unifying factor. Because body-genres are presumed to stimulate physical reactions by depicting bodies in graphic detail, body-genres are associated with 'base' pleasures, which reveal 'our undignified animality, the natural beneath the cultural' (Bernstein, 2004: 9; see also Shaviro, 1993: 100; Hawkins, 2007). Suppositions regarding audiences' ignobleness lead various pundits to contend that body-genres – like bodiliness itself – ought to be policed. That desire to regulate is evident in Christopher Hart's (2009) assessment of *Antichrist*: 'its mingling of sex and violence, the cheapest and nastiest trick in the book, is usually one which the BBFC pounces on'. Following Hart's logic, since 'torture porn' suggests a confluence of unruly elements that require restriction, any film categorised as such should be 'pounce[d] on' by censors.

Hart's insinuation is representative of the impeditive tone adopted in the majority of torture porn criticism, which stifles debate. One way of stimulating discussion is to approach that porn-horror convergence from the opposite direction. The 'porn' paradigm has been employed to evince torture porn's 'extremity'. However, 'torture porn' discourse can also be utilised to understand why some porn has been dubbed 'extreme'. Contemplating the differences and similarities between extreme porn and torture porn will illuminate what is meant by 'extremity'. In contrast to torture porn, some extreme porn reifies the anxieties that undergird both anti-porn and anti-torture porn discourses: sex is overtly merged with forms of violence. Indeed, that interruption of horrific violence into the sexual setting disrupts conventional understandings of 'the pornographic' itself.

'That was *too* much':[6] *Meatholes*

The sheer quantity of porn produced every year renders the genre difficult to handle in a limited space. For this reason, an indicative example of extreme porn has been selected as a case-study: Tusion's *Meatholes* series. Nikki Hunter's scene in *Meatholes 2* is examined in detail because it epitomises Tusion's modus operandi. *Meatholes* includes the kind of conventional acts, verbal exchanges, and formal aesthetics that are characteristic of extreme porn. What makes the series distinctive – and therefore worth detailing as a case study – is Tusion's coupling of physical punishment with intense verbal interrogation. *Meatholes'* female participants are degraded in a fashion that strikingly resembles the humiliation and psychological breakdown techniques used in torture. Those combinations push *Meatholes's* dynamics of subservience and 'mastery' beyond just BDSM porn, into the realm of 'torture pornography'. Simultaneously, *Meatholes* is so unlike torture porn, it throws into relief what is at stake in applying the terms 'porn' and 'extreme' to mainstream horror films. *Meatholes* is extreme in the sense that it exceeds the porn genre's conventional remit of portraying sex. The series fuses intercourse, degradation, and physical violence in ways that flout contemporary censorial standards.

Unlike extreme porn auteur Max Hardcore, for example, Tusion has been overlooked in critical responses to extreme porn. That disparity may have arisen from their divergent personas. Max Hardcore gained a reputation for courting controversy and starring in his productions.[7] Tusion instead remains off-screen/faceless, even in interview circumstances.[8] Tusion does lay claim to extremity however, stating that he is an outsider even in the porn industry. According to Tusion (in Pipe, 2000), other producers fear that his films 'will destroy pornography as we know it'. Although hyperbolic, the assessment has some grounding insofar as Tusion seeks to deconstruct pornographic conventions. Tusion's method derives from his dissatisfaction that 'ninety eight per cent' of porn is 'not real' (in Pipe, 2000). In this sense, Tusion's attitude is antithetical to James Atlas's (1999: 63) contention that porn must be 'highly contrived', since it is 'exciting only because it *isn't* anything like real life'. Tusion bemoans porn's routines and staged productions. He does not redress his dissatisfaction by differing from the norm, as many other extreme porn filmmakers have. Tusion actively attacks generic conventionality itself. Nevertheless this critique is constantly brought into tension by his other goal: to create pornography.

Meatholes is not devoid of convention, then. The series' vignettes usually present one woman engaging in rough sex with two men, occurring over one continuous take. The sex typically consists of oral, vaginal, and anal penetration, as well as 'extreme' sex acts: spitting, cock-gagging, mild choking, breast slapping, and so forth. *Meatholes* has its own routines, and more broadly conforms to gonzo-porn's aesthetic conventions. Tusion's porn is not formally experimental. The 'extreme' acts themselves are conventional inasmuch as BDSM involves ritualised behaviours, established practices, and consent apparatuses (safe-words, for instance), even if those mechanisms are not apparent on-screen. As Laura Kipnis (1999: 61) and Gayle Rubin (1993) have urged, eroto-degradation scenarios may be misinterpreted as violent and thus 'extreme' by those unfamiliar with their mores. Some viewers may find it strange that many BDSM participants look upon bruises with pride rather than as signifiers of violence, for example (see *Graphic Sexual Horror*). Any discussion of BDSM porn's 'extremity' must remain sensitive to that context. *Meatholes*'s sex acts are not extreme per se; the films are only 'extreme' because they contravene contemporary legal standards regarding what is considered permissible in the porn context. *Meatholes* contrasts with torture porn in that respect. This relationship is crucial to understanding what 'extreme porn' implies. Extremity is measured against legal edicts and by comparing objects to one another.

The inclusion of 'extreme' sex acts is only one way in which *Meatholes* is set apart from 'banal' porn. Tusion's formal approach also unveils porn's inauthenticity and conventionality. The series adheres to a gonzo verité style, being constituted by spontaneous handheld camerawork and long uninterrupted takes. The gonzo mode contrasts with non-extreme feature-pornography's stagy shooting and editing techniques, which emulate the glossy panache of contemporary Hollywood's aesthetic standards. In comparison, Tusion's porn looks unprofessional. For instance, during Kelly Wells's scene (*Meatholes 6*), the camera operator momentarily runs off set. In doing so, the camera reveals how constructed the series is by displaying the lights, sound equipment and so forth that surround *Meatholes*'s sex-setting. This incident also posits that *Meatholes* has nothing to hide. Paradoxically, in uncovering *Meatholes*'s mediated nature, Tusion fosters the impression of transparency and authenticity. The same process is evident in Bianca Pureheart's scene (*Meatholes 5*), which is constantly broken by background chatter.

Tusion's requests to the crew ('let's get this light over here please') and performers ('look to the camera to your right'), are coupled with tangential, non-sex related conversation about topics such as Tusion's height. These inclusions illuminate the mundane profession under porn's fantasy-façade by flagging up technical details, the production process, and even collegiate interactions. These elements are usually masked in porn to maintain the fantasy that the performers personally enjoy the sex, rather than perceiving it as a vocational routine.

Despite Tusion's idiosyncrasies, these formal properties befit gonzo's reality-based ethos. The formal divulgences alone are not enough to create gaps between conventions and content or to expose porn's banality. Tusion's critique of porn arises from coupling this formal disposition with the deconstruction of female performers' personas. Tusion seeks to portray the 'identit[ies] and soul[s] of the young ladies doing pornography' (in Pipe, 2000), as well as sexual acts. As he puts it to Hunter in *Meatholes 2*, 'the camera comes on and you get that look like... "here I am"... I'm going to expose you'. The realist aesthetic facilitates this aim, connoting that the women are genuinely unmasked. Tusion's efforts to deconstruct female stars' feigned performances are intertwined with his attempts to unveil porn's genre conventions.

Meatholes is not point-of-view porn, which is shot from and puts the viewer 'in' the performer's position to amplify pleasure. Outside of the occasional spank, Tusion does not participate in the sex itself. Tusion is the camera-operator and speaks directly to female performers throughout the scenes, showering them with verbal abuse and intimate inquiries. He posits that his intention is to 'ask a small and pointed question at an awkward time so that they are defenseless', to obtain 'an honest response... so you can see a real person' (in Pipe, 2000). His questions are highly personal. For example, in *Meatholes 5* Tusion asks Bianca Pureheart the name of her first boyfriend. In *Meatholes 3*, he asks Nautica Thorn how over-weight her mother is. This attack on their performative personas is disquieting because it does not follow the usual conventions of BDSM verbal degradation.

Although he does not have sex on camera, Tusion is not 'just an observer' as he claims in *Meatholes 2*. As Hunter retorts, 'it doesn't look like [he is] just observing', since his interrogative role directly involves him in the ensuing action. *Meatholes* magnifies the same witness-torture dynamic found in torture porn, inasmuch as Tusion is a participatory witness. His interrogation assails the female performer, and the camera itself adds to their degradation. This is apparent later in Hunter's scene when Tusion interjects 'ask [all your friends] if they're watching, whore'.

Hunter's to-camera response is the half-whisper 'you're all watching'. The camera – usually just part of the porn shoot scenery from the performers' perspective – is made strange by Tusion's interpolation. Once she envisages the camera as a conduit for viewership, Hunter incriminates the consumer, spitting to camera '[w]hat do you feel right now watching this? Damn you'. Her reaction bridges the gap between the moment in which the sex act occurs and the moment in which it is consumed. In tandem with that collapse, Hunter breaks down entirely, slapping male performer Dirty Harry and sobbing uncontrollably.

Hunter's anguish is of an entirely different order to that found in torture porn's overtly dramatised renditions of suffering. The differences stem from how intimate *Meatholes*'s incursions are. Contrasting with the agony actors simulate in torture porn films, *Meatholes*'s performers physically endure. The aim – to disarm female performers' usual psychological barriers – is emotionally impactful. This difference does not imply that *Meatholes* is not staged. BDSM porn can 'shock' because the edited footage might not 'reflect the reality of how it was made', as BDSM performer Lorelei Lee states (in *Graphic Sexual Horror*). Tusion (in Pipe, 2000) proffers that he is 'not interested in degrading anyone who doesn't derive pleasure from it'.[9] Although Hunter's distress does not appear to be contrived, the extent to which it is consensual is ultimately unknowable. *Meatholes* cannot evince what 'really happened' by supplying 'visible proof', as infamously articulated by Linda Williams (1989: 230), because it is a priori mediated and constructed.

Hunter's to-camera accusation – implicating the viewer's pleasure in her suffering – reveals that Tusion's approach cannot exhibit any 'truth' about performers or sex. In dissecting conventions, Tusion only unveils porn's representational mode. The acts depicted are not 'extreme' in the sense that they are obscene per se since they are not illegal when consenting adults engage in those same acts privately. The acts only become indecent when they are committed to film, exhibited, and consumed as porn. The representation and commoditisation of those acts makes that difference. Performance is not separated from the transactional context that requires such performances in *Meatholes*.[10] As part of her self-derogation, for instance, Hunter declares that she is 'a whore for hire ... that's all I'm good for'.

This emphasis on porn's commercial and representational underpinnings also lays bare *Meatholes*'s power-biases. Tusion's adherence to porn conventions abets this uncovering. As the series' highly offensive title suggests, *Meatholes* unabashedly contravenes anti-porn feminists' primary objection to hardcore heterosexual sex films: that porn

Figure 8.1   Dirty Harry comforts Nikki Hunter during her breakdown in *Meatholes 2* (2005, USA, dir Khan Tusion)

objectifies women (see Bronstein, 2011: 131). Unlike torture porn, *Meatholes* is severely gender-biased. Tusion patently aims to expose only the *female* stars. While the female performers are physically and mentally laid bare, Tusion is never presented on-screen. When he does accidentally stray too far into frame, black boxes appear to block him from view. This happens during Kelly Wells's scene in *Meatholes 6*, for example. *Meatholes*'s male performers are not interrogated. Additionally, during Hunter's breakdown, Dirty Harry tries to comfort her, turning away from the camera to whisper 'it's just a performance'. His comment elucidates that *he* was acting even if her response was not feigned. This does not mean that *Meatholes*'s men are 'soulless, unfeeling, amoral life-support systems for erect penises', as Gail Dines (2010: xxiv) characterises male porn performers. They instead play anonymous meatpoles. This provides some protection that *Meatholes*'s women do not share.

Tusion seeks to disrupt performances that usually offer female performers some defence. These performances also facilitate objecti-fication, since the performers' real personalities are masked by unreal nymphomaniac personas. *Meatholes*'s power-biased representations personalise the female performers. That outcome is problematised by Tusion's desire to critique porn. Since Tusion finds porn trite and seeks to rectify that shortcoming by breaking down only female performers' personas, women are held culpable for porn's banality. Tusion posits that porn is prosaic *because* female performances of sexual pleasure are inauthentic. *Meatholes* thus propagates Williams's (1989: 230) notion that pornographers seek to but cannot visually capture female sexual pleasure on film. Women are personalised and humiliated in *Meatholes* as punishment and in compensation for that inability. Tusion therefore unmasks porn's conventionality because he so appositely consolidates what porn is and does. *Meatholes*'s extremity arises from reflecting porn's expected aims and conventions in a way that makes them strange. In *Meatholes*, porn is unflinchingly limned as a kind of horror.

'[A] juxtaposition most people find simply unacceptable':[11] horror-porn features

Tusion is not alone in interrogating porn's conventions in this period. While torture porn was peaking in popularity at the box-office, another genre-branch – horror-porn – also increased in production. Horror-porn films literalise the hybridity that 'torture porn' implies, but which torture porn does not deliver. In horror-porn, conventional horror facets are incorporated into the porn context. Developing porn's long-established tradition of appropriating plot structures from other genres (see Hunter, 2006), horror-porn films such as *Fuckenstein*, *The Human Sexipede*, and *BoneSaw* include their origin texts' violence alongside explicit sexual images. In many cases, that merging of sex and violence marks these films as 'extreme' by contemporary standards.

This kind of appropriation does not *always* render horror-porn 'extreme', however. For instance, porn-slasher films – such as *Camp Cuddly Pines Powertool Massacre* and Zero-Tolerance's *Friday the 13th: A XXX Parody* – intensify the stereotyped horror-slasher motif of teens having sex in the woods then being killed, showing intercourse at-length and in genitally-explicit detail. In that regard, the porn versions develop organically from their horror originators. The horror-porn genre bridge is further naturalised by including formal conventions associated with horror in the porn context. For example, *Camp Cuddly Pines*'s point-of-view camera-shots mimic the original *Friday the 13th*'s stalking sequences. Yet neither of these porn parodies is extreme, because the horror plots are principally assumed as a framework to drive sex-action. The violence that is included is fleeting, is often comic in tone, and is secondary to the films' sex rather than being integrated throughout. In both *Camp Cuddly Pines* and *Friday the 13th: A XXX Parody*, ejaculation closes the porn sequences, distinguishing the sex episode from any adjoining horror. Resultantly, the porn-horror intermix remains within accepted censorial boundaries.

Multiple horror-porn films more fully integrate the two genres, however. As a result of that slippage, horrific acts – mutilation, rape, murder – are eroticised. Horror-porn starkly contrasts with torture porn in this respect. The sex–violence amalgamation contravenes contemporary censorial standards, marking these films as 'extreme'. *Re-Penetrator* is an illustrative example. Based (very loosely) on the horror film *Re-Animator*, *Re-Penetrator*'s plot involves Dr. Herbert Breast resurrecting a female cadaver with a serum designed to incite her sexual passion. The 20 minute film (excluding credits) is constituted by approximately 17 minutes of sex. While plainly pornographic then, *Re-Penetrator*'s hardcore sex and violence are fully imbricated. Stock audio–visual devices – dry ice, green lighting, and organ music – are employed to create horror atmospherics throughout, naturalising gory-sex in the diegetic context. Furthermore, horror is unified with sexual activity itself. (Fake) blood emanates from the female performer's crotch during intercourse. After Herbert ejaculates, his zombie beau bites his jugular and pulls out his innards. She rides his dying body, which is exhibited via a series of genitally explicit penetration shots. The sequence ends with a pan over Herbert's torso, which is covered in his own entrails. Failing to coax his flaccid member (hidden amidst his innards) into erection, the female zombie discovers the reanimation serum and smiles to camera. It is Herbert's turn to become a sex-zombie. Herbert's death and her agency close the text, and the pop-shot's sovereignty is usurped by its gore-climax. *Re-Penetrator*'s horror consequently debunks the notion that porn is structured around male sexual pleasure (see Williams, 1989: 101; Dines, 2010: xxvi). By combining sex and violence, *Re-Penetrator* upsets porn's normative conventions.

Porn-horror coalescence thereby invalidates the sense that these films are just 'porn', casting doubt over the notion of distinct genre boundaries. Moreover, like *Camp Cuddly Pines Powertool Massacre*, *XXXorcist*, *A Wet Dream on Elm Street*, and Zero Tolerance's horror-parodies, *Re-Penetrator*'s tone is primarily comedic. If, as McRoy (2010: 93) proposes, 'it is the [porn] genre's very *excessiveness* that generates much of its affect', the three-genre fusion – horror, porn, and comedy – is apt: these films are genre-excessive. Genre is usually a 'stabilising' factor that delimits meaning. Genre merging threatens to destabilise the coherence of 'porn' as a category. To this end, feature-based horror-porn is usually self-conscious in tone and typically includes self-deprecating jokes about the film's status *as* porn.

Figure 8.2   Lexi Belle must spell 'fellatio' correctly to survive her trap in *Saw: A Hardcore Parody* (2010, USA, dir Hef Pounder)

Zero Tolerance's *Saw* parody epitomises that ethos. The film stars porn-veteran Ron Jeremy as its Jigsaw-style evil mastermind, who ensnares porn performers. The film takes 'torture porn' literally, transforming porn performance pressures into torture-games. When Evan fails to maintain his erection for forty minutes, for instance, he is killed by an exploding pacemaker. Additionally, Ron is motivated by dissatisfaction with contemporary porn: 'I was on top of the business when it meant something ... Have you seen the filth that's come out of this industry? It's lost its passion ... its artistic attitude'. The *Saw* parody's own distinct artlessness is subject to self-mockery here, yet horror-parody is also used to evoke extreme porn (termed 'filth'). The parody jokingly critiques extreme porn's violent degradation-spectacles while also contributing to that body of 'filth'. That contradiction is resolved by casting Ron Jeremy in the lead antagonist role. Jeremy is arguably America's most successful video era male porn performer.[12] His presence flags that porn's traits have changed since his heyday in the 1980s. Nevertheless, he also signifies the continuities that exist between past and present. The differences Ron refers to – that which has been 'lost' and replaced by 'filth' according to his dialogue – have developed organically within the genre over time. Rather than scapegoating extreme porn as a separate entity, the whole genre – 'the business ... the industry' – is critically reflected upon.

By utilising a torture porn plot-line, the *Saw* parody implicates another genre in the same arguments. Rather than scapegoating torture porn or suggesting that torture porn is degrading and extreme, the comparison between porn and horror indicates that torture porn is not pornographic, ultimately re-establishing the genre boundaries that 'torture porn' bridges. The film suggests that only pornographic filmmakers can really produce 'torture pornography'. Simultaneously, the *Saw* parody is not quite 'extreme', because its violence is primarily comedic. In contradistinction to torture porn's prevailing po-faced seriousness – which critics have interpreted as a marker of torture porn's alleged 'extremity' – comedy dispels the threatening tone of the *Saw* parody's violence. The notion that torture porn's seriousness is a signifier of extremity is debunked: although openly humorous, the parody version is a priori more taboo than *Saw* because the parody contains genitally explicit portrayals of sex. By inviting such comparisons, the parody conveys that extremity is a relative scale and raises questions about what is considered extreme in different genre contexts.

Not all horror-porn films are comedic however. Unlike other horror-porn parodies, Rob Rotten's films *Porn of the Dead* and *Texas Vibrator Massacre* are grave enterprises.[13] Rotten's films epitomise the porn-horror melding that 'torture porn' implies. His films share torture porn's reputedly humourless tone, yet the sexually explicit, violent content is far removed from the multiplex-friendly horror offered in movies such as *Wolf Creek*, for instance. *Texas Vibrator Massacre*'s grimness illustrates that difference. As with other hillbilly-tinged imprisonment-themed porn movies of the era, such as *Squealer* and *Stranded*, the atmosphere of Rotten's porno-*The Texas Chainsaw Massacre* is palpably forbidding. The film's aesthetic is infused with horror convention, even during sex scenes. *Texas Vibrator Massacre*'s characteristic yellow hues and grainy film-stock effects hark back to 1970s exploitation horror aesthetics. Visual techniques such as image distortion and blurry slow-motion are also employed. These are unusual, since they interfere with the conventional goal of pornography: displaying the performers' bodies. *Texas Vibrator Massacre*'s formal attributes confirm that the film is not only a vehicle for exhibiting sex. The soundscape consolidates *Texas Vibrator Massacre*'s porn-horror melding. Fly-buzzing noises recur throughout and are stereo hard-panned to create a pervasive aura of disgust. In contrast to *Re-Penetrator*'s comic-book organ music, *Texas Vibrator Massacre*'s extra-diegetic score assimilates the kind of bass drones used to establish dread-atmospheres in contemporary horror.

The action is similarly grisly. Emphasis is placed on rape and murder. Once *Texas Vibrator Massacre*'s protagonists are killed, shots linger on their corpses. The stress usually placed on bodies in pornography is adapted to incorporate images more conventionally found in horror. That logic is apparent in *Texas Vibrator Massacre*'s closing scene, in which lead female Vanessa is beaten to death with a monkey-wrench. The murder is intercut with shots of her naked genitals. The final pan-out epitomises the film's porn-horror balance: Vanessa's upper-body is covered with a bloody sheet, and her exposed lower half is nude. That framing renders Vanessa as just a crotch. Numerous anti-porn feminists have asserted that such diminution is commonplace in porn and objectifies women (Dworkin, 1989: xxxiii; Caputi, 1992: 212). According to such arguments, reducing the female body to fragmented, sexualised parts is a form of symbolic violence. Vanessa's death literalises that emblematic violence. *Texas Vibrator Massacre* thus reverses Williams's (1989: 164) vision of porn as a 'separated utopia', in which sexual pleasure overrides what, in other contexts, would appear to be coercion and suffering.

Texas Vibrator Massacre's extremity stems from its tone, which accentuates the film's taboo elements. Horror facets and sex are integrated rather than juxtaposed in *Texas Vibrator Massacre*. The film's nudity-bloodshed combinations demonstrate just how far torture porn films are from delivering on the genre-hybridity and extremity promised by 'torture porn' discourse. *Texas Vibrator Massacre*'s aesthetic compound disturbs its pornographic conventionality. The BBFC was one organisation evidently disquieted by that mixture since they banned *Texas Vibrator Massacre* in 2008. Its prohibition underscores the film's 'extremity', which is rooted in its sex-horror union.

Unlike gonzo-porn – in which fabrication is masked via realist aesthetics – *Texas Vibrator Massacre*'s genre construction is pronounced because Rotten draws on such a famous horror text (*The Texas Chainsaw Massacre*). Motifs inspired by *The Texas Chainsaw Massacre* – such as lead antagonist Leatherface's costume – continually remind the viewer of *Texas Vibrator Massacre*'s constructedness. In practice, the narrative functions as a horror film, intersected with lengthy, sexually explicit sequences. These scenes are aberrant inasmuch as they are not present in *The Texas Chainsaw Massacre*. Sex incidents hinder the narrative progression as the *The Texas Chainsaw Massacre*-familiar viewer comprehends it. Although *Texas Vibrator Massacre*'s aesthetic naturalises its porn-horror hybridity then, its *The Texas Chainsaw Massacre*-based plot constantly brings its foundational genres into tension. Rotten's *Porn of the Dead* operates differently. Narrative is eschewed in favour of an episodic, disconnected vignette structure. *Porn of the Dead*'s structural organisation thereby follows gonzo porn's practices. However, those structural conventions are disrupted by horrific devices that are not typically found in porn, such as castration, flesh shredding, and bodily grotesquery. Hilary Scott's lengthy dialogue regarding her 'ass juices' is representative of the latter, for example. Together, Rotten's films suggest that successful porn-horror combination is capable of unbalancing genre's stabilising effect. Gestures towards porn production within both films corroborate this tacit assault on genre conventionality. Before Vanessa is beaten to death in *Texas Vibrator Massacre*, she is photographed by her captor. At his request, Vanessa tilts her head and spreads her legs, while he photographs her genitals in close-up. The sequence is reminiscent of a porn photo-shoot, albeit a nightmarish one. Vanessa's confinement is paralleled by her abductor 'capturing' images of her body. That Vanessa is subsequently bludgeoned to death implies that pornographic representation has destructive effects. *Porn of the Dead*'s third scene offers a similarly acerbic commentary on porn from a producer's perspective. The scene opens with a crew filming Trina Michaels copulating with an unidentified male performer. One crew member picks his nose as an expression of boredom, underscoring that porn is constituted by facile routines. *Porn of the Dead* is postulated to be exciting and 'extreme' in comparison, because the zombie-horror that unfolds contravenes pornography's conventional limitations. In the lull before the zombie attack, the tension between porn as concept (taboo) and porn as genre (commercial, conformist) is established. The faux-director's proclamation that his male performer should 'grab those titties...not too hard!' illustrates the prevailing industrial pressure to self-censor rather than push conventional boundaries. Cussing is rampant elsewhere in the film, but is noticeably censored in this sequence. That conspicuousness is hammered home by mis-bleeping some words ('**** her doggiestyle, yeah fuck her doggiest***'). Censorship, it is propounded, is both erroneously and arbitrarily imposed on porn. Rotten's disdain for the censorial impetus is evinced not only by that mockery, but also via the excessive, censorship-breaching images that follow.

Like Tusion then, Rotten's 'extremity' and hybridity stem from his overt critique of porn's genre conventions. This attack is palpable in supplementary advertising material for Rotten's company, Punx Productions. Trailers for Rotten's films boast that they have 'been approved for NO ONE' and are 'rated GFY: Go Fuck Yourself'. The name Punx Productions consolidates this 'outsider' spirit, aligning his films with 'alternative' subcultures. Rotten's own numerous tattoos and the hardcore metal music that plays throughout *Porn of the Dead* confirm Rotten's anti-mainstream stance. The porn-horror intermix is contextualised as part of this integral status, which marks Rotten as an 'outsider', even in porn circles. In stark contrast, torture porn is centred within the horror genre, and is far less controversial than 'torture porn' implies. Those comparisons demonstrate why torture porn could profit at the box-office, while Rotten's and Tusion's films are 'extreme' and peripheral, even by porn's standards.

'How bad can it be?':[14] conclusion

The question that remains is precisely what does 'extremity' mean, and how does it relate to 'porn'? Rotten's approach hints that extreme porn may have emanated from industrial circumstances, specifically the need to stand out in porn's crowded marketplace. By branding himself as an outsider, Rotten characterises his films as an 'alternative' to more mainstream porn. This separation entails critiquing vanilla pornography. Tusion shares Rotten's ethos, as is evident from his comments about mainstream porn. According to Tusion (in Pipe, 2000), 'ninety per cent of [porn] is banal' because acts that were deemed outrageous '[t]wenty years ago', have become 'so commonplace that [they] no longer hold any interest'.[15]

One interpretation of Tusion's comment is that 'extreme' connotes 'worse'. In this view, if previously taboo acts have become 'banal' and have been replaced, porn will continue to become increasingly 'extreme' in the future. Commensurate with contemporary anxieties, this means porn's content will become more violent and degrading. However, such a construal misunderstands the relational nature of 'extremity'. Extreme porn films that dwell on rape-fantasy – such as those made by Extreme Associates in the mid-2000s – are strikingly similar to 1970s rape-themed porn films such as *Forced Entry* (1973). The most compelling evidence for change is that several practices that were rarely exhibited in earlier pornography have become commonplace in contemporary hardcore porn. These include throat-gagging, bukkake, gangbanging, and double-anal penetration. These behaviours are certainly less exceptional than they once were, and there is little doubt that these acts are both symbolically degrading and eroticised. However, it does not follow that this transposition in particular traits has altered the conceptual meanings of 'porn'. An increase in the prevalence of these specific acts does not displace what 'porn' 'is'. The modifications *do* reflect a shift in what is considered to epitomise 'extremity'. That does not necessarily mean that porn is becoming 'worse'.

These particular acts are vilified because they so clearly violate contemporary acceptability standards. The benchmark for acceptability is established via the regulatory structures that surround porn. Material that breaches 'community standards' is curbed by obscenity law, for example. Porn that pushes those boundaries has resultantly been labelled 'extreme'. If this is the criteria for such labelling however, it is not immediately apparent why past porn that violated *its* contemporaneous 'community standards' is not also dubbed 'extreme'. One possible explanation is that 'extreme porn' refers to the present, and as such, much of the discourse surrounding the label fails to account for how 'extremity' gradually changes.

This problem is compounded by obscenity law's vagueness. As Supreme Court Justice Potter Stewart's (1964)[16] famous declaration 'I know it when I see it' conveys, obscenity law is based on imprecise presumptions rather than finite criteria. Since 'extremity' is also defined against acceptability standards, it is just as difficult to pin down as obscenity is. Stewart's proclamation reveals that community standards are mutable and subjective as opposed to universal, fixed and objective. This is apt given that both 'extremity' and obscenity are relative and ever-evolving. The problem arises from their employment in discursive contexts *as if* they are fixed standards. Much like deontic moral principles then, it does not matter which standards are breached and how. What matters is that recognised standards exist in discourse, and that those standards have been knowingly violated.

'Extreme porn' is a problematic term because conceptually, 'porn' itself is synonymous with taboo. The specific acts that characterise porn's 'extremity' manifest what is currently unacceptable. Yet, the need to specify that some pornography is 'extreme' signals that 'porn' is correlated with genre conventions, ideas, and representational modes that are no longer gauged to be obscene. That is, the label 'porn' has come to intimate only spectacle, rather than unacceptability. As Nina Martin (2011) has it, pornographic representations are excessive rather than sexual, and so 'porn' has become a signifier without a referent. 'Extreme porn' has facilitated that confusion, because it creates a disparity between 'porn' as genre-label and 'porn' as conceptual framework. The 'extreme' in 'extreme porn' stands for the concept-version of 'porn', while the 'porn' in 'extreme porn' refers to genre. This distinction is vital. Conceptually, porn qua porn *epitomises* what is obscene at any given juncture. 'Extreme porn' is tautological then, since porn *is* the standard by which acceptability and taboo are measured.

With this distinction in mind, the discursive purposes of 'porn' and 'extremity' become apparent. The legal recourse that has followed porn-producers' breaching of censorial boundaries concretises extreme porn's 'extremity'. In the UK, legislation has sought to restrict the public's ability to consume pornography by outlawing extreme porn (see Jones and Mowlabocus, 2009). Moreover, two of porn's infamous 'extreme' producers – Rob Black and Max Hardcore – were both imprisoned, impeding production.[17] Such incidents bring 'porn' into disrepute, concretising the idea that most porn is 'extreme' and needs to be curbed. 'Extremity' was used to illegitimate porn at an interval when hardcore porn was becoming increasingly culturally acceptable. Rob Black and Max Hardcore were prosecuted because, unlike Tusion, they were particularly vocal about their 'extreme' output. Indeed, Black (in Javors, 2010) refers to his incursion on the mainstream – his appearance on a PBS Frontline Special entitled *American Porn* – as the trigger for his prosecution.

The 'extreme porn' furore may have been damaging to porn as a commercial genre, yet the legal resistance to extreme porn is inherent to what porn is, conceptually. Referring to porn as 'extreme' has meant reinvigorating the concept with its appropriate taboo status. Legal cases test and restate the boundaries of community standards as they change over time. The push–pull between porn and law is necessary so as to maintain the conceptual meaning of 'porn'. Specific acts, images, films and directors have been pilloried under the rubric of 'extreme porn', yet the term has been evoked in legal contexts to delimit acceptability standards more broadly. The idea that porn is 'worsening' – becoming 'extreme' – is a means of discursively containing the genre's ever-shifting prevalent facets.

This is where extreme porn and torture porn diverge. Torture porn's detractors borrow from 'porn' rhetoric to evince the subgenre's extremity, yet they commonly fail to account for the cultural and industrial differences between the two genres. Torture porn operates within legitimated boundaries, being distributed via high-profile, regulated commercial channels, be they the multiplex or the DVD market. Even in its most acceptable forms, hardcore porn is limited to distribution paths that are both less visible and harder to monitor than those torture porn occupies. Much hardcore porn is internet-distributed and streamed online, making it difficult to police. Pushing porn to commercial filmmaking's outskirts is one way of symbolically illegitimating porn. Labelling films as 'porn' and propagating the notion that 'porn' is synonymous with 'badness' is another.

'Torture porn' discourse aids those causes, circumscribing lines between legitimate and illegitimate cultural forms. Content differences aside, 'torture porn', 'extreme porn', and 'horror-porn' are underpinned by the same anxieties. In discourse if not in practice, all three terms insinuate that these subgenres contain unacceptable fusions of sex and violence. Generic slippage is also a source of tension as the discourse surrounding 'torture porn' and 'gorenography' denotes. Hybridity causes alarm because it reveals that such labels are incapable of delineating meaning. As a label that disparages via implied hybridity, 'torture porn' is self-defeating in that sense. A compound label is apparently needed to encompass torture porn's content, but the label's hybridity exposes an inability to delimit torture porn's content and render it 'safe'.

Unlike 'torture porn', which implies a kind of genre synthesis that is not delivered by the subgenre's content, extreme porn films are excessive insofar as they sometimes contain images that are too akin to horror to easily fit under the genre-heading 'porn'. As this chapter's case studies illustrate, that plurality frequently manifests as attacks on porn's genre conventions. Yet extreme porn is not the only site for such questioning. As the next chapter will demonstrate, horror too has its 'extreme' branch. Hardcore horror's manifestations of extremity, spectacle, and unacceptability further elucidate the tensions that arise from the multiple connotations of 'porn'.

9
'You Will Not Believe Your Eyes...or Stomach':[1] Hardcore Horror

Torture porn's detractors have commonly sought to illegitimate the subgenre by claiming that its presence in the multiplex is inappropriate. Edelstein's (2006) complaint that 'scenes of torture and mutilation were once confined to the old 42nd Street...whereas now they...[hold] a place of [honour] in your local multiplex' is indicative of that context-based unease (see also Cochrane, 2007; Skenazy, 2007). Such derogation intimates that horror should return to its 'rightful' place on film-culture's peripheries. Yet, marginalising these ostensibly 'extreme' and consequently contentious depictions means dismissing rather than scrutinising and understanding them. These complaints imply that once banished to the fringes of culture, such artefacts do not require appraisal.

Accordingly, little critical attention has been paid to non-mainstream horror. Simon Kinnear's (2010) position that torture porn took 'the stigma out of hardcore horror' leaving 'the genre's extreme wing looking rather toothless' paints torture porn as 'hardcore', and thus conveys Kinnear's inattentiveness to horror that exists outside of the mainstream. Kinnear's idea of 'hardcore horror' does not account for independent, micro-budgeted horror movies such as Fred Vogel's *August Underground* series and Lucifer Valentine's 'Vomit Gore' trilogy, which were released concomitant to torture porn's boom-period in the multiplex. In this chapter, that recent surge in American hardcore horror filmmaking will be analysed. Anglo-American critics have chiefly conceived of 'torture porn' as an American multiplex phenomenon. American hardcore horror is a counter-movement that operates in parallel to and reacts against torture porn's box-office profitability, illuminating what torture porn's mainstream status means.

Although this chapter's case studies are films made in the 'torture porn' era, that is not to suggest that hardcore horror is uniquely a 21st century phenomenon. Internet and digital technologies have made reproduction, editing, and distribution more affordable for budding filmmakers than in previous decades, but micro-budget indie horror has flourished since the advent of home-video technology. Tamakichi Anaru, Jorg Buttgereit, Andreas Schnaas, and Daisuke Yamanouchi are among the filmmakers who gained international renown for releasing sexually-driven gore-movies on VHS in the 1980s and 1990s, for example. Like those precursors, contemporary hardcore horror films are precluded from mainstream distributional routes to market because they are not certificated by bodies such as the MPAA or BBFC. In that sense, hardcore horror is defined against studio distributed, and in particular theatrically released, horror.

Perhaps because of that exclusion from the mainstream, hardcore horror filmmakers commonly embrace images that rile censors, incorporating graphic sexual depictions within primarily violent narrative contexts. That is, hardcore horror filmmakers have used their relative censorial freedom to 'push the envelope', conflating sex and violence. Although torture porn has been hyperbolically termed 'extreme' for allegedly blending sex and violence, hardcore horror filmmakers have exploited that combination while also evading critics' disdainful responses. These films remain under-analysed and neglected as a result of their marginality, however. Acknowledging the relationships and differences between torture porn, extreme porn, and hardcore horror elucidates what is at stake in evoking the terms 'porn' and 'extremity' to describe torture porn.

'There's only one rule – anything goes':[2] mainstream versus hardcore

The boundaries between mainstream and peripheral genres are typically demarcated by differences in their cultural–commercial contexts. For instance, American pornographers mainly operate out of a distinct settlement, based in Los Angeles's San Fernando Valley. Topographically, porn is distinguished from mainstream filmmaking, which is associated with the Hollywood hills. The line between porn and regular feature-filmmaking – between legitimate and illegitimate – is thus circumscribed geographically. American hardcore horror filmmaking is not collectivised in the same way, and so the differences between hardcore and mainstream horror filmmaking require clarification. For example, director

Shane Ryan submits that the shooting budget for his film *Amateur Porn Star Killer* was only $45.[3] Micro-budget filmmakers commonly downplay their production costs to explicate their divergence from the inflated budgets associated with Hollywood studio filmmaking (see Schamus, 1998; Berra, 2008: 15–26). Lack of funding intimates independence from commercial/industrial pressures, and therefore signifies integrity. Off-Hollywood films are customarily characterised as more 'gritty' and authentic than mainstream studio productions or even lower budget films that emulate Hollywood cinema's glossy aesthetics. Torture porn ordinarily falls into the latter category.

Budget is only one signifying device hardcore horror filmmakers employ in writing their own cultural marginality. For instance, the 'Underground' of hardcore horror film *August Underground* encodes the series as 'alternative', a construction substantiated by filmic content. *August Underground*'s protagonists sport tattoos and piercings, and the films feature scenes set in tattoo and piercing parlours. Much like Rob Rotten's auto-constructed 'alternative' image, these inclusions indicate the filmmakers' subcultural affiliations. Furthermore, all three *August Underground* movies feature sequences filmed at hardcore metal concerts, and Frank 'Killjoy' Pucci – vocalist for death metal band Necrophagia – stars in *August Underground's Mordum*. These musical associations evince the filmmakers' subcultural credibility. The to-camera insert-shot of a masked man at a concert venue exclaiming 'fuck commerciality' in *August Underground's Mordum* ties those subcultural mores into production company Toetag Pictures's indie-pride. These inclusions encapsulate and unambiguously articulate hardcore horror's ethos.

Moreover, *August Underground's Penance* features at least two fans playing targets, validating the filmmakers' grass-roots outlook. Collapsing the gap between producer and consumer fosters a sense of consumer loyalty, creating genuine links between fan and filmmaker that starkly contrast with Lionsgate's inaccessible corporate image, for instance. Hardcore horror's commercial viability is contingent on forming such connections. Hardcore horror filmmakers are reliant on word-of-mouth to form a reputation since their distributors do not have the advertising budgets most torture porn distributors do. The Internet has allowed fans to access and spread word about hardcore horror films on a global scale. Independent production/distribution companies also utilise this route to market. Unearthed Films, who released Valentine's hardcore horror 'Vomit Gore' trilogy, are one such net-based company. Hardcore horror films are clearly differentiated from their mainstream counterparts via those distributional differences. Like pornography, hardcore horror is mostly consumed in the home. With the exception of festival screen-ings, hardcore horror is not exhibited theatrically, being excluded from the certificated multiplex setting.

Numerous horror films are barred from major commercial routes-to-market altogether. Banning denotes that films are hardcore, inasmuch as they are officially outlawed. The BBFC has recently rejected *Murder-Set-Pieces*, *Grotesque*, and *The Bunny Game*, for example.[4] In each case, combinations of sex and violence – 'unacceptable content' – were cited as the impetus for censorship. Moreover, the films were described as being constituted by said content. *Grotesque* was deemed to offer 'little more than ... unrelenting and escalating ... humiliation, brutality and sadism', for instance (BBFC, 2009). The description makes *Grotesque* sound like pornography in which sex is replaced by torture. Such descriptions mirror concerns the press raised over torture porn movies like *The Devil's Rejects*, *Martyrs*, or *The Hills Have Eyes*. That these films were not banned demonstrates that the outcry against torture porn's content was unfounded. What is remarkable is that banned films such as *Murder-Set-Pieces* have not garnered more attention from torture porn's detractors, who expressed alarm over an alleged increase in sexual/ised violence. One reason banned films have not been subject to such scru-tiny is precisely because 'torture porn' discourse is punitive. Because banned films have already been prohibited from mainstream distribu-tion, torture porn's depreciators have no need to address them. Films that have been cut in order to allow their commercial release – such as *A Serbian Film* and *The Human Centipede II* – straddle the boundary between legitimacy and illegitimacy by existing in uncut (illegal) and censored (legal) states. The sanctioned versions of these films have commonly been dubbed 'torture porn', a mode of categorisation that makes the films understandable (and 'safe') by aligning them with existing disci-plinary discursive structures.

Prohibition may severely hinder a film's commercial prospects, but in the case of hardcore horror it also enhances reputation. Banning verifies that the movie contains material 'not found in the average Hollywood film' (Schaefer, 1999: 124). Outlawing also confirms that distribution must occur via 'alternative' routes, bypassing the censor's castigatory gaze. Since censors reflect dominant values (see Harries, 2002; White, 2006; Cole, 2012), exclusion becomes a sign of unconformity. Regardless of their veracity, these assumptions evince that hardcore horror's appeal derives from its polarisation to the mainstream. Interdiction enhances hardcore horror's other established integrity markers. Obtaining these illicit films – in spite of the lack of advertising and having to overcome censorial restrictions – requires effort and therefore augments the ownership some fans feel over these films. In some cases, illicit appeal is corroborated by filmic content. For instance, *Murder Collection V.1* is centred on a contrived 'morally reprehensible web show', which is said to broadcast 'murders caught on camera'. Although the footage is fabricated, *Murder Collection V.1* consolidates its hardcore status by appearing to supply 'morally reprehensible' uncensored death footage.

Torture porn shares some of that constructed unacceptability. In spite of the subgenre's comparatively uncontroversial content and mainstream status, torture porn advertising and packaging frequently gestures towards kinship with hardcore horror's censor-baiting controversy. For example, following the banning of its poster, *Captivity*'s trailers boasted that the film is 'so intense' that it was 'punished by the public'.[5] Despite being distributed through mainstream commercial channels, torture porn's marketing typically cultivates the impression that the films have pushed censorial boundaries, most notably via DVD packaging declaring that the films are 'unrated', 'uncut', or 'extreme'. Technicolor Home Entertainment employed a different embellishment tactic when promoting *Walled In* and *Pig Hunt* in the UK. Both films were classified '15' by the BBFC, yet were released onto the market with '18' certificates. This was achieved by packaging the DVD with an extra feature – a single trailer – that was classified '18'. '18' certification is usually undesirable inasmuch as it limits the available market. These instances of certificate-bumping are clearly purposeful attempts to advertise both films as 'stronger' horror,[6] aligning the films with the reputedly 'hard' content torture porn became infamous for.

Various torture porn film distributors utilise similar marketing techniques, turning critical controversy to their advantage. The US trailer for After Dark's Horrorfest DVD label professes that the company 'def[ies] the system' by releasing movies 'too graphic...disturbing... [and] shocking for general audiences'. This rhetoric implies that theatrically released films are usually heavily censored to fit majority sensibilities. After Dark's target audience, in contrast, are positioned as being able to handle and attain 'hard' content via their Horrorfest DVDs. In other cases, overblown avowals are made about graphic content to sell torture porn. For instance, *Penance*'s official website (penancefilm.com) boasts that the film's auto-castration sequence is 'the most outrageously graphic scene in movie history'. *Chaos*'s tagline is equally hyperbolic, proclaiming that it is the 'most brutal movie ever made'. By promising to provide salacious content, these taglines construct the idea that these films are illegitimate. Nevertheless, because the subgenre's films are not prohibited, torture porn is also abundantly accessible. The appearance of controversy is intended to boost rather than hinder sales.

Similar mechanisms are utilised by hardcore horror filmmakers, although hardcore horror does not share torture porn's commercial power. *ReGOREgitated Sacrifice*'s opening disclaimer cautions that '[t]he material herein will definitely offend most viewers', for example, constructing the film's audience as a privileged niche who are unlike 'most viewers'. However, since this warning is played out via the subsequent content, the statements' purpose is different to the exaggerated proclamations found in marketing materials for torture porn films. The warning reveals that *ReGOREgitated Sacrifice*'s appeal is necessarily limited. Exclusivity is a marker of credibility, but it also means that hardcore horror films are of diminished profitability by design. Being defined by their inability to fit into certificated or multiplex contexts as torture porn films do, hardcore horror movies are illegitimate. This is not to suggest that hardcore horror's only purpose is to shock. The status 'hardcore' – like extreme porn's 'extremity' – discloses little about the films themselves. In order to understand what makes hardcore horror affronting or 'extreme', hardcore horror's content must be examined.

'Humiliation. Rape. Murder. You Know the Drill':[7] hardcore horror conventions

Much contemporary American hardcore horror adheres to a visual style that is fashioned after the mythic 'snuff' film. Among the most notorious examples of such movies are Vogel's *August Underground* franchise (2003–7) and Ryan's *Amateur Porn Star Killer* series (2006–10). Although more formally experimental, Valentine's 'Vomit Gore' trilogy (2006–10) is also modelled after snuff-fiction.[8] Like torture porn films, these hardcore horror narratives dwell on abduction and torture motifs. However, the combination of verité, first-person camerawork and humiliation themes mean these hardcore horror films also share commonalities with gonzo porn. This kind of hardcore horror thus bridges between extreme porn and torture porn, and those contexts inform the analysis that follows.

In one sense, the verité faux-snuff approach allows hardcore horror filmmakers to pay homage to and ride on the coattails of notorious banned snuff-themed predecessors such as *Cannibal Holocaust* (1980), but there are other more significant reasons why hardcore horror filmmakers so commonly utilise that mode. Mythically, snuff films are envisaged as being made for private niche consumption rather than broad public dissemination.[9] The form thereby connotes illicitness, feeding hardcore horror's reputation as uncensored, anti-mainstream material. Moreover, the verité aesthetic implies plausibility. These films are shot on home-video cameras since amateur killers would not usually own professional recording-equipment. The faux-snuff narrative is a popular mode because its cheap look marries the diegetic context with hardcore horror's budgetary restrictions. Although the 'found footage' device has become increasingly popular in mainstream horror following the financial success of *The Blair Witch Project* and *Paranormal Activity*,[10] hardcore horror particularly benefits from the mode's ostensible unmediated spontaneity, which is antithetical to studio horror's typically glossy professionalism. The aesthetic thereby authenticates hardcore horror filmmakers' claims to cultural credibility.

Like that reputation, hardcore horror's realism is carefully constructed. For example, *August Underground* begins with blank video static and residual footage that supposedly occupied the tape prior to the killing spree that supplants it. The grainy/ghosted picture and sloppy handheld camerawork progresses as home-shot footage would, without the air of technical forethought. Real-time continuous shooting and improvised dialogue are utilised in *Amateur Porn Star Killer 3* to foster the impression that the footage is genuine. More than 30 minutes of the film is constituted by innocuous conversation between the killer and his target before any threat becomes apparent, for instance, and a 30 second sequence in which the camera remains unfocused further intimates amateurish authenticity. Extra-diegetic music is avoided in these films for the same reason. As in gonzo porn, these realist facets substantiate the action's (pseudo)veracity. In porn, realism authenticates the action, confirming that sex occurred and connoting that the performers' sexual pleasure is genuine. In hardcore horror, the reality-aesthetic is used to verify suffering, thereby amplifying the horror. Form facilitates suspension of disbelief in both genres,[11] but the emphasis on realistic threat rather than pleasure renders hardcore horror 'extreme'.

Where hardcore horror is non-realist, its formal 'extremity' is validated in other ways. Reality-aesthetic elements (handheld cameras) and everyday spaces (such as bedrooms and bathrooms) are incorporated into Valentine's 'Vomit Gore' trilogy, but the form is dominated by contrasting non-realist modes. Blank white studio spaces are occasionally occupied. Unexpected imagery such as microscope-based sperm and ovum stock-footage interrupts the action, for example. Slow motion, distortion, and coloured filters are employed, as are radical shifts between natural light, torchlight, and stark over-lighting. The sound is frequently detached from the images, and includes children laughing, low demonic growls, pitch-shifted voices, and reversed singing. The editing is rapid, intercutting between these modes. The result is an audio–visual onslaught. The series' bodily, diegetic violence is matched by formal excess. Additionally, Valentine eschews conventional narrative structuring. The lead protagonist (Angela) is played by several actors within each film. What is revealed about Angela – that she was sexually abused by her father, became a bulimic prostitute, and committed suicide – is ascertained via fragments of dialogue, flashbacks, and symbolic imagery. The series' disorientating aesthetic barrage is paralleled by elliptical storytelling. Both traits are unconventional, and their excessive use marks the series as 'extreme'.

Numerous hardcore horror filmmakers share Valentine's disavowal of traditional narrative structures, opting for fragmented surfing and episodic events. *Stockholm Syndrome* and *Diary of a Sex Offender* are built around sexually violent set-pieces, for instance. The plot movement is sparse in both cases, meaning narrative incidents are only loosely connected. *August Underground* consists of collected atrocities with little character development. *Murder Collection V.1*'s clip-show format is expressly episodic, each vignette being demarcated by the host Balan's voice-over. The resolution-based, causal narrative structures and character arcs that epitomise Hollywood's storytelling strategies (see Bordwell and Thompson, 2011: 127–8) are rejected in these hardcore horror films. Eschewing such structures is a further sign of anti-mainstream 'extremity'.

In contrast, torture porn filmmakers predominantly follow standard Hollywood storytelling conventions, despite their reputation. Torture porn filmmakers have been reproached for foregrounding violence to the detriment of narrative and characterisation (see Lim, 2009; Beckford, 2008; Puig, 2008). Such indictments imply that torture porn films are structured like gonzo porn. Even though torture porn filmmakers often opt for bleak, unresolved denouements, torture porn's violent set-pieces are imbedded in narrative structures and are contextualised by goal-driven characters' motives. Indeed, torture porn filmmakers regularly refer to such mechanisms to defend their portrayals of violence (see Chapter 3). The fragmented set-pieces that characterise hardcore horror, on the other hand, are akin to gonzo porn's wall-to-wall sex episodes. That is not to say that the narrative methods employed in hardcore horror are thoughtless, inappropriate, or purposeless as detractors have suggested of torture porn. Hardcore horror's atrocities are made all the more horrific by their lack of causal contextualisation. In *August*

Underground, for example, neither the killers' nor their targets' backstories are detailed. That device magnifies the film's terror by creating the impression that violence can happen to anyone, without reason.

Hardcore horror films befit many of the accusations inappropriately levelled at torture porn, demonstrating how inapt it is that torture porn has been scapegoated. Furthermore, although those attributes appear in hardcore horror films, depreciators' objections to those traits remain invalid. For instance, unlike torture porn, hardcore horror films mainly depict violence from the perpetrators' perspectives. The associations various critics make between point-of-view camerawork and pleasurable sadistic identification are still debunked in such cases. Hardcore horror antagonists' motives are seldom clear, meaning the torturer-position is alienating. For example, *August Underground's Mordum*'s most disturbing aspect is that the tortureds' suffering is met with laughter throughout. The torturers' blatant joy is profoundly horrifying because their delight is neither rationalised nor made accessible by the narrative. Antithetically, the captives' fear and suffering are understandable because those are instinctive responses to torment.

'Mere sex doesn't do it':[12] sexual violence as extremity

Degradation themes are emphasised in hardcore horror, torture porn, and extreme porn. However, virtually all sex acts are intertwined with rape, murder, and mutilation in hardcore horror films. Much of extreme porn's sex may be horrific, but the emphasis remains primarily on at least one participant's sexual pleasure in the majority of extreme porn, because sex is allotted more screen-time than violence. Antithetically, sex is principally limned as violence in hardcore horror: sexual pleasure is eschewed, and carnage is displayed in greater detail than sex. Hardcore horror also differs from torture porn, since hardcore horror films tend to intensify and more frequently employ the sexual-horror motifs found in torture porn, such as rape and castration. Moreover, hardcore horror films are tonally distinguished from torture porn by their genital explicitness and realist aesthetics. To illustrate, *August Underground's Mordum*'s torturers demand that a male captive cut off his own penis with scissors. They subsequently place the penis in his fellow captive's vagina to rot. *Maskhead*'s climactic scene is devoted to its eponymous torturer raping a woman with a wooden plank strap-on, which is depicted in genitally-explicit detail. Although these extractions are inadequate to explain what such imagery means in the hardcore horror context, they elucidate the taboo-breaking nature of hardcore horror's sexual violence.

Rape and castration are not the only taboos hardcore horror filmmakers draw upon. Another example is the presence of simulated pederasty. The focus on child abuse in hardcore horror films – such as the molestation and murder of a 13-year-old in *Amateur Porn Star Killer*[13] – plays off contemporary worries regarding young people and sexualisation (see Kammeyer, 2008; Mills, 2010; Duits and Zoonen, 2011; Oppliger, 2008). Again hardcore horror differs from extreme porn and torture porn in such cases. For example, female performers routinely don early teen fashionwear in Max Hardcore's extreme porn. Clothing is utilised to infantilise the women, connoting that they are innocent and vulnerable (see Dines, 2009: 137–8).[14] Max Hardcore's diametric role as sexual aggressor is resultantly exaggerated, and that power difference is eroticised. In hardcore horror, the tone is dictated by its prevalent abductions and murders. The power-bias between adult predator and juvenile prey is designed to embellish the terror inherent to hardcore horror's violent exchanges. Child abuse also drives several torture porn plots, including *Hamal_18*, *Hard Candy*, *Dungeon Girl*, and *7 Days*, yet the difference between torture porn and hardcore horror is evident in the respective approaches to violence. Where minors are subjected to abusive violence in torture porn, those acts are not shown on-screen:[15] instead, the consequences arising from those acts provide narrative focus. In contrast, hardcore horror's 'extremity' is evinced via the graphic presentation of such deeds.

When these themes are approached in the hardcore horror context, they manifest in a grisly fashion. Many hardcore horror films – including *August Underground's Penance* and *Stockholm Syndrome* – feature forced abortions, for example. As with threats against minors in torture porn, the idea that children are innocent and vulnerable means that such incidents are controversial. However, in the hardcore horror context, the violation is augmented by (a) carrying the threat through into explicit, on-screen violence, (b) harming two parties (mother and foetus) simultaneously rather than just a minor, and (c) exacting violence on an unborn foetus, which is utterly incapable of self-defence. In other cases, foeticide is coupled with additional taboos. *Slow Torture Puke Chamber*'s forced-abortion necrophilic-pederasty is especially offensive, not only because it intermixes taboos, but also because it is so prolonged. The sequence spans across 24 minutes, nearly a third of the film's duration. During this time, the attacker uses the baby's limbs to self-induce vomiting, rapes the foetus, refers to the infant as a 'fucking hooker', then dismembers, blends and drinks its appendages.

This latter sequence confirms how excessive hardcore horror can be, and as one of hardcore horror's most provocative instances of sexual

violence, it is worth scrutinising. However shocking it may be, the foeticide has a symbolic function. The trilogy is constituted by metaphoric
incidents that reify lead protagonist Angela's suffering as a self-punishing
bulimic and as someone affected by childhood sexual abuse. The foetus
signifies her helplessness. The sequence is intercut with images of
Angela (played both by Hope Likens and Ameara Lavey) vomiting, and
is overlaid with a voice-over in which Angela describes her experiences
of rape. As the trilogy's climactic event, this episode does not shy from
how damaging molestation and rape are. Although images cannot ever
capture the emotional devastation that sexual assault causes, *Slow Torture
Puke Chamber* is an extremely affecting attempt to manifest that horror.

No matter how distasteful its images are, Angela's anguish is not trivi-
alised in the series. Valentine's trilogy is entirely devoted to one characters' plight. Rather than charting her history as a linear narrative, all
three films illuminate Angela's suffering and fear. Rarely does horror
film invest so heavily in one protagonist's experiences. Being marginal,
hardcore horror provides a space in which such a protracted emotional
reconnoitring can occur. This space also permits Valentine to explore
controversial subject matter without flinching from its horror. Taboo
is used to engage the audience with the character's trauma. The series
does not exhibit Angela's abuse as it happened. Instead the films dwell
on abstracted images of violence – such as the foeticide sequence – that
incarnate her *experiences*. It would be a mistake to assume that hardcore
horror's only function is to limn grotesque acts just because ugly deeds
are shown.

Yet, this is not to suggest that hardcore horror is unproblematic. Most
questionably, Valentine fails to paint Angela as anything *other* than a
victim. Her abuse recurs endlessly. Beyond the first film (*Slaughtered
Vomit Dolls*), she is always-already dead. The links made between Angela's
sexual abuse and her helplessness are indicative of a tendency to render
injured parties unknowable outside of their torture in hardcore horror.
Frequently, the wounded are utterly disempowered; they are bound from
the moment they are presented, then they suffer and die. Torture porn's
tortured, in contrast, are usually situated by backstory prior to torture (if
not capture), and they predominantly fight back against their torment.
Compared with hardcore horror's essentialised victims, torture porn's
tortured have agency, and their narrative roles are dynamic.

Another related problem hampering Valentine's trilogy is that because
Angela's plight is pivotal, she is the series' sole subject of violence. Several
women take on the role of Angela across the trilogy, and her torment
is played out via sequences in which various women – each of whom

teen porn star

Figure 9.1   One of the archetypal stand-ins for Angela in *ReGOREgitated Sacrifice* (2008, Canada/USA, dir Lucifer Valentine)

stand-in for Angela – are physically attacked. Virtually all of the trilogy's violence is aimed at females then, because those acts refer to Angela's abuse. Where women are agents in the series, they abuse other women or themselves. In *ReGOREgitated Sacrifice*, the casualties are labelled 'teen porn star', 'daughter', 'whore', and so forth. Angela's persona is thereby broken down into what Valentine terms 'archetypes'.[16] This combination of multiple casting, archetypal female roles, and unambiguously gendered sexual violence is highly problematic, since it represents 'Angela' as an everywoman. That is, Valentine's approach risks implying that all women are (potential) Angelas.

Although some hardcore horror films such as the *August Underground* series and *Maskhead* include both male and female torturers and balance their sufferers' genders, others such as the *Amateur Porn Star Killer* films are solely centred on female targets being harmed by men. As with torture porn however, this is not to propose that the films themselves should be deemed misogynistic just because they depict misogynistic characters. For instance, *Murder-Set-Pieces* was rejected by the BBFC in 2008 on the grounds that it might 'eroticise or endorse sexual assault', and 'may encourage a harmful association between violence and sexual gratification' (BBFC, 2008). As such, *Murder-Set-Pieces* was marked as unacceptable because the narrative was interpreted as ratifying its antagonists' 'harmful' sexual attitudes. There is certainly no doubt that the film's antagonist is a despicable, misogynistic figure. The primary focus of *Murder-Set-Pieces* is its nameless killer – the Photographer – who spends the film talking to prostitutes, strippers, and nude models, or raping and murdering them. Here, the emphases on sexual violence and disempowerment that characterise hardcore horror are fused with portrayals of women as sex objects, fatalities, or (usually) both. Thus, female characters are represented as sexually vulnerable in *Murder-Set-Pieces*. The killer's macho muscularity only serves to exacerbate this gendered power-bias. He is an unassailable aggressor, and is not brought to justice in the narrative.

However, this is not to say that the film is misogynistic per se. In fact, the film could be interpreted as an exercise in misandry. The Photographer is presented as hyper-masculine, but that masculinity is hardly limned in a favourable light. The Photographer's sexual violence denotes his abnormality. The narrative is driven by his actions, but his deviancy makes the Photographer difficult to engage with. Indeed, his namelessness creates distance between audience and character. He is limed as a narcissistic, misogynistic, raping, murdering, cannibalistic Nazi. His deeds are contextualised via that characterisation. *Murder-Set-Pieces* does not promote sexual torture, since the film's horror derives from the Photographer's sexual cruelty, and is intertwined with his other unacceptable traits. *Murder-Set-Pieces* is 'extreme' insofar as the representations contravene social taboos regarding flagrant displays of misogyny in culture. The filmmakers rely on viewers understanding that misogyny is anathema in order to manufacture shock. Consequently, *Murder-Set-Pieces* implicitly endorses the idea that misogyny is objectionable, despite its antagonists' behaviour. *Murder-Set-Pieces*'s 'extremity' is contingent on the norm that is infringed: if misogyny and representations of sexual violence were acceptable, its imagery would fail to shock.

This distinction applies to hardcore horror films more broadly, particularly where sex is characterised as 'extreme'. Hardcore horror's sex acts breach acceptability standards, particularly those enshrined by censorial guidelines. For example, *Slow Torture Puke Chamber* features scenarios in which urine, menstrual blood, and (unsurprisingly) vomit are brought into conjunction with sexual violence. In other films, sex is combined with additional distasteful elements. *Stockholm Syndrome* features a raping, murdering priest, for instance. The sexual homicide he commits is doubly anomalous since it is sacrilegious, directly belying his pious vocation. Two of *August Underground's Mordum*'s killers are marked as deviant because they are incestuous siblings. Other interdicted forms of sex such as necrophilia are evoked in *Murder-Set-Pieces, Amateur Porn Star Killer 2,* and *Blood and Sex Nightmare* to underline how abnormal their antagonists are. Most significantly, and in opposition to torture porn, virtually no consensual sex acts are offered in hardcore horror. In this context, sex is painted as deplorable, being correlated with murder and violence. Again, the shock evoked via such acts is contingent on the norms that are reacted against. Although hardcore horror imagery violates accepted standards of decency, unless those standards remain stable, hardcore horror will no longer be 'hardcore'.

Representations of sex in hardcore horror create discordances, then. In hardcore horror, aberrant forms of sex are predominantly associated with immoral violence. That characterisation conflicts with hardcore horror's 'alternative' ethos: the celebration of commercial, industrial, and aesthetic non-normativity. Rather than just gainsaying established standards, however, hardcore horror filmmakers revel in dissonance. Hardcore horror's imagery is provocative not because it is transgressive, but rather because it is founded on resistances and tensions.

In that light, an important distinction needs to be made between two types of sex act that epitomise 'extremity'. Some of the acts drama- tised in hardcore horror violate acceptability standards because they are plainly immoral and illegal. Rape is one example. However, other acts – those involving bodily wastes, for example – are 'abnormal' because they are distasteful. Immorality and distaste are habitually treated as if they are interchangeable (Kelly, 2011; Schnall et al., 2008; Kekes, 1992). The illegal acts depicted in hardcore horror – such as rape and murder – are simulated. As such, the images do not capture deeds that are properly immoral, because they are only dramatised representations. In contrast, the distasteful acts exhibited – such as sexually contextualised urination – are authentic, yet they are only immoral because they are committed to film: the acts themselves are not illegal, but the representations of those acts *are.* This discrepancy is vital because where subjected to censorial scrutiny, hardcore horror films themselves are treated as immoral and are censured because they display that which is distasteful.

'Sensation+Perception=Affect':[17] offensive purposes

The pleasures associated with both horror and porn are problematised by the candid commingling of sex and horror. The representations of sexual degradation contained within hardcore horror invert vanilla pornogra- phy's carnal utopias. Unlike in exploitation horror films, where nudity (especially female nudity) is casually presented as titillating spectacle and does not problematise the narrative flow, hardcore horror's sex–violence confluences are disquieting. Hardcore horror's gore-fantasies expose the body in ways that horror and porn do not typically. The acts of urination, vomiting, and bleeding found in Valentine's 'Vomit Gore' films are pornographic inasmuch as they render the body's inner secrets visible. The sex–violence convergences offered in hardcore horror open the body in an unlimited fashion.

Censors' active suppression of and critics' inclination to ignore these films demonstrate that taboo-contravention is unsettling. Accordingly, it may be hard to comprehend why anyone finds hardcore horror appealing. Bernstein's (2004: 11) explication of the 'pornographic gaze' – which grips audiences in a state of simultaneous 'fascinat[ion] and repuls[ion:] we cannot bear to look and we cannot stop looking' – is one account of the compulsion to view forbidden material. However, that explanation does not elucidate what such fascinated revulsion *means*. Hardcore horror films show bodies engaged in sex and violence, and many hardcore horror filmmakers seek to stimulate physical responses to such portrayals. For instance, Vogel comments that he intends Toetag Pictures's productions to be sensorially provocative: 'I wanted the audience to put themselves in that place ... [to] imagine what it would smell like'. In Vogel's *Murder Collection V.1*, the narrator directly prompts such engagement, asking the viewer, 'why are you watching? ... with what you are about to observe you ... will ask "could this happen to me?"'. Horror and porn share this capacity for visceral stimulation, which 'incise[s] those imaginings in [the audience's] very flesh' (Shaviro, 1993: 100). The propensity to 'move' viewers is powerful. The instance of visceral affect indicates that one's values have been disturbed. Viewers therefore contribute to hardcore horror's meanings if they physically respond to its content. Hardcore horror is fiction. Even so, physical reactions expose one's attitudes towards bodies, sex, violence, and decency. Hardcore horror films challenge those constructed views as well as the processes via which particular practices are deemed unacceptable.

One such process is the condemnation of genres that test acceptability thresholds. Both porn and horror are considered 'base' genres that are undeserving of intellectual study because they stir on a corporeal level. Neither pornography nor horror films are customarily regarded as prompting philosophical contemplation. Both genres are typically considered to be disposable culture of simple pleasures and fleeting appeal. Given this predisposition towards envisaging porn as transient culture, it is unsurprising that porn's history has been neglected by so many commentators who use 'porn' in the scornful, metaphoric sense.

Prior to the nineteenth century, porn was politically subversive. Its 'primary role [was as a] social critic', offering 'a space in which cultural anxieties over sexuality, gender, race, and class could be worked through' (Garlick, 2010: 600; see also Hunt, 1993: 42; Sigel, 2002). Extreme porn, hardcore horror, and horror-porn befit this conception of porn. Their taboo-flouting sex–violence combinations re-politicise porn and horror. Re-politicising entails rethinking how these genres operate as sites of contestation against which acceptability standards are formed and disputed.

Such political challenges do not arise from the particular acts, themes, or aesthetics found in contemporary hardcore horror or extreme porn per se, since what is considered indecent alters over time. These subgenres are politically charged because of their relative 'extremity'. Since they are taboo, the representations of sex and violence found in hardcore horror and extreme porn rebut concurrent uses of 'porn' elsewhere in culture. The 'porn' metaphor voids that term of its conceptual function: demarcating what is indecent. 'Torture porn' is a prime example of 'porn' being misused in that way. As comparisons to extreme porn and hardcore horror prove, torture porn films are not extreme or pornographic by contemporary standards, despite detractors' protests against the subgenre.

The first infamous snuff-style horror films made in the late 1970s and into the 1980s attracted attention for their sex–violence blends, especially from anti-pornography feminists.[18] It is startling that hardcore horror films – which flagrantly blur those lines – have not been subject to the same scrutiny. This is a major oversight, since these sidelined texts hinge on sexual taboo. Hardcore horror dramatises culturally, socially, and/or politically unacceptable subject matter. Because various sexual taboos are expressly explored in hardcore horror, these films are a rich resource for anyone interested in contemporary sexual politics. Since these marginalised texts epitomise what is indecent according to contemporary standards, ignoring them means failing to decipher what those taboos mean or how unacceptability is demarcated.

Labels such as 'porn' and 'extreme' are principally utilised to denigrate subgenres. The upshot of this dismissive usage, as 'torture porn' elucidates, is critical confusion. Misassessment of torture porn's 'extremity' reveals pundits' limited grasp of what is happening on the peripheries of commercial filmmaking. Without that context, torture porn's place both within culture and on the 'extremity' scale remain unclear. These confusions are exacerbated by the incongruous results of remonstrative campaigning against torture porn. The term 'porn' conveys that torture porn films can and should be dismissed. However, 'porn' also indicates that the subgenre is controversial. Torture porn garnered attention precisely because of those connotations. Simultaneously, critical failure to apprehend what is happening on commercial filmmaking's fringes has permitted hardcore horror filmmakers to create the very 'extreme' images that torture porn's detractors express concern about.

Conclusion: 'Will You Continue?':[1] Beyond 'Torture Porn'

Although it is too early to accurately predict torture porn's future, torture-themed horror continues to be produced; *Nailed Down*, *Rogue River*, and *Would You Rather* are just three films scheduled for release in 2012 that follow in torture porn's footsteps. Scholars are only just beginning to take significant steps beyond the limiting allegorical approach to 'torture porn' (see Hills, 2011; Walliss and Aston, 2012; Reyes, 2012). The label has been proliferated in the press and adopted by horror fans to such an extent that 'torture porn' is likely to endure as part of popular horror's lexis, in the same way that the slasher and splatter subgenres – from which torture porn evolved – have. 'Torture porn' arose in response to a boom in production, most notably between 2003 and 2007. During this era, particular motifs – abduction, torture, and graphic violence – were dubbed 'extreme'. As more films concurrently displayed these traits, critics began treating those qualities as characteristic attributes that could be used to identify 'torture porn' as a discrete category. Now that those elements have been established as properties of torture porn, the next wave of popular multiplex horror accused of presenting graphic violence, pushing acceptability boundaries, or being titillating is also likely to be termed 'torture porn'.

For the moment, torture porn has shifted towards the DVD market, and this movement has been accompanied by two trends post-2008. The first pertains to torture porn's visceral content. Some recent *Saw*-like test-based horror films such as *Die*, *Exam*, and *Choose* are less overtly violent than their torture porn predecessors, and have been allocated '15' certificates by the BBFC as a result. This trend may indicate that some filmmakers and producers are either consciously moving away from what has been branded as controversial content or are self-censoring. The trend may equally convey that in a saturated area of horror, it has

187

become necessary to opt for lower certification in order to widen the available market, boosting potential profitability. The second trend, as mentioned in Chapter 7, is that some post-2008 direct-to-DVD torture porn has boasted more sexual violence than earlier theatrically released torture porn films. Unlike hardcore horror, which bypasses censors, torture porn's higher profile and mainstream distribution have meant that increased sexual violence has been met with increased censorship. Torture porn films such as *A Serbian Film*, *The Bunny Game*, and *The Human Centipede II* have been banned or cut by the BBFC due to their sexually violent imagery. Both trends constrain torture porn's content, and mirror recent shifts away from 'extremity' in hardcore pornography.

Several implications follow. First, increased censorship demonstrates that torture porn films were not originally as sexually orientated as has been contended, since as soon as sexual violence increased, censors have restricted that content. Second, these trends may come to be remembered as the press's victory over torture porn. Various press reviewers demanded torture porn's relegation from the multiplex context and called for increased censorship in response to the subgenre's content. Regardless of how influential those complaints were for producers and censorship bodies, since these desires have been fulfilled, detractors appear to have conquered torture porn. This development also consolidates torture porn's reputation as a bubble of violent horror that necessitated such action, substantiating objectors' pejorative assessments of the subgenre. Third then, torture porn's reputation as sexually violent, boundary pushing horror may be sealed by the subgenre's subsequent displacement from the multiplex and subjection to censorship. Although the 'torture porn' paradigm established in press discourse did not befit torture porn's content, because resultant developments correlate with their desires, it may seem as if decriers were right about torture porn all along.

Hilden's (2007) trepidation regarding the sex–violence analogy being 'used not to convince the MPAA to ease up on [sex], but rather to justify a crackdown on [violence]' was well-founded. In another sense, increased censorship and self-censorship later in torture porn's trajectory has less to do with the subgenre's reputation than it does larger motions towards cultural illiberalism. Indeed, as Peter Bradshaw (2011) observes, recent film bans have been interpreted as a movement towards a 'new Conservative era'. 'Torture porn' is part of an advancement towards cultural regulation that is evinced by, for example, clampdowns on internet file-sharing – notably the Stop Online Piracy Act (SOPA) – in 2011, a development that has been seen as potentially detrimental to freedom of expression by many (see Wong, 2011). File-sharing is a key avenue for disseminating peripheral media, and so SOPA's obstructions to copyright infringement also impede the distribution of various marginal forms of audio–visual cultural expression. The hegemony of dominant cultural forms such as studio-produced, theatrically released films is thereby facilitated. Additionally, pornography has also faced increased systemic pressure in the UK, following proposals that online video should be 'locked behind paywalls' (see Melonfarmers, 2012b). The idea that sex has become acceptable in mainstream culture led to the coining of pejorative terms such as 'torture *porn*' with reference to non-sexual content. More explicit calls to restrict depictions of sex have followed. For instance, in a UK government-commissioned report, Reg Bailey (2011) – head of the campaign group The Mothers' Union – warns that the cultural ubiquity of sexual imagery is socially damaging, and ought to be more harshly regulated. Such advances towards cultural restriction may impact on the meanings of 'torture porn'. The combination of torture porn's relative box-office success and its hyperbolic reputation may mean that the torture porn boom could come to be regarded as a liberal 'golden age' in horror. A swing towards cultural conservatism may augment rather than diminish the subgenre's lasting cultural status.

'Torture porn' thus reveals much about how popular horror film is treated within culture's shifting terrain, and what those negotiations signify more broadly. The furore surrounding torture porn has emanated from critical anxieties about 'extreme' material entering mainstream popular contexts such as the multiplex. Special FX technologies have progressed since cinema's advent, and modes of depicting violence alter across time, but 'extremity' implies that popular horror's content has radically shifted towards impropriety. Those fears affirm that popular cultural texts have more power than is typically assumed. Furthermore, to deem that horror has become 'uncontrolled' is to fail to acknowledge the wider historical patterns that situate unacceptability or the specific forms taboo takes at any juncture.

The overarching failure to adequately bridge between concepts and particularities severely hampers torture porn discourse. As exemplified in Chapter 1, the subgenre's depreciators customarily segregate torture porn from its generic antecedents. In this view, torture porn is the antithesis of past genre classics that have 'stood the test of time'. That proposal is underpinned by tension: while genre continuities are downplayed, established discursive paradigms are simultaneously sustained. Via this imbalance, it is insinuated that torture porn evinces horror's declining standards, and that critical paradigms, in contrast, have perpetual value. However, the opposite is also implied: that these critical structures are inapposite, and torture porn exposes that inaptness. Like genre conventions, critics' attitudes gradually evolve over time. Torture porn films stand accused of being shallow and transient, yet superficial and faddish *responses* to torture porn undercut that position.

'Torture porn' discourse is typically reactionary in tone. The subgenre's disparagers predominantly concentrate on current film releases, and ubiquitously portray torture porn as urgently alarming. This discursive refrain is not entirely inappropriate given that imminent peril is one of torture porn's prevailing leitmotifs. Torture porn's diegetic situations are emotionally fraught, meaning protagonists negotiate the balance between their subjective interests (particular) and moral principles (conceptual). However, as Chapter 6 illustrated, reactionary, personally-invested responses are recurrently critiqued in torture porn narratives. In these films, relinquishing to immediate pressures leads to immoral deeds, psychological devastation, and death. Torture porn thematically warns against the kind of narrow, of-the-moment thinking that its detractors so often employ. The same kind of exigency is evident in scholars' attempts to connect these films to concurrent political circumstances, particularly those related to 9/11. 'Torture porn' discourse is characterised by an over-privileging of the immediate, and a disregard for the organic nature of change. By focusing on the present and ignoring torture porn's likenesses to the past, such argumentation risks overlooking how pressing 'now' seems at *every* interval, whenever it is experienced.

These flaws indicate a lack of engagement with torture porn on a conceptual level. Without analysing detail as a springboard to conceptual thinking, a gap forms between signifier ('torture porn') and what the term is meant to signify (torture porn's narrative content). In fact, the wording 'torture porn' elucidates that the category formed not around the films, but around the idea that torture porn's content violates standards of acceptability. The particular – the standards by which acceptability is defined, for example – continually evolves. Deciphering the significance of such developments entails referring to conceptual contexts. Those conceptual contexts – that there are acceptability standards that can be violated, for instance – remain comparatively constant. 'Torture porn' discourse's key concepts – 'extreme', 'pornographic', and 'horrific' – all signify breaches of standards, but torture porn is only a new configuration of specific tropes, not a radical shift in what those concepts mean.

Approached from this angle, it becomes clear that labels such as 'torture porn' are flawed in two significant ways. First, 'torture porn' generalises, masking a host of particularities including contextual circumstances, acceptability standards, conventional facets, characters' actions, and critics' attitudes, for example. Those attributes are fluid and become meaningful by clashing against one another. The label 'torture porn' cannot pin down these connotations, because torture porn is in motion. What 'torture porn' discourse does is to bring a host of traits, values and interpretations together. Second, labelling entails demarcating boundaries by pointing towards differences. That is, 'torture porn' implies a delimited, static category, yet the label's meanings cannot remain fixed because the subgenre's content and the discourse surrounding these films are continually evolving.

Critics have commonly treated 'torture porn' as delineating rigid dichotomous binaries, thereby facilitating pejorative discourses. For example, torture porn is alleged to be 'extreme', 'immoral', or 'trash', which implies that the subgenre is not 'acceptable', 'moral', or 'classic'. By approaching those dichotomous poles as contested concepts, however, it becomes apparent that they are approximate and relative, rather than objective and permanent. The very notion of dichotomous poles implies a spectrum of states in-between those apparently oppositional conditions. Values that are painted as stark dichotomous poles do not just imply their relation to the 'diametric' pole then, but also to the infra-dichotomous shades in-between. When considering morality, for example, it is not enough to label one act 'wrong'. It is also necessary to consider that act's apparent divergence from 'right', and the flux in-between those poles, both of which inform one's assessment of immorality. These in-between stages are infinitely divisible. As such, separating right from wrong, torturer from tortured, or extreme from acceptable become matters of asking where precisely the tipping points are. It also means being attentive to how such assessments are made, and according to what conditions. Although useful for grasping patterns and for throwing points of contestation into relief, one's thinking should not finish at categorising or demarcating difference. The general should not replace engagement with the particular. By scrutinising the tensions that arise from categorisation, we can learn about the dichotomy paradigms themselves.

When envisaged as a dynamic process in which meaning is contested rather than as a way of finalising meaning, labelling can be utilised to uncover how particularity is intertwined with broader conceptual frameworks. In dealing with both torture porn and 'torture porn', this book has aimed to break down and unfurl rather than reductively define and fix what 'torture porn' means. 'Torture porn' is a nexus at which numerous concepts converge. Only by recognising its multifaceted, variable nature can one comprehend what torture porn is now and begin to account for how 'torture porn' will evolve in the future.

Notes

Introduction: 'Welcome to Your Worst Nightmare'

1. *Hostel* tagline.
2. For Edelstein's first use of the term, see Edelstein, 2005.
3. Lowenstein (2011) for example, has claimed that '"torture porn" does not exist'.
4. 2010 Entertainment One DVD release.
5. 2012 Left Films DVD release.
6. 2008 Film 2000 DVD release.
7. Director interview featurette (*Martyrs* 2009 Optimum Releasing DVD release). Further reference to any DVD commentaries or featurettes cited throughout the book will refer to release initially cited for each film.
8. For example, on *Antichrist*, see Tookey, 2009; Hunter, 2009; and on *The Killer Inside Me* see Phillips, 2010; Anna Smith, 2010.

1 'The Past Catches Up to Everyone': Lineage and Nostalgia

1. *Choose* tagline.
2. Major International English language publications were searched via LexisNexis UK. The 45 films are: *Antichrist, Captivity, The Collector, Deadgirl, The Devil's Rejects, Donkey Punch, Dying Breed, Embodiment of Evil, The Final, Frontier(s), Funny Games, Grindhouse, The Hills Have Eyes, Hostel, Hostel: Part II, The Human Centipede, The Human Centipede II, I Know Who Killed Me, I Spit on Your Grave, Irreversible, The Last House on the Left, The Loved Ones, Martyrs, Meat Grinder, Mum and Dad, P2, Saw, Saw II, Saw III, Saw IV, Saw V, Saw VI, Saw 3D, Scar, A Serbian Film, Shadow, Switchblade Romance, The Texas Chainsaw Massacre, The Texas Chainsaw Massacre: The Beginning, Timber Falls, Turistas, Untraceable, Vacancy, Wolf Creek, Wrong Turn,* and *wΔz.*
3. 39 had at least limited theatrical runs in the UK.
4. *The Texas Chainsaw Massacre: The Beginning* tagline.
5. See, for instance, DVD director commentaries by Aja (*Switchblade Romance* 2005 Optimum Releasing release); Ryan Nicholson (*Live Feed* 2008 Film 2000 release); and Dave Parker (*The Hills Run Red* 2009 Warner Home Video release).
6. Bryan in *Carver*.
7. There are some exceptions. While not as 'innocent' or 'boyish' as Clover's Final Girl (1993: 40), Tammi in *Donkey Punch*, Jordan in *Hunger*, and Beth in *Hostel: Part II* are female torture porn protagonists who are clearly marked as exceptional and likely to out-survive their peers.
8. See the following DVD commentaries: Aja (*Switchblade Romance*); Dunstan (*Saw 3D* 2011 Lionsgate Home Entertainment release); Schmidt (*Wrong Turn* 2004 20th Century Fox release).

9. *Shaun of the Dead* (2004), *Zombie Strippers!* (2008), and *Cockneys vs Zombies* (2011) are just three examples of zom-edy films.
10. Gordon, 2009.
11. The same sentiment is echoed by Tom Long (2008) regarding *Untraceable*, and by Nathan Lee (2008) about *Saw V*.
12. Gatiss's BBC series *A History of Horror* (2010), from which the quote is taken, covers no horror films beyond the late 1970s.

2 'Bend to Our Objectives': 'Torture Porn' as Press Discourse

1. Riley in *The Killing Room*.
2. *Nine Dead* tagline.
3. It is worth clarifying that these certificates are not entirely equal, even if they carry similar connotations. PG-13 is distinguished from an R-rating in the same way the '15' certificate is from '18', the former in each pair being 'soft', the latter being 'hard'. However, numerous R-rated torture-related films were allotted 15 certificates in the UK, including *The Killing Room*, *Roadkill*, and *The Strangers*.
4. *Captivity* tagline.
5. The figures were collated from LexisNexis UK, searching for 'torture porn' across all major world publications in English. The same search across all languages and all news sources yielded similar results: 599 articles in 2007; 746 articles in 2008; 685 articles in 2009; 658 articles in 2010; and 559 articles in 2011. Usage peaks in 2007–9, and declines thereafter.
6. Although these 'extreme' versions are packaged to foster the impression that they are more violent, it is not always the case that they are significantly gorier than the theatrical cuts. For example, although the 'unrated' DVD version of *The Texas Chainsaw Massacre: The Beginning* is over five minutes longer than the R-rated theatrical release, only around 30 seconds of that restored footage portrays physical violence. The rest is constituted by extended dialogue sequences.
7. Elmer in *Untraceable*.
8. *Cannibal Holocaust* was released in the UK in 2001 with nearly six minutes of cuts. In 2011, the film was passed with only 15 seconds excised.
9. See Zombie in McClintock (2006), Berman (*Borderland* 2010 Momentum Pictures release DVD commentary), and Aja (*The Hills Have Eyes* 2006 20th Century Fox release DVD commentary).
10. Archie in *Tortured*.

3 'No-one Approves of What You're Doing': Fans and Filmmakers

1. Sylvie in *7 Days*.
2. Alexa in *The Hills Run Red*.
3. A documentary about these filmmakers entitled *The Splat Pack* was released in 2011.

4. Jerod Hollyfield (2009) also notes that '*Hostel*'s reception was atypically scathing'.
5. Indeed, in his director commentary for *Hostel* (2006 Sony Pictures DVD release), Roth admits that 'it's hard to shut [him] up' when it comes to talking about horror.
6. Roth (*Hostel: Part II* 2007 Sony Pictures release DVD commentary).
7. Shankland (*wΔz* 2008 Entertainment One release DVD commentary). See also Laugier (*Martyrs*, interview featurette).
8. Blanks (*Storm Warning* 2008 Optimum release DVD commentary). Devi Snively's short film *I Spit on Eli Roth* (2009) similarly singles out Roth.
9. Mason (*Broken* 2007 Revolver Entertainment release DVD commentary). Mason states he did not enjoy *Saw*, and jokes that someone should rape and torture whoever coined the term. While Laugier states that he 'love[d] *Hostel*', and was 'influenced by' it, he is quick to distance *Martyrs* from torture porn: 'I don't think my film bears any relation to *Saw* or *Hostel*. The films don't have the same intention or the same style…*Martyrs* was like an anti-*Hostel*' (*Martyrs* interview featurette).
10. See the following DVD commentaries: Lynch (*Wrong Turn 2* 2007 20th Century Fox release); Smith (*Creep* 2005 Pathé Distribution release); Berman (*Borderland*).
11. *The Tortured* 2010 Entertainment One release 'Behind the Scenes' featurette. Zombie offers similar observations regarding *The Devil's Rejects* (2005 Momentum Pictures release DVD commentary).
12. Shankland (*wΔz* DVD commentary) proffers that 'unlike the usual project' for such films (displaying 'sadism or cruelty'), violence 'reveals love' in *wΔz*. Zombie states that violence should be uncomfortable to watch, because it is inherently disquieting (*30 Days in Hell*).
13. Roth (*Hostel: Part II* DVD commentary).
14. Roth (*Hostel* DVD commentary).
15. Bousman (*Saw IV* 2008 Lionsgate release DVD commentary).
16. *Mum and Dad* 2008 Revolver Entertainment release.
17. Ramon in *Killing Words*.
18. In order to gather information without imposing an agenda, already existing stand-alone discussions on horror community sites were consulted. I neither instigated nor intervened in discussions quoted here. The responses quoted are publically accessible, and users will only be identified by their on-screen usernames.
19. Users Gargus and Slates81 respectively (Miska, 2009).
20. See comments made by user Aoiookami regarding *Hostel*'s 'weak premise', and his or her acceptance of the label's aptness in that case (N.a. 2009). Later in the conversation, Ash28M notes the pattern that 'people who don't like those films tend to like the term ["torture porn"]'.
21. User Ash28M (N.a. 2009).
22. User Thedevilyouknow (N.a. 2008d).
23. See user Itiparanoid13 and Napalmfuzz's comments following Miska (2007). See also user DemonToSome's comment (N.a. 2007c): 'That name ["torture porn"] is to lure non horror fans in'.
24. Jacques in *5150 Elm Way*.

Part II   Introduction

1. These ideas are expounded in full in Kant's *Groundwork of the Metaphysics of Morals* and *The Metaphysics of Morals*. The summation that follows provides the essential ideas that will be drawn upon in Chapter 6.
2. Some may misread Kant's (1998: 55) insistence that moral consciousness is a priori, for example, as proposing that individuals are slaves to moral imperatives.
3. The original *The Texas Chainsaw Massacre*'s redneck horror stereotypes regarding 'inbred types doing...dastardly things' in the outback (*Shocking Truth*) is mimicked by more than thirty torture porn films.

4   'Your Story's Real, and People Feel That': Contextualising Torture

1. Joyce in *Saw 3D*.
2. Even Edelstein concurs that *Hostel* has a 'political subtext' (Johnson, 2007).
3. See, for example, Martin and Porter (1986: 60). Various scholars – including Gregory Currie (1995: 174–5) and Peter Hutchings (2004: 195–6) – have objected to those assumptions.
4. Brady, 2010a.
5. Other 9/11-torture porn parallels are offered by Wetmore (2012) and Rod Buxton (2011).
6. See Lynch (*Wrong Turn 2* DVD commentary), Zombie (*30 Days in Hell*), and Berman (*Borderland* DVD commentary).
7. Inoue in *Deathtube*.
8. *Penance, The Butcher, The Poughkeepsie Tapes*, and *The Great American Snuff Film* are rare examples of 'found footage' torture porn films, which utilise a realist aesthetic.
9. *A Serbian Film* tagline.
10. *Untraceable, I Know Who Killed Me*, and *Train* are among the only torture porn films where a lead captive unambiguously defeats their captors without becoming a physical and emotional wreck. Thus, some moral resolution is provided in these films. That is not to say that such resolution is unproblematic: see the analysis of *Untraceable* in Chapter 5.
11. On the difference between 'destroyed' and 'deconstructed' (as it is used here), see Scarry, 1985: 20.
12. Wilson in *The Hills Run Red*.
13. *Broken* tagline.

5   'Some are Victims. Some are Predators. Some are Both': Torturous Positions

1. *She's Crushed* tagline.
2. Bridget in *The Final*.
3. Secondary characters in *Captivity* and *Live Animals* also switch in this way.
4. *Storm Warning* tagline.

5. The discussion of *Captivity* here refers to the US Unrated version. The UK release is the same as the US R-Rated version, and misses the epilogue. Another edit (known as the 'original' or 'thriller' version) differs greatly. Police are shown investigating Jennifer's disappearance throughout, and most of the torture set-pieces are excluded, since the latter were reputedly edited in to sell the film as torture horror. The technique of cutting to black when protagonists lose consciousness is also found in, for instance, *Dying Breed*, *The Hills Run Red*, *Manhunt*, and *Vacancy 2*. The same technique is employed in *Hard Candy* and *I Spit on Your Grave* where the male sexual predators are knocked out by Haley and Jennifer respectively. The principle is the same inasmuch as the tortured's point-of-view is reflected in the mise-en-scene, although cutting to black signals a power exchange in these cases.
6. In her book-length study of self-defence, Fiona Leverick (2006) stresses the need to uphold the right to life above all else. While her rights-based approach is undermined by her acceptance of homicide in some circumstances, she does suggest that killing is justified only 'where an aggressor poses an unjust immediate threat, *and there is no other way in which the threat can be avoided* by the victim' (65–6). The 'morally preferable option' is to retreat where possible, as this 'promotes maximum respect for the right to life' (76).
7. As Daniel Batson et al. (2009: 155) warn, '[m]oral outrage – anger at violation of a moral standard – should be distinguished from anger at the harm caused by standard-violating behaviour'. On the issue of balance, retributivists argue 'that it is a matter of *duty* that [proportionate] retribution occur' (Rosebury, 2009: 18).
8. *7 Days* tagline.
9. *Kill Theory* tagline.
10. *The Task* tagline.
11. The same is true of *Deathtube*'s online witnesses, who are torn between supporting and condemning the tortured they watch suffer. *Deathtube* collapses the witness/tortured distance since the snuff website's targets are constituted by abducted Deathtube watchers.
12. On group witnessing and responsibility diffusion, see Darley and Latané (1970).
13. The same applies to Haneke's *Funny Games*: for critiques of Haneke's apparent hypocrisy, see Schneller, 2008; Fern, 2008; Kermode, 2008b.
14. Creely in *The Poughkeepsie Tapes*.

6 'In the Land of the Pig, the Butcher Is King': Torture, Spaces, and Power

1. Vincent in *The Unforgiving*.
2. *The Killing Room* tagline.
3. *Vacancy* tagline.
4. Other examples include *The Collector*, *Funny Games*, *Kidnapped*, and *The Strangers*.
5. They are, in this sense, reminiscent of the 'terrible places' found in slasher films (Clover, 1993: 30), exposing another aspect of torture porn's genre lineage.

6. *Gag* tagline.
7. Law is not directly a list of moral obligations, and moral practice is partially context-relative. Many moral philosophers offer divergent takes on this issue. For a critique of moral universality and a discussion of context dependency, see Johnson, 2011: 3 and 12.
8. On morality and the phenomenon of renormalisation, see Luban, 2006: 50–1; Correia et al., 2007: 37.
9. On the inalienability of rights see Uniacke, 2000; Leverick, 2006: 61–2.
10. CJ in *Stash*.
11. *Kill Theory* and *House of 9* similarly pit captives against one another in this way.
12. On morality, self-realisation, and devotion to principle, see Varga, 2011.
13. On morality and self-judgement, see Westphal, 1984: 77–8; Rosenthal, 2011: 160.
14. Kojima in *Grotesque*.

Part III Introduction

1. This focus on misogyny means Part III will be principally centred on male–female interactions. Accordingly, the analysis of porn in Chapter 8 will only account for heterosexual porn, since this is most relevant to the misogyny debate.

7 'Ladies First'?: Torture Porn, Sex, and Misogyny

1. Ridley in *Matchdead*.
2. Caption in *Death Factory: Bloodletting*.
3. 2010 Icon Home Entertainment DVD release.
4. Shankland (*wΔz* DVD commentary), Roth (*Hostel* DVD commentary).
5. However, *Scream Bloody Murder's* (1972) advertising claimed that it was 'the first motion picture to be called gore-nography!!!' For a replication of the poster, see Thrower, 2008: 64.
6. For arguments against the notion that slasher films are misogynistic, see Cowan and O'Brien, 1990: 187; Gunter, 2002: 122.
7. The torturer in *Grotesque*.
8. The 134 'zombie' deaths that feature in the *Planet Terror* section of *Grindhouse* have been excluded from the statistics that follow, since these are almost exclusively coded male. To include these would skew the numbers in an unrepresentative way. These statistics only refer to the press's 45-film torture porn canon since these films have been explicitly accused of belonging to 'torture porn' (in the pejorative sense). The qualitative discussion will extend beyond these 45 films to explore torture porn's sexual politics more broadly.
9. The same is true of those films in which women are the sole or lead torturers – including *Branded*, *The Loved Ones*, and *She's Crushed* – as well as those that present women as part of a group of torturers, such as *The Devil's Rejects*, *Farmhouse*, and *Tortura*. Women may be strong in such cases, but strength manifests as cruel violence. *Neighbor's* female torturer easily overpowers the men she encounters for instance, yet she is callous and brutal. She is coded

as inherently unappealing rather than as a positive exemplar of gendered strength.

10. Jim in *Creep*.
11. Despite its art-film credentials – in comparison with torture porn's reputation as cultural trash – *Irreversible* is built around a rape-revenge structure. As such, *Irreversible* has been ill-received as an art-film. *Irreversible* is included here alongside other torture porn films in the spirit of arguing that torture porn deserves to be taken as seriously as films belonging to more culturally credible genres. *Irreversible* bridges that gap.
12. On the moral legitimacy of murder in return for rape, see Leverick, 2006: 143.
13. On the phallocentricism inherent to such discourse, see Rooney, 1993: 93.
14. For recent research on male rape and inequalities in the evaluation of male and female rape, see Weiss, 2010. On the legal issues surrounding definition of female sexual assault and rape, see Bourke, 2007: 212–3.
15. Interjections in rape-studies have explicitly probed the question of essentialised male–female difference via evolutionary theory: see Thornhill and Palmer, 2000; Travis, 2003.
16. Dennis in *Sympathy*.
17. For the purposes of this discussion, and because they are coded as such in the narratives, the insertion of foreign objects into orifices is considered to be rape. Laws in different countries disagree on whether foreign object insertion is defined as rape: see Kahn et al., 2003.
18. On this, and the disproportionate attention paid to castration in horror scholarship, see Hutchings, 2004: 65.
19. Roth (*Hostel: Part II* DVD commentary).
20. Steven Monroe (in Hays, 2010) on rape in *I Spit on Your Grave*.

8 'Why Are You Crying? Aren't You Having Fun?': Extreme Porn

1. Jamie in *Texas Vibrator Massacre*.
2. Hailey in *Hard Candy*.
3. Miller v. California 413 U.S. 15 (1973).
4. Wendy Hesford (2004: 119) is among the many scholars who have refuted this anti-porn argument.
5. These assumptions have been widely contested: see O'Toole, 1999: 334–5; Segal, 1993: 8–15; Vance, 1990. Despite inconclusive evidence – see Prince, 2000: 20–4; Rothman, 2001: 37; Hill, 1997: 104–6 – media effects still influences legislation surrounding visual imagery. In rejecting *The Human Centipede II*, for instance, the BBFC cited 'the likelihood of any harm that may be caused to the viewer or, through their behaviour, to society' (BBFC, 2011).
6. Tusion in *Meatholes 2*.
7. See, for example, Dines, 2010; Maddison, 2013. In this sense, Max Hardcore is akin to Eli Roth: both have been scapegoated for being too vocal.
8. Max Hardcore and Tusion are captured in these divergent ways in *Hardcore* (2000).

9. Regan Starr, who appeared in Tusion's *Rough Sex 2*, claims otherwise. For Starr's and Tusion's conflicting reports on the scene, see Amis, 2001 and Ross, 2000.
10. Indeed, fellow extreme porn filmmaker Max Hardcore places onus on the consumer-led nature of porn to explain content: 'the public has spoken, and what they want is extreme material' (in Cachapero, 2006).
11. O'Toole, 1999: 359.
12. In his autobiography, Jeremy and Spitznagel (2008: 168) claims to have starred 'in over seventeen hundred adult movies' since the late 1970s.
13. On generic fluctuation and gender in *Porn of the Dead*, see Jones, 2011b.
14. Jason in *Saw: A Hardcore Parody*.
15. This sentiment was shared by Rob Black (*Frontline*) and Lizzie Borden (*Porn Shutdown*) (both of Extreme Associates) before they were imprisoned on obscenity charges. Black claimed that he made extreme porn to 'stand out' in the marketplace (*Louis Theroux's Weird Weekends*).
16. Jacobellis v. Ohio, 378 US 184 (1964).
17. Black was indicted in 2003, and served a ten month jail-sentence (2009–10). Hardcore was indicted in 2007, began serving a 46 month jail-sentence in January 2009, and was released in January 2011. The gambit appears to have worked insofar as on his release Hardcore (in Kernes, 2011) claims to have 'sanitised' his output, and unveiled plans to move away from porn. Although Black denies that he has been 'tamed', he has dubbed extreme porn 'silly' and is currently directing porn aimed at the couples market (*Louis Theroux: Twilight of the Porn Stars*). The Manwin Group are following a similar course, closing the rough sex website PornstarsPunishment.com as part of the company's move towards 'high end adult production' (Warren, 2012).

9 'You Will Not Believe Your Eyes ... or Stomach': Hardcore Horror

1. *Slaughtered Vomit Dolls* tagline.
2. Cowboy in *Maskhead*.
3. 'Interview with Filmmakers' on 2007 Cinema Epoch DVD release.
4. The BBFC also required cuts to several films: *A Serbian Film* (cut by just over four minutes), *Break* (cut by 53 seconds), and *I Spit on Your Grave* (cut by 43 seconds). This is not quite the same as outright banning, although films do not have to be officially banned to still be considered illegitimate. For a list of films that have not been formally rejected by the BBFC but are still effectively banned, see Melonfarmers, 2012a.
5. The trailers are available at *Captivity*'s (2007) official website.
6. Such certification issues gain additional symbolic weight the UK context, as it feeds into the way ex-Video Nasties have been marketed as 'illicit' products since the bans on those films were lifted. That history is evident in the way stronger horror is marketed to UK audiences (see Walker, 2011).
7. *Amateur Porn Star Killer 2* tagline.
8. Lavey and Valentine discuss realism in the *Slaughtered Vomit Dolls* 'making of' DVD featurette (2010 Unearthed Films release).

9. A wealth of literature is available concerning the origins and development of snuff fiction (see Kerekes and Slater, 1995; Petley, 2000; Carol, 1993, to name just a few examples), so that topic is not dwelt upon here. On faux-snuff and hardcore horror, see Jones, 2011a.
10. Recent examples include *Cloverfield*, *Apollo 18*, and *The Last Exorcism*.
11. In fact, because its horror hinges on the film's reality aesthetics, the faux-snuff film's formal properties are foregrounded. On realism and horror, see Chouliaraki, 2006: 24; Freeland, 1995.
12. George in *Trunk*.
13. The 13 year-old was played by a 19 year-old (Michiko Jimenez).
14. On children and connotations of innocence, see Vanobbergen, 2004.
15. Movies such as *A Serbian Film* straddle that boundary. (Fake) erect penises are displayed in its censored edit, yet explicit sexual wounding – such as Jeca's mother biting Milos's penis, and Layla being suffocated by a penis – have been excised from the BBFC's certificated version. The same is true of *The Human Centipede II*'s barbed-wire rape, sandpaper masturbation, and a newborn baby being crushed to death under a car accelerator pedal, which were all removed to attain certification.
16. 2010 *ReGOREgitated Sacrifice* Unearthed Films release DVD commentary.
17. Balan in *Murder Collection V.1*.
18. The closing scene of *Snuff* has been specifically scrutinized, since it begins as a sex sequence and culminates in murder (see Labelle, 1992: 189, for example).

Conclusion: 'Will You Continue?': Beyond 'Torture Porn'

1. The Man in *Broken*.

Bibliography

Aftab, Kaleem (2009) 'Don't Lose Your Head', *Arts & Book Review*, June 5.

Amis, Martin (2001) 'A Rough Trade', *The Guardian*, March 17.

Andén-Papadopoulos, Kari (2009) 'Body Horror on the Internet: US Soldiers Recording the War in Iraq and Afghanistan', *Media Culture Society*, 31:6.

Anderson, Jason (2007) 'From Horror Film to Torture Porn', *The Globe and Mail*, July 13.

Anderson, John (2007a) '1408', *Variety*, June 18.

—— (2007b) 'Frontier(s)', *Variety*, September 24.

—— (2007c) 'Subtly Terrifying, Just Like Real Life', *The New York Times*, December 30.

—— (2008) 'Horrormeister Sinks His Teeth into Cruelty of Film Culture', *The Washington Post*, February 16.

—— (2009) 'Retrofitting That Hockey Mask', *The New York Times*, February 8.

Andrews, Nigel (2007) 'The Great and Grisly Tradition', *Financial Times*, June 28.

Antonucci, Mike (1998) 'Anime Magnetism Drawing Power of Japanese Animation Tapes', *San Jose Mercury News*, February 8.

Atlas, James (1999) 'The Loose Canon', *The New Yorker*, March 29.

Bailey, Reg (2011) 'Letting Children Be Children', https://www.gov.uk/government/uploads/system/uploads/attachment_data/file/175418/Bailey_Review.pdf date accessed 19 June 2012.

Barnes, Brookes (2009) 'Audiences Laughed to Forget Troubles', *The New York Times*, December 30.

Batson, C. Daniel, David A. Lishner, Amy Carpenter, Luis Dulin, Sanna Harjusola-Webb, E. L. Stocks, Shawna Gale, Omar Hassan, and Brenda Sampat (2003) '"... As You Would Have Them Do Unto You": Does Imagining Yourself in the Other's Place Stimulate Moral Action?' *Personality and Social Psychology Bulletin*, 29:9.

Batson, C. Daniel, Mary Chao, and Jeffery Givens (2009) 'Pursuing Moral Outrage: Anger at Torture', *Journal of Experimental Social Psychology*, 45.

BBFC (2008) 'Murder Set Pieces', http://www.bbfc.co.uk/AVV245696/ date accessed 19 April 2012.

—— (2009) 'Grotesque', http://www.bbfc.co.uk/AVV261504/ date accessed 3 September 2011.

—— (2011) 'The Human Centipede II', http://www.bbfc.co.uk/BVV278459/ date accessed 21 October 2011.

Beale, Lewis (2009) 'Like *Terminator*, Film Franchises Will Be Back', *Chattanooga Times Free Press*, May 22.

Beckford, Martin (2008) 'Film Violence Led to Knife Crime, Says Attenborough', *The Daily Telegraph*, July 25.

Benson-Allott, Caetlin (2008) '*Grindhouse*: An Experiment in the Death of Cinema', *Film Quarterly*, 62:1.

Bentley, Rick (2011) 'Scandals and Skunks', *Pittsburgh Post-Gazette*, December 29.

Bernstein, J. M. (2004) 'Bare Life, Bearing Witness: Auschwitz and the Pornography of Horror', *Parallax*, 10:1.

Berra, John (2008) *Declarations of Independence* (Bristol: Intellect).

Billson, Anna (2008) 'Crash and Squirm', *The Guardian*, October 31.

Blake, Linnie (2008) *The Wounds of Nations: Horror Cinema, Historical Trauma and National Identity* (Manchester: Manchester University Press).

Booth, William (2008) 'Critics Everywhere Agree', *The Washington Post*, September 12.

Bor, Michael (2007) 'Is There a Link Between "Torture Porn" and Real Sexual Violence?' *The Guardian*, May 3.

Bordwell, David, and Kristin Thompson (2011) *Minding Movies: Observations on the Art, Craft, and Business of Filmmaking* (London: University of Chicago Press).

Bourke, Joanna (2007) *Rape: A History from 1860 to the Present* (London: Virago).

Bowles, Scott (2009) 'Classic Horror Films Come Back to Life, Profitably', *USA Today*, February 13.

Bradshaw, Peter (2007) 'Captivity', *The Guardian*, June 22.

—— (2010) 'The Collector', *The Guardian*, June 25.

—— (2011) 'Don't Ban This Filth', *The Guardian*, June 9.

Brady, Tara (2010a) 'It Came, It Sawed, It Conquered', *The Irish Times*, October 26.

—— (2010b) 'It Is Hell. It Is Not an Entertainment', *The Irish Times*, December 9.

Brett, Vicki (2007) 'Gore-Fest Revisited in House of Horrors', *The Sunday Mail*, June 10.

Brodesser-Anker, Claude (2007) 'Why "Torture Porn" Is the Hottest (and Most Hated) Thing in Hollywood', *Advertising Age*, May 21.

Bronstein, Carolyn (2011) *Battling Pornography: The American Feminist Anti-Pornography Movement, 1976–1986* (Cambridge: Cambridge University Press).

Brown, Annie (2009) 'Battle to Ban Extreme Porn', *Daily Record*, January 19.

Brownmiller, Susan (1976) *Against Our Will: Men, Women and Rape* (New York: Bantam).

Buxton, Rod (2011) '*The Texas Chainsaw Massacre: The Beginning*: A Cultural Critique of the Bush-Cheney Administration', *Jump Cut*, 53.

Cachapero, Joanne (2006) 'Hardcore Content', http://www.xbis.com/articles/15635 date accessed 12 February 2012.

Captivity (2007) *Captivity* Website, http://www.captivitythemovie.com date accessed 1 December 2011.

Caputi, Jane (1992) 'Advertising Femicide: Lethal Violence against Women in Pornography and Gorenography', in Jill Radford and Diana E. H. Russell (eds) *Femicide: The Politics of Woman Killing* (Buckingham: Open University Press).

Carol, Avendon (1993) 'Snuff: Believing in the Worst', in Alison Lassiter and Avendon Carol (eds) *Bad Girls and Dirty Pictures: The Challenge to Reclaim Feminism* (London: Pluto).

Carroll, Noel (1990) *The Philosophy of Horror, or, Paradoxes of the Heart* (London: Routledge).

Cashmore, Pete (2010) 'The Worst Film Movement Ever Has Hit Rock Bottom', *The Guardian*, August 28.

Catt, Lizzie (2010) '"Scary" Boyfriend Fears for Peaches', *The Express*, March 25.

Charity, Tom (2007) 'Vacancy', *The Times*, June 16.

Chen, Ya-Ru, Xiao-Ping Chen, and Rebecca Portnoy (2009) 'To Whom Do Positive Norm and Negative Norm of Reciprocity Apply? Effects of Inequitable Offer,

Relationship, and Relational-Self Orientation', *Journal of Experimental Social Psychology*, 45.

Cheney, Victor (2006) *A Brief History of Castration* (Bloomington: AuthorHouse).

Chittenden, Maurice and Matthew Holehouse (2010) 'Boys Who See Porn More Likely to Harass Girls', *Sunday Times*, January 24.

Chouliaraki, Lilie (2006) *Spectatorship of Suffering* (London: Sage).

Cieply, Michael (2007) 'Report Says the Young Buy Violent Games and Movies', *The New York Times*, April 13.

Clover, Carol (1993) *Men, Women and Chainsaws* (London: BFI).

Cochrane, Kira (2007) 'For Your Entertainment', *The Guardian*, May 1.

Cole, Stephen (2007) 'He Came, He Saw, He Tortured the Audience', *The Globe and Mail*, October 29.

Cole, Tom (2012) 'Let the Banned Play On', http://www.radiotimes.com/news/2012–02–01/let-the-banned-play-on-how-uk-film-censorship-works-in-practice date accessed 1 February 2012.

Conner, Shea (2009) 'Oh, the Horror', *St. Joseph News-Press*, October 30.

Conroy, John (2000) *Unspeakable Acts, Ordinary People: The Dynamics of Torture* (Berkeley: University of California Press).

Correia, Isabel, Jorge Vala, and Patrícia Aguiar (2007) 'Victim's Innocence, Social Categorisation, and the Threat to the Belief in a Just World', *Journal of Experimental Social Psychology*, 43.

Cowan, Gloria, and Margaret O'Brien (1990) 'Gender and Survival vs Death in Slasher Films', *Sex Roles*, 23:3/4.

Cumming, Serena Davis, Michael Deacon, Mark Monahan, Clive Morgan, Ceri Radford, Benjamin Secher, Patrick Smith, and Rachel Ward (2010) 'The Week's Best Films', *The Daily Telegraph*, June 19.

Currie, Gregory (1995) *Image and Mind: Film, Philosophy and Cognitive Science* (Cambridge: Cambridge University Press).

Dalton, Stephen (2009a) 'Film Choice', *The Times*, October 17.

—— (2009b) 'Film Choice', *The Times*, October 22.

Danquah, Paul (2010) 'The Movies and the Issue of Morality', *Africa News*, August 2.

Darley, John, and Bibb Latané (1970) *The Unresponsive Bystander: Why Doesn't He Help?* (New York: Appleton-Century-Crofts).

Davis, Blair and Kial Natale (2010) '"The Pound of Flesh Which I Demand": American Horror Cinema, Gore, and the Box Office, 1998–2007', in Steffen Hantke (ed.) *American Horror Film: The Genre at the Turn of the Millennium* (Mississippi: University Press of Mississippi).

Dawar, Anil (2011) 'Jo's Killer Watched "Torture" Videos of Women Being Strangled During Sex', *The Express*, October 29.

De Lauretis, Teresa (1987) *Technologies of Gender: Essays on Theory Film and Fiction* (Basingstoke: Macmillan).

Debruge, Peter (2008) 'Deadgirl', *Variety*, September 15.

Derakhshani, Tirdad (2007) 'Numbing Sequel Lacks Sympathy', *The Philadelphia Inquirer*, June 8.

Di Fonzo, Carla (2007) 'Gross Cinema', *Intelligencer Journal*, October 26.

Dimanno, Rosie (2011) 'Why Obama Is Right About the Photos', *The Toronto Star*, May 6.

Dines, Gail (2009) 'Childified Women: How the Mainstream Porn Industry Sells Child Pornography to Men', in Sharna Olfman (ed.) *The Sexualisation of Childhood* (Westport: Praeger).

—— (2010) *Pornland: How Porn Has Hijacked Our Sexuality* (Boston: Beacon Press).

—— (2011) 'The New Lolita: Pornography and the Sexualisation of Childhood', in Melinda Tankard Rhist and Abigail Bray (eds) *Big Porn Inc.: Exposing the Harms of the Global Pornography Industry* (Victoria: Spinifex Press).

Dipaolo, Marc (2011) *War, Politics and Superheroes: Ethics and Propaganda in Comics and Film* (Jefferson: McFarland).

Douthat, Ross (2007) 'Punch the Director!', *National Review*, July 9.

Driscoll, Rob (2007) 'Violence Is the New Sex', *The Western Mail*, June 29.

Duits, Linda, and Liesbet Van Zoonen (2011) 'Coming to Terms with Sexualisation', *European Journal of Cultural Studies*, 14:5.

Dworkin, Andrea (1974) *Woman Hating* (New York: Dutton).

—— (1989) *Pornography: Men Possessing Women* (London: Dutton).

Edelstein, David (2005) 'On Socialised Criticism', http://www.slate.com/articles/arts/the_movie_club/features/2005/the_movie_club_2005/on_socialised_criticism.html date accessed 18 November 2011.

—— (2006) 'Now Playing at Your Local Multiplex: Torture Porn', http://nymag.com/movies/features/15622/ date accessed 2 December 2008.

—— (2010) 'The Selfish Altruist', *New York Magazine*, May 3.

Edwards, David (2007) 'Gore Bore Is Total Torture', *The Mirror*, June 22.

Egan, Kate (2007) *Trash or Treasure? Censorship and the Changing Meanings of the Video Nasties* (Manchester: Manchester University Press).

Errigo, Angie (2009) 'A Family in Grief', *Mail on Sunday*, March 29.

Everywoman (1988) *Pornography and Sexual Violence: Evidence of the Links* (London: Everywoman).

Felperin, Leslie (2008) 'Mum & Dad', *Variety*, July 14.

Fern, Ong Sor (2008) 'Not at All Fun and Games', *The Straits Times*, April 16.

Fletcher, Phoebe (2009) 'Apocalyptic Machines: Terror and Anti-Production in the Post-9/11 Splatter Film', in Leanne Franklin and Ravenel Richardson (eds) *The Many Forms of Fear, Horror and Terror* (Oxford: Inter-Disciplinary Press).

Floyd, Nigel (2007) 'Could Critics of "Torture Porn" at Least Watch the Movies?' *Time Out*, June 20.

Forster-Towne, Claudia (2011) *Terrorism and Sexual Violence* (Pretoria: Africa Institute of South Africa).

Foucault, Michel (1995) *Discipline and Punish: The Birth of the Prison*, Alan Sheridan (trans.) (London: Vintage).

Fox, Killian (2007) 'Get Ready for the Gorefest', *The Observer*, June 10.

Freeland, Cynthia (1995) 'Realist Horror', in Cynthia Freeland and Thomas Wartenberg (eds) *Philosophy and Film* (New York: Routledge).

Friend, Tad (2009) 'Inside a Movie Marketer's Playbook', *The New Yorker*, January 19.

Garlick, Steve (2010) 'Taking Control of Sex?: Hegemonic Masculinity, Technology, and Internet Pornography', *Men and Masculinities*, 12:5.

Gillis, Stacy, Gillian Howie, and Rebecca Munford (eds) (2004) *Third Wave Feminism: A Critical Exploration* (London: Palgrave).

Ginbar, Yuval (2008) *Why Not Torture Terrorists? Moral, Practical and Legal Aspects of the 'Ticking Bomb' Justification for Torture* (Oxford: Oxford University Press).

Goldberg, Barbara (1989) 'Anti-Porn Activists Fight Obscenity Charges', *United Press International*, April 17.

Goldstein, Patrick (2010) 'The Big Picture', *Los Angeles Times*, November 2.

Goodwin, Christopher (2007) 'Sitting Comfortably?' *The Sunday Times*, April 15.

Gordon, Bryony (2009) 'Torture Porn Should Have No Place in a Theme Park', *The Daily Telegraph*, April 16.

Gordon, Devin (2006) 'Horror Show', *Newsweek*, April 3.

Govier, Trudy (2002) *Forgiveness and Revenge* (New York: Routledge).

Graham, Jane (2009a) 'Caught in a Trap, and I Can't Back Out', *The Guardian*, October 16.

—— (2009b) 'Extreme Torture Films Grate on Saw Nerves', *The Sydney Morning Herald*, October 19.

Gray, Carmen (2008) 'Frontier(s)', *Sight and Sound*, 18:3.

Gray, Kurt, and Daniel M. Wegner (2010) 'Torture and Judgments of Guilt', *Journal of Experimental Social Psychology*, 46:1.

Gunter, Barrie (2002) *Media Sex: What Are the Issues?* (London: Lawrence Erlbaum).

Hardy, Ernest (2010) 'Deep Zombie Throat', *LA Weekly*, January 7.

Hardy, Simon (2004) 'Reading Pornography', *Sex Education*, 4:1.

Hare, Breeanna (2010) 'The Most Disturbing Movie Ever Made?' http://articles.cnn.com/2010–05–10/entertainment/centipede.torture.movie_1_movie-torture-stars-don-t-shine?_s=PM:SHOWBIZ date accessed 21 September 2010.

Harlow, John (2011) 'Hollywood Biteback', *The Sunday Times*, January 2.

Harries, Dan (2002) 'Watching the Internet', in Dan Harries (ed.), *The New Media Book* (London: BFI Publishing).

Hart, Christopher (2009) 'What Does It Take for a Film to Get Banned These Days?' *Daily Mail*, July 20.

Hawkins, Joan (2007) 'Sleaze Mania, Euro-Trash and High Art', in Mark Jancovich (ed.) *Horror: The Film Reader* (London: Routledge).

Hayes, Katy (2010) 'We Must Be Masochists to Bear This Pain', *The Sunday Times*, October 31.

Hays, Matthew (2010) 'Rape-Revenge Remake Cranks Up the Volume', *The Globe and Mail*, July 10.

Heal, Clare (2007) 'Are We Adult Enough to Decide What to Watch for Ourselves?' *Sunday Express*, October 28.

Hesford, Wendy S. (2004) 'Documenting Violations: Rhetorical Witnessing and the Spectacle of Distant Suffering', *Biography*, 27:1.

Hicks, Tony (2009) 'Horror Films Reflect the Times', *San Jose Mercury News*, October 21.

Hilden, Julie (2007) 'Free Speech and the Concept of "Torture Porn": Why Are Critics So Hostile to *Hostel II*?' http://writ.news.findlaw.com/hilden/20070716.html date accessed 21 September 2010.

Hill, Annette (1997) *Shocking Entertainment: Viewer Response to Violent Movies* (Luton: University of Luton Press).

Hill, Claire (2007) 'Welcome to the Meat Factory', *The Western Mail*, June 22.

Hills, Matt (2005) *The Pleasures of Horror* (New York: Continuum).

—— (2011) 'Cutting into Concepts of "Reflectionist" Cinema? The *Saw* Franchise and Puzzles of Post-9/11 Horror', in Aviva Briefel and Sam Miller (eds) *Horror After 9/11: World of Fear, Cinema of Terror* (Austin: University of Texas Press).

Holden, Stephen (2008) 'Brutal, Painful Death, Just a Mouse Click Away', *The New York Times*, January 25.

—— (2009) 'Cultures and Sexes Clash in the Aftermath of a Rape in Turkey', *The New York Times*, August 7.

Hollyfield, Jerod Ra'Del (2009) 'Torture Porn and Bodies Politic: Post-Cold War American Perspectives in Eli Roth's *Hostel* and *Hostel: Part II*', *Cineaction*, 78.

Horeck, Tanya, and Tina Kendall (eds) (2011) *The New Extremism in Cinema: From France to Europe* (Edinburgh: Edinburgh University Press).

Hornaday, Ann (2008a) 'Snared in Its Own Sordid Trap', *The Washington Post*, January 25.

—— (2008b) 'Watching Is Sheer Torture', *The Washington Post*, June 6.

—— (2009) 'A Beast for the Senses', *The Washington Post*, October 23.

Howell, Peter (2009) 'Going to Bat for Tarantino', *The Toronto Star*, August 21.

Huddleston, Tom (2010) 'Film – Spiderhole', *Time Out*, October 28.

Hulse, Ed (2007) 'Directing New Brands of Horror', *Video Business*, March 12.

Hunt, Lynn (1993) 'Obscenity and the Origins of Modernity, 1500–1800', in Lynn Hunt (ed.) *The Invention of Pornography: Obscenity and the Origins of Modernity, 1500–1800* (New York: Zone Books).

Hunt, Carol (2007) 'Right, Girls, Let's Get Mutilated for the Boys', *The Sunday Independent*, June 10.

Hunter, Allan (2009) 'Weekend Films', *The Express*, July 24.

—— (2010) 'Greek Tragedy as Brand Hits Rock Bottom', *The Express*, June 25.

Hunter, Ian Q. (2006) 'Tolkien Dirty', in Ernest Mathijs (ed.) *The Lord of the Rings: Popular Culture in Global Context* (London and New York: Wallflower Press).

Huntley, Jacob (2007) '"I Want to Play a Game": How to See *Saw*', *Irish Journal of Gothic and Horror Studies*, 3.

Hutchings, Peter (2004) *The Horror Film* (Harlow, Pearson).

Ide, Wendy (2008a) 'All Mammoth and No Trousers', *The Times*, March 13.

—— (2008b) 'Pain, Angst and Abba', *The Times*, February 9.

—— (2009) 'The Life before Her Eyes', *The Times*, March 26.

Jackson, Craig (2012) 'I Fear This Cynical Celebration of Violence Will Inspire More Young Killers', *Daily Mail*, April 4.

Jacobellis v. Ohio, 378 US 184 (1964).

Javors, Steve (2010) 'Rob Black Released Early from Prison', http://business.avn.com/articles/video/Rob-Black-Released-Early-From-Prison-401081.html date accessed 12 February 2012.

Jensen, Robert (2007) *Getting Off: Pornography and the End of Masculinity* (Cambridge, MA: South End Press).

Jeremy, Ron, and Eric Spitznagel (2008) *The Hardest (Working) Man in Showbiz* (London: HarperCollins).

Johnson, Kevin (2007) 'Dissecting Torture', *St. Louis Post-Dispatch*, October 26.

Johnson, Mark (2011) 'There Is No Moral Faculty', *Philosophical Psychology*, 25:3.

Jones, Alan (2006) 'The New Blood', *Total Film*, 113.

Jones, Steve (2010) '"Time Is Wasting": Con/sequence and S/pace in the *Saw* Series', *Horror Studies*, 1:2.

—— (2011a) 'Dying to Be Seen: Snuff-Fiction's Problematic Fantasies of "Reality"', *Scope*, 19.

—— (2011b) '*Porn of the Dead*: Necrophilia, Feminism, and Gendering the Undead', in Christopher Moreman, and Cory Rushton (eds) *Zombies Are Us: Essays on the Humanity of the Walking Dead* (Jefferson: McFarland).

Jones, Steve and Sharif Mowlabocus (2009) 'Hard Times and Rough Rides: The Legal and Ethical Impossibilities of Researching "Shock" Pornographies', *Sexualities*, 12:5.

Kahn, Arnold, Jennifer Jackson, Christine Kully, Kelly Badger, and Jessica Halvorsen (2003) 'Calling It Rape', *Psychology of Women Quarterly*, 27:3.

Kammeyer, Kenneth C. W. (2008) *A Hypersexual Society: Sexual Discourse, Erotica, and Pornography in America Today* (London: Palgrave).

Kant, Immanuel (1979) *Lectures on Ethics*, Louis Infield (trans.) (Kent: Methuen).

——— (1998) *Critique of Pure Reason*, Paul Guyer and Allen Wood (eds) (Cambridge: Cambridge University Press).

——— (2000) *Groundwork of the Metaphysics of Morals*, Mary Gregor (ed.) (Cambridge: Cambridge University Press).

——— (2003) *The Metaphysics of Morals*, Mary Gregor (ed.) (Cambridge: Cambridge University Press).

Kattelman, Beth (2010) 'Carnographic Culture: America and the Rise of the Torture Porn Film', in Mikko Canini (ed.) *Domination of Fear* (New York: Rodopi).

Kehr, David (2003) 'Film in Review', *The New York Times*, October 17.

Kekes, John (1992) 'Disgust and Moral Taboos', *Philosophy*, 67:262.

Kellner, Douglas (2010) *Cinema Wars: Hollywood Film and Politics in the Bush-Cheney Era* (Oxford: Wiley-Blackwell).

Kelly, Daniel (2011) *Yuck! The Nature and Moral Significance of Disgust* (Cambridge: MIT Press).

Kendall, Nigel (2008) 'A Tangled Web', *The Times*, March 1.

Kendrick, James (2009) 'Razors in the Dreamscape: Revisiting *A Nightmare on Elm Street* and the Slasher Film', *Film Criticism*, 33:3.

Kerekes, David, and David Slater (1995) *Killing for Culture: An Illustrated History of Death Film From Mondo to Snuff* (London: Creation Books).

Kermode, Mark (2007) 'This Is Pure Torture', *The Observer*, June 24.

——— (2008a) 'It's Gross, Gory and Rather Good', *The Observer*, October 13.

——— (2008b) 'Scare Us, Repulse Us, Just Don't Ever Lecture Us', *The Observer*, March 30.

——— (2010) 'A Confederacy of Dunces', *The Observer*, December 26.

Kern, Laura (2008) 'Film in Review', *The New York Times*, June 27.

Kernes, Mark (2011) 'Max Hardcore Introduces...the New Max Hardcore', http://business.avn.com/articles/legal/Max-Hardcore-Introduces-The-New-Max-Hardcore-458729.html date accessed 7 February 2012.

Killingbeck, Tom (2011) 'The Man Who Watches Gorno for a Living', http://www.vice.com/en_uk/read/the-man-who-watches-gorno-for-a-living date accessed 15 June 2011.

Kinnear, Simon (2010) 'The BBFC vs A Serbian Film', http://www.kinnemaniac.com/2010/08/26/the-bbfc-vs-a-serbian-film/ date accessed 30 August 2010.

Kinsella, Warren (2007) 'Torture Porn's Dark Waters', *National Post*, June 7.

Kipnis, Laura (1999) *Bound and Gagged: Pornography and the Politics of Fantasy in America* (Durham: Duke University Press).

Kirkland, Bruce (2008a) 'Lust Is a Must', *The Toronto Sun*, March 16.

——— (2008b) 'Something About *The Girl Next Door*', *The Toronto Sun*, January 21.

Kline, Salli J. (1992) *The Degeneration of Women: Bram Stoker's* Dracula *as Allegorical Criticism of the Fin-de-Siècle* (Rheinbach-Merzbach: CMZ-Verlag).

Labelle, Beverly (1992) 'Snuff – The Ultimate in Woman Hating', in Jill Radford and Diana E. H. Russell (eds) *Femicide: The Politics of Woman Killing* (Buckingham: Open University Press).

Lacey, Liam (2007) 'The New Brutality', *The Globe and Mail*, November 10.

—— (2009) 'There's a Reason for All This Torture Porn: It Makes Money', *The Globe and Mail*, October 30.

Lake Crane, Jonathan (1994) *Terror and Everyday Life: Singular Moments in the History of the Horror Film* (California: Sage).

Lee, Nathan (2008) 'Grand Guignol, by Way of the Tool Shed', *The New York Times*, October 25.

Leith, Sam (2010) 'Freddy Krueger Had the Third-Best Melty Face in Film', *The Guardian*, May 3.

Leupp, Thomas (2010) 'Sex and the City 2', http://www.hollywood.com/movie/Sex_and_the_City_2/5599559/reviews date accessed 18 October 2011.

Leverick, Fiona (2006) *Killing in Self Defence* (Oxford: Oxford University Press).

Leydon, Joe (2007) 'Captivity', *Variety*, July 23.

Lim, Dennis (2009) 'Death Lives a Fourth Time to Ply His Trade', *The New York Times*, August 23.

Lidz, Franz (2009) 'Limbs Pile Up, and Money, Too', *The New York Times*, October 25.

Lockwood, Dean (2008) 'All Stripped Down: The Spectacle of "Torture Porn"', *Popular Communication*, 7:1.

Long, Tom (2008) 'Cyber-Sick: Grisly Torture Flick Embodies What It Pretends to Expose', *The Detroit News*, January 25.

Longsdorf, Amy (2011) 'New on DVD', *Herald News*, December 30.

Longworth, Karina (2010) 'The Human Centipede', *LA Weekly*, May 6.

Lovece, Frank (2010) 'A Final Cut?' *Newsday*, October 24.

Lowe, David (2010) 'DVDs', *The Sun*, October 22.

Lowenstein, Adam (2005) *Shocking Representations: Historical Trauma, National Cinema and the Modern Horror Film* (New York: Columbia University Press).

—— (2011) 'Spectacle Horror and *Hostel*: Why "Torture Porn" Does Not Exist', *Critical Quarterly*, 53:1.

Luban, David (2006) 'Liberalism, Torture and the Ticking Bomb', in Karen J. Greenberg (ed.) *The Torture Debate in America* (Cambridge: Cambridge University Press).

MacAllister, Pat (2003) *Death Defying* (New York: Continuum).

MacDougall, David (2006) *The Corporeal Image: Film, Ethnography and the Sense* (Princetown: Princetown University Press).

MacKinnon, Catharine (2007) *Women's Lives, Men's Laws* (Cambridge: Harvard University Press).

Macnab, Geoffrey (2011) 'The Book of Eli', *The Guardian*, July 27.

Maddison, Stephen (2013) '"It's Gonna Hurt a Little Bit. But That's Okay – It Makes My Cock Feel Good" Extreme Porn, Max Hardcore and the Limits of Pleasure', in Feona Attwood, Vincent Campbell, Ian Q. Hunter and Sharon Lockyer (eds) *Controversial Images* (London: Palgrave Macmillan).

Maher, Kevin (2007) 'Please, Let's Not Have More of the Same', *The Times*, December 27.

—— (2009a) 'Embodiment of Evil', *The Times*, July 2.

—— (2009b) 'General Release: Drag Me to Hell', *The Times*, July 18.

—— (2010a) 'Gloom Raiders', *The Times*, October 2.

—— (2010b) 'The Tourist Is Cartoonish', *The Times*, December 10.

Mangan, Lucy (2007) 'Cable Girl', *The Guardian*, July 10.

Martin, Mick and Marsha Porter (1986) *Video Movie Guide 1987* (New York: Ballantine Books).

Martin, Nina (2011) 'Porn: It's Not Just About Sex Anymore', *Jump Cut*, 53.

McCartney, Jenny (2007a) 'Cut It Out', *The Sunday Telegraph*, July 1.

—— (2007b) 'The Films Get Sicker – So Does Society', *The Sunday Telegraph*, April 22.

—— (2008) 'Our Attitude to Violence Is Beyond a Joke', *The Sunday Telegraph*, July 27.

McClintock, Pamela (2006) 'Blood Brothers', *Variety*, December 25.

McCoy, Alfred W. (2006) *A Question of Torture* (New York: Owl Books).

McEachen, Ben (2010) 'Plenty of Guts but No Glory', *Sunday Herald Sun*, October 31.

McGlynn, Clare (2007) 'Is there a Link between "Torture Porn" and Real Sexual Violence?' *The Guardian*, May 3.

McKie, Andrew (2008) 'Science Fiction', *The Daily Telegraph*, June 14.

McLean, Gareth (2007) 'Watch This', *The Guardian*, July 11.

McRoy, Jay (2010) 'Parts Is Parts: Pornography, Splatter Films and the Politics of Corporeal Disintegration', in Ian Conrich (ed.) *Horror Zone: The Cultural Experience of Contemporary Horror Cinema* (New York: I. B. Tauris).

Melonfarmers (2012a) 'Banned or Unavailable', http://www.melonfarmers.co.uk/banned.htm date accessed 5 July 2012.

—— (2012b) 'ATVOD Watch', http://www.melonfarmers.co.uk/me_atvod_12a.htm date accessed 5 July 2012.

Middleton, Jason (2010) 'The Subject of Torture: Regarding the Pain of Americans in *Hostel*', *Cinema Journal*, 49:4.

Miller v. California 413 U.S. 15 (1973).

Miller, Craig (2012) 'Real Time', *Hobart Mercury*, January 28.

Mills, Eleanor (2010) 'Too Much Too Young?' *The Sunday Times*, December 19.

Miska, Brad (2007) 'Torture Porn, Where Were You All This Time?' http://www.bloody-disgusting.com/news/9388/ date accessed 21 October 2010.

—— (2009) '00's Retrospect: 2005, the Birth of So-called "Torture Porn"', http://bloody-disgusting.com/news/18512/00s-retrospect-2005-the-birth-of-so-called-torture-porn/ date accessed 21 October 2010.

—— (2011) 'Lucky McKee's *The Woman* Causes Outrage!', http://www.bloody-disgusting.com/news/23164 date accessed 24 January 2011.

—— (2012) 'October Now Owned by *Paranormal Activity* Franchise. The End', http://www.bloody-disgusting.com/news/27781 date accessed 7 February 2012.

Molitorisz, Sacha (2012) 'Cinema's New Love Interest', *The Sun Herald*, February 12.

Monahan, Mark (2010) 'Why I Love Gore-Free Scary Movies', *The Daily Telegraph*, October 29.

Morris, Jeremy (2010) 'The Justification of Torture Horror: Retribution and Sadism in *Saw*, *Hostel* and *The Devil's Rejects*', in Thomas Fahy (ed.) *The Philosophy of Horror* (Lexington: University Press of Kentucky).

Muir, Kate (2010a) 'Hammer Returns with Chilling Vampire Tale', *The Times*, October 15.

—— (2010b) 'It's LA, Jim, but Not as We Know It', *The Times*, June 11.

Mullen, R. N. (2007) 'When You Can Read in the Irish Times That Paedophilia Is Not All Bad, It's Time for Moral Outrage', *Daily Mail*, June 6.

Mundell, Ian (2008) 'Euros Face H'wood Onslaught', *Variety*, June 16.

Murphy, Jeffrie (1990) 'Getting Even: The Role of the Victim', *Social Philosophy & Policy*, 7:2.

Murray, Gabriele (2008) '*Hostel II*: Representations of the Body in Pain and the Cinema Experience in Torture Porn', *Jump Cut*, 50.

N.a. (2001) 'Current Releases', *Time Out*, August 29.

N.a. (2007a) 'Charming Fly Boys Pull Out of a Nosedive', *Daily Mail*, June 1.

N.a. (2007b) 'I Was Paid to Sit through This Obscenity but Why Should You?' *Daily Mail*, June 29.

N.a. (2007c) 'Saw Franchise Is Not Torture Porn!', http://www.horror-movies.ca/Forum/viewtopic.php?id=5836 date accessed 21 October 2010.

N.a. (2008a) 'Something for the Weekend', *The Sun*, November 7.

N.a. (2008b) 'Gore-fest Is Just Torture', *Daily Mail*, December 26.

N.a. (2008c) 'Torture Porn: A Serious Discussion', http://www.joblo.com/forums/showthread.php?s=f68388f632b054f408739356fcb5557f&t=124551 date accessed 21 October 2010.

N.a. (2008d) 'Torture Porn Discussion', http://rue-morgue.com/boards/showthread.php?t=22008 date accessed 21 October 2010.

N.a. (2009) 'The Torture Porn Debate Poll', http://www.horrordvds.com/vb3forum/showthread.php?t=38671 date accessed 21 October 2010.

N.a. (2010a) 'Always a Little Horror', *Sunday Express*, October 10.

N.a. (2010b) 'Saw 3D', *Variety*, November 14.

N.a. (2010c) 'Saw 3D: Last Slash Is a Slight Cut Above', *The Toronto Star*, October 31.

N.a. (2010d) 'Fright Plan for All Seasons', *Variety*, October 24.

N.a. (2010e) 'What to See in the Arts This Week', *The Sunday Times*, July 18.

N.a. (2011) 'Bird Had "Fixation with Porn"', *The Express*, March 15.

Nathan, Sara (2010) 'Peaches and "A Night of Drugs and Debauchery" with a Stranger That Ended Up All over the Net', *Daily Mail*, March 27.

Nelson, Rob (2007) 'The Torturer Talks', *LA Weekly*, June 7.

Nelson, Robert (2004) 'Drains the Imagination', *The Age*, May 12.

Newman, Kim (1996) 'Journal of the Plague Years', in Karl French (ed.) *Screen Violence* (London: Bloomsbury).

—— (2008) 'On the Fright Train', *The Times*, August 9.

—— (2009a) 'Horror Will Eat Itself', *Sight and Sound*, 19:5.

—— (2009b) 'My Bloody Valentine 3-D', *The Times*, January 17.

O'Hagan, Sean (2009) 'When I Show a Film, I am Showing Myself', *The Observer*, July 12.

O'Sullivan, Michael (2009) 'Working Both Sides of the Camera', *The Washington Post*, August 21.

O'Toole, Laurence (1999) *Pornocopia: Porn, Sex, Technology and Desire*, 2nd edn (London: Serpent's Tail).

Ochoa, George (2011) *Deformed and Destructive Beings: The Purpose of Horror Films* (Jefferson: McFarland).

Onstad, Katrina (2008) 'Horror Auteur Is Unfinished with the Undead', *The New York Times*, February 10.

Oppliger, Patrice A. (2008) *Girls Gone Skank: The Sexualisation of Girls in American Culture* (Jefferson: McFarland).

Orange, Michelle (2009) 'Taking Back the Knife', *The New York Times*, September 6.

Ordona, Michael (2010a) 'A Stake in the Grass', *Los Angeles Times*, October 8.

—— (2010b) '"Saw" Has Seen Better Days', *Los Angeles Times*, October 30.

Otterman, Michael (2007) *American Torture: From the Cold War to Abu Ghraib and Beyond* (London: Pluto Press).

Patterson, John (2007) 'If Only...', *The Guardian*, June 23.

—— (2010) 'Movie Violence Used to Thrill and Inform by Breaking Taboos', *The Guardian*, June 19.

Pauley, John (2011) 'The Problem of Evil and the Possibility of Nihilism', *International Journal of Philosophical Studies*, 19:1.

Paust, Jordan (2007) *Beyond the Law: The Bush Administration's Unlawful Responses in the 'War' on Terror* (Cambridge: Cambridge University Press).

Penance (2009) *Penance* Website, http://www.penancefilm.com/ date accessed 2 April 2011.

Petley, Julian (2000) 'Snuffed Out: Nightmares in a Trading Standards Officer's Brain', in Xavier Mendik and Graeme Harper (eds) *Unruly Pleasures: The Cult Film and Its Critics* (Surrey: FAB Press).

Phelan, Laurence (2009) 'New Films', *The Independent*, July 25.

—— (2010) 'Film', *The Independent*, December 11.

—— (2011) 'New Films', *The Independent*, January 22.

Philips, Kendall R. (2005) *Projected Fears: Horror Films and American Culture* (Westport: Praeger).

Phillips, Melanie (2010) 'BAFTA Fawns over Tarantino, but His Stomach-Churning Film Is Still Giving Me Nightmares', *Daily Mail*, February 22.

Piepenburg, Erik (2012) 'Testing Horror's Threshold for Pain', *The New York Times*, September 16.

Pipe, Roger (2000) 'Kahn [sic] Tusion Interview', http://www.rogreviews.com/26943/interview-kahn-tusion/ date accessed 5 June 2012.

Platell, Amanda (2008) 'A Punch in the Face of Decency', *Daily Mail*, July 17.

Prince, Stephen (2000) 'Graphic Violence in the Cinema', in Stephen Prince (ed.) *Screening Violence* (New Brunswick: Rutgers University Press).

—— (2009) *Firestorm: American Film in the Age of Terrorism* (New York: Columbia University Press).

Projansky, Sarah (2001) *Watching Rape: Film and Television in Postfeminist Culture* (New York: New York University Press).

Puig, Claudia (2008) 'Don't Bother Looking for It, Cybercrime Film Is Virtually Unwatchable', *USA Today*, January 25.

—— (2009) '"Last House" is Condemnable', *USA Today*, March 13.

Rechtshaffen, Michael (2010) 'Ratings System Needs a Revise', *The Toronto Sun*, November 10.

Reyes, Xavier Aldana (2012) 'Beyond Psychoanalysis: Post-Millennial Horror Film and Affect Theory', *Horror Studies*, 3:2.

Riegler, Thomas (2010) 'We're All Dirty Harry Now: Violent Movies for Violent Times', in Mikko Canini (ed.) *Domination of Fear* (New York: Rodopi).

Robey, Tim (2007a) 'Drew's Luck Runs Out', *The Daily Telegraph*, June 22.

—— (2007b) 'It's Not Scary – Just Revolting', *The Daily Telegraph*, June 27.

Roby, Wendy (2008) 'It's a Scream!', *The Guardian*, October 29.

Rockoff, Adam (2002) *Going to Pieces* (Jefferson: McFarland).

—— (2010) 'Freak Shows Reloaded'. *Sunday Tasmanian*, May 16.

Rooney, Ellen (1993) 'A Little More Than Persuading', in Lynn A. Higgins and Brenda R. Silver (eds) *Rape and Representation* (New York: Columbia University Press).

Rosebury, Brian (2009) 'Private Revenge and Its Relation to Punishment', *Utilitas*, 21:1.

Rosenthal, Abigail L. (2011) 'Defining Evil Away: Arendt's Forgiveness', *Philosophy*, 86:2.

Ross, David (2002) *The Right and the Good* (Oxford: Oxford University Press).

Ross, G. (2000) 'Khan Tusion Interview', http://business.avn.com/articles/video/Khan-Tusion-Interview-34233.html date accessed 17 September 2010.

Rothman, William (2001) 'Violence and Film', in J. David Slocum (ed.) *Violence and American Cinema* (New York: Routledge).

Rubin, Gayle (1993) 'Misguided, Dangerous and Wrong: An Analysis of Anti-Pornography Politics', in Alison Assister and Avedon Carol (eds), *Bad Girls and Dirty Pictures: The Challenge to Reclaim Feminism* (London: Pluto Press).

Russell, Ken (2007) 'Death of Two Masters', *The Times*, August 2.

Safire, William (2007) 'As Gorno Ankles, Zitcoms Roll Out', *The New York Times*, November 11.

Sandhu, Sukhdev (2007) 'Film on Friday', *The Daily Telegraph*, June 29.

—— (2009) 'On the Run from Reality', *The Daily Telegraph*, December 23.

Sandler, Kevin R. (2002) 'Movie Ratings as Genre: The Incontestable R', in Steve Neale (ed.) *Genre and Contemporary Hollywood* (London: BFI).

Saner, Emine (2007) 'Everything but the Ghoul', *The Guardian*, April 6.

Sapolsky, Barry, and Fred Molitor (1996) 'Content Trends in Contemporary Horror Films', in James B. Weaver and Ron Tamorini (eds) *Horror Films: Current Research on Audience Preferences and Reactions* (New Jersey: Lawrence Erlbaum).

Sapolsky, Barry, Fred Molitor, and Sarah Luque (2003) 'Sex and Violence in the Horror Film: Re-examining the Assumptions', *Journalism and Mass Communication Quarterly*, 80:1.

Sarracino, Carmine and Kevin Scott (2008) *The Porning of America* (Boston: Beacon).

Scarry, Elaine (1985) *The Body in Pain: The Making and Unmaking of the World* (Oxford: Oxford University Press).

Schaefer, Eric (1999) *Bold! Daring! Shocking! True! A History of Exploitation Films, 1919–1959* (London: Duke University Press).

Schamus, James (1998) 'To the Rear of the Back End: The Economics of Independent Cinema', in Steve Neale and Murray Smith (eds) *Contemporary Hollywood Cinema* (London: Routledge).

Schembri, Jim (2010) 'Horror with a Conscience', *The Age*, November 26.

Schiesel, Seth (2009) 'No Mercy and Ample Ways to Die', *The New York Times*, October 12.

Schnall, Simone, Jonathan Haidt, Gerald L. Clore, and Alexander H. Jordan (2008) 'Disgust as Embodied Moral Judgment', *Personality and Social Psychology Bulletin*, 34:8.

Schneller, Johanna (2003) 'Hungry for Blood? Gore Porn's for You', *The Globe and Mail*, October 31.

—— (2008) 'The Torture Merchants' Not-so-Funny Game', *The Globe and Mail*, March 22.

Schopenhauer, Arthur (1909) *The World as Will and Idea: Volume II*, 6th edn, R. B. Haldane and J. Kemp (trans.) (London: Kegan Paul).

Schwartz, Missy (2010) 'Battle of the Horror Sequels', *Entertainment Weekly*, 1088.

Scott, Paul (2010) 'Why Can't "Saint" Bob Save Peaches from Herself?' *Daily Mail*, April 3.

Segal, Lynne (1993) 'Does Pornography Cause Violence? The Search for Evidence', in Pamela Church Gibson and Roma Gibson (eds) *Dirty Looks: Women, Pornography, Power* (London: BFI Publishing).

Shaviro, Steven (1993) *The Cinematic Body* (Minneapolis: University of Minnesota Press).

Shoard, Catherine (2004) 'Good and Evil Not so Black and White Cinema', *Sunday Telegraph*, September 19.

Sigel, Lisa Z. (2002) *Governing Pleasures: Pornography and Social Change in England, 1815–1914* (New Brunswick: Rutgers University Press).

Silwinski, Sharon (2006) 'Camera War, Again', *Journal of Visual Culture*, 5:1.

Sinfield, Alan (2004) *On Sexuality and Power* (Columbia: Columbia University Press).

Sipos, Thomas (2010) *Horror Film Aesthetics: Creating the Visual Language of Fear* (Jefferson: McFarland).

Skal, David J. (1993) *The Monster Show: A Cultural History of Horror* (London: Plexus).

Skenazy, Lenore (2007) 'It's Torture! It's Porn! What's Not to Like? Plenty, Actually', *Advertising Age*, May 28.

Slaymaker, Gary (2008) 'Film Reviews', *The Western Mail*, May 23.

Slotek, Jim (2009a) 'Collector Missing a Big Piece – The Plot', *The Toronto Sun*, October 30.

—— (2009b) 'Welcome Back, Sam!', *The Toronto Sun*, May 29.

Smith, Anna (2010) 'Anna Smith Film Critic', *The Observer*, June 13.

Smith, Theresa (2010) 'Torture Porn Is a Turn-Off', *Cape Argus*, April 12.

Strossen, Nadine (2000) *Defending Pornography* (New York: New York University Press).

Tait, Sue (2008) 'Pornographies of Violence? Internet Spectatorship on Body Horror', *Critical Studies in Media Communication*, 25:1.

Tallon, Philip (2010) 'Through a Mirror Darkly: Art Horror as a Medium for Moral Reflection', in Thomas Fahy (ed.) *The Philosophy of Horror* (Lexington: University Press of Kentucky).

Tapper, Jake (2006) 'Blood Lust', *ABC News Transcripts*, April 21.

Taylor, Gary (2002) *Castration: An Abbreviated History of Western Manhood* (London: Routledge).

Teeman, Tim (2010) 'I Have a Gun. It's Wise to Keep It Close When I am in Remote Places', *The Times*, September 18.

Terrell, Lacey (2009) 'The Brutal and the Banal Become Us', *The Star-Ledger*, March 8.

Terry, Geraldine (ed.) (2007) *Gender-Based Violence* (Oxford: Oxfam).

Thompson, Luke (2007) 'Why "Torture Porn" Isn't', *LA Weekly*, September 6.

—— (2008) 'Bad Blood', *LA Weekly*, January 3.

Thomson, Desson (2008a) 'Horror without the Gore', *The Washington Post*, January 5.

—— (2008b) 'If these Walls Could Talk, They'd Scream', *The Washington Post*, January 4.

Thornhill, Randy, and Craig Palmer (2000) *A Natural History of Rape: Biological Bases of Sexual Coercion* (Massachusetts: MIT Press).

Thrower, Stephen (2008) *Nightmare USA* (Surrey: FAB Press).

Tookey, Chris (2006) 'Thank Heaven for Sunshine', *Daily Mail*, December 29.

—— (2007a) 'Mayan Mayhem from Macho Mel', *Daily Mail*, January 5.

—— (2007b) 'Viggo's Mobster Delivers on His Promise', *Daily Mail*, October 26.

—— (2008a) 'If You Go down to the Woods Today, Beware the Hillbillies', *Daily Mail*, May 23.

—— (2008b) 'Old Meat Head Is Back!', *Daily Mail*, February 22.

—— (2008c) 'Parking Can Be a REAL Nightmare', *Daily Mail*, May 2.

—— (2008d) 'What's so Great About Wallowing in Squalor?' *Daily Mail*, March 14.

—— (2009) 'The Man Who Made This Horrible, Misogynistic Film Needs to See a Shrink', *Daily Mail*, July 24.

—— (2011) 'It's Not Just the Internet That's Full of Violent Porn – So Are the Cinemas', *Daily Mail*, November 1.

Travis, Cheryl B. (ed.) (2003) *Evolution, Gender and Rape* (Massachusetts: MIT Press).

Tyler, Meagan (2010) '"Now That's Pornography!"': Violence and Domination in *Adult Video News*', in Karen Boyle (ed.) *Everyday Pornography* (London: Routledge).

Uniacke, Suzanne (2000) 'Why Is Revenge Wrong?' *The Journal of Value Inquiry*, 34:1.

Upadhyay, Chandra Mohan (1999) *Human Rights in Pre-Trial Detention* (New Delhi: S. B. Nangia).

Utichi, Joe (2012) 'A Buffy-Style Kicking for Torture Porn', *The Sunday Times*, April 15.

Vance, Carole S. (1990) 'The Pleasures of Looking: The Attorney General's Commission on Pornography versus Visual Images', in Carol Squiers (ed.) *The Critical Image: Essays on Contemporary Photography* (London: Lawrence and Wishart).

Vanobbergen, Bruno (2004) 'Wanted: Real Children About Innocence and Nostalgia in a Commodified Childhood', *Studies in Philosophy and Education*, 23:2.

Varga, Somogy (2011) 'Self-Realisation and Owing to Others: An Indirect Constraint?' *International Journal of Philosophical Studies*, 19:1.

Vaughan, Johnny (2007) 'Captivity', *The Sun*, June 22.

Ventre, Michael (2009) '"Saw" Franchise Creates Buzz, but Is It Any Good?', http://today.msnbc.msn.com/id/33455422/ns/today-entertainment/t/saw-franchise-creates-buzz-it-any-good/ date accessed 28 October 2009.

Vera, Noel (2002) 'Spider under Glass', *BusinessWorld*, September 20.

Walker, Johnny (2011) 'Nasty Visions: Violent Spectacle in Contemporary British Horror Cinema', *Horror Studies*, 2:1.

Walliss, John and James Aston (2012) '"I've Never Murdered Anyone in My Life. The Decisions Are up to Them"': Ethical Guidance and Cultural Pessimism in the *Saw* Series', *Journal of Religion and Popular Culture*, 24:3.

Warren, Peter (2012) 'Manwin Shutters Brazzers Site PornstarsPunishment.com', http://business.avn.com/articles/technology/Manwin-Shutters-Brazzers-Site-PornstarsPunishment-com-481930.html date accessed 19 July 2012.

Weiss, Karen G. (2010) 'Male Sexual Victimisation: Examining Men's Experiences of Rape and Sexual Assault', *Men and Masculinities*, 12:3.

Westphal, Merold (1984) *God, Guilt and Death: An Existential Phenomenology of Religion* (Bloomington: Indiana University Press).

Wetmore, Kevin (2012) *Post-9/11 Horror in American Cinema* (New York: Continuum).

White, Michele (2006) *The Body and the Screen: Theories of Internet Spectatorship* (Cambridge: MIT Press).

Whittle, Peter (2007) 'Here's Blood in Your Eye', *The Sunday Times*, June 10.

Wigley, Samuel (2007) 'Captivity', *Sight and Sound*, 17:8.

Wilhelm, Peter (2009) 'Sly Descent into Horror', *Financial Mail*, October 23.

Williams, Alex (2006) 'Up to Her Eyes in Gore, and Loving It', *The New York Times*, April 30.

Williams, Linda (1989) *Hard Core: Power, Pleasure, and the 'Frenzy of the Visible'* (Berkeley: University of California Press).

Williamson, Kevin (2007a) 'Pure Torture', *The Toronto Sun*, July 14.

——— (2007b) 'Room for Change', *The Toronto Sun*, June 20.

——— (2007c) 'Tortured Soul', *The Toronto Sun*, July 8.

——— (2010a) 'Funny? We're Not Laughing', *The Toronto Sun*, March 14.

——— (2010b) 'Scorsese, De Niro Back in the Mob?' *The Toronto Sun*, February 21.

Wilson, David (2012) 'We Must Vet Screen Violence', *The Sun*, April 4.

Wise, Damon (2011) 'House of Pain', *The Guardian*, April 23.

Wloszczyna, Susan (2007) '"Saw" Has Its Teeth Firmly in Halloween', *USA Today*, October 22.

——— (2009) 'Move Over, Movie Vampires', *USA Today*, January 22.

Wong, Cynthia M. (2011) 'US Piracy Laws Could Threaten Human Rights', http://www.indexoncensorship.org/2011/11/usa-sopa-human-rights-internet/ date accessed 7 February 2012.

Yong, Shu Hoong (2010) 'Many Sides of Porn', *The Straits Times*, October 21.

Zane, Alex (2010) 'The Collector', *The Sun*, June 25.

Zeitchik, Steven (2010) 'Two Films, Two Sex Scenes, Two Ratings', *Los Angeles Times*, December 4.

Zinoman, Jason (2007) 'A Bloody Cut above Your Everyday Zombie Film', *The New York Times*, June 10.

——— (2011) 'How to Fix Horror', http://www.slate.com/articles/arts/culturebox/features/2011/how_to_fix_horror/part_i_stop_trying_to_be_so_respectable.html date accessed 10 July 2011.

Zoc, Iloz (2008) 'Torture Porn in Horror Today', http://blogcritics.org/video/article/lott-d-roundtable-torture-porn-in/ date accessed 21 March 2009.

Filmography

1408 (2007, USA, dir Mikael Håfström).
2001 Maniacs (2005, USA, dir Tim Sullivan).
24 (2001–10, USA, dir Stephen Hopkins et al.).
30 Days in Hell: The Making of the Devil's Rejects (2005, USA, dir Craig Weaver).
5150 Elm Way (5150 Rue des Ormes) (2009, Canada, dir Eric Tessler).
7 days (Les 7 Jours du Talion) (2010, Canada, dir Daniel Grou).
7th Hunt, The (2009, Australia, dir Jon Cohen).
9 Songs (2004, UK, dir Michael Winterbottom).
99 Pieces (2007, USA, dir Anthony Falcon).
9to5: Days in Porn (2008, USA/Germany, dir Jens Hoffman).
Abominable Dr. Phibes, The (1971, UK/USA, dir Robert Fuest).
Alive or Dead (2008, USA, dir Stephen Goetsch).
Amateur Porn Star Killer (2007, USA, dir Shane Ryan).
Amateur Porn Star Killer 2 (2008, USA, dir Shane Ryan).
Amateur Porn Star Killer 3 (2009, USA, dir Shane Ryan).
American Crime, An (2007, USA, dir Tommy O'Haver).
Anniversary at Shallow Creek, The (2010, USA, dir Jon D. Wagner).
Antichrist (2009, Denmark/Germany/France/Sweden/Italy/Poland, dir Lars Von Trier).
Apollo 18 (2011, USA/Canada, dir Gonzalo López-Gallego).
Are You Scared? (2006, USA, dir Andy Hurst).
August Underground (2001, USA, dir Fred Vogel).
August Underground's Mordum (2003, USA, dirs Fred Vogel, Cristie Whiles, and Michael Schneider).
August Underground's Penance (2007, USA, dir Fred Vogel).
Basement (2010, UK, dir Asham Kamboj).
Blair Witch Project, The (1999, USA, dirs Daniel Myrick and Eduardo Sánchez).
Blood and Sex Nightmare (2008, USA, dir Joseph B. Kolbeck).
BoneSaw (2006, USA, dir Jett Blakk).
Bonnie and Clyde (1967, USA, dir Arthur Penn).
Book of Revelation, The (2006, Australia, dir Ana Kokkinos).
Borderland (2007, Mexico/USA, dir Zev Berman).
Boy Meets Girl (1994, UK, dir Ray Brady).
Branded (2006, USA, dir Darla Enlow).
Break (2009, Germany, dir Matthias Olof Eich).
Breaking Nikki (2009, Argentina, dir Hernan Findling).
Breathing Room (2008, USA, dirs John Suits and Gabriel Cowan).
Broken (2006, UK, dirs Simon Boyes and Adam Mason).
Bunny Game, The (2010, USA, dir Adam Rehmeier).
Butcher, The (2009, South Korea, dir Jin Won Kim).
Caged (Captifs) (2010, France, dir Yann Gozlan).
Callback (2009, USA, dir Ben Ross).
Camp Cuddly Pines Powertool Massacre (2005, USA, dir Jonathan Morgan).

Cannibal Ferox (1981, Italy, dir Umberto Lenzi).
Cannibal Holocaust (1980, Italy, dir Ruggero Deodato).
Captivity (2007, USA/Russia, dir Roland Joffe).
Carver (2008, USA, dir Franklin Guerrero Jr).
Casino Royale (2006, UK/Czech Republic/USA/Germany/Bahamas, dir Martin Campbell).
Cellar Door, The (2007, USA, dir Matt Zettell).
Chaos (2005, USA, dir David DeFalco).
Cherry Tree Lane (2010, UK, dir Paul Andrew Williams).
Chitty Chitty Bang Bang (1968, UK, dir Ken Hughes).
Choose (2011, USA, dir Marcus Graves).
Chronicles of Narnia, The: The Lion, the Witch and the Wardrobe (2005, USA/UK, dir Andrew Adamson).
Clockwork Orange, A (1971, UK/USA, dir Stanley Kubrick).
Cloverfield (2008, USA, dir Matt Reeves).
Cockneys vs Zombies (2011, UK, dir Matthias Hoene).
Collector, The (2009, USA, dir Marcus Dunstan).
Creep (2004, UK/Germany, dir Christopher Smith).
Dark Reality (2006, USA, dir Christopher Hutson).
Darker Reality, A (2008, USA, dir Chris Kazmier).
Deaden (2006, Canada/USA, dir Christian Viel).
Deadgirl (2008, USA, dir Marcel Sarmiento).
Death Factory: Bloodletting (2008, USA, dir Sean Tretta).
Death Tunnel (2005, USA, dir Philip Adrian Booth).
Deathbell (Gosa) (2008, South Korea, dir Yoon Hong-Seung).
Deathtube (2010, Japan, dir Yohei Fukuda).
Deep Throat (1972, USA, dir Gerard Damiano).
Detour (Snarveien) (2009, Norway, dir Severin Eskeland).
Devil's Rejects, The (2005, USA/Germany, dir Rob Zombie).
Dexter (2006–present, USA, dirs Michael Cuesta, et al.).
Diary of a Sex Offender (2010, USA, dir John Niflheim).
Die (2010, Canada/Italy, dir Dominic James).
Donkey Punch (2008, UK, dir Oliver Blackburn).
Dracula (1931, USA, dir Tod Browning).
Dread (2009, UK/USA, dir Anthony DiBlasi).
Dungeon Girl (2008, USA, dir Ulli Lommel).
Dying Breed (2008, Australia, dir Jody Dwyer).
Embodiment of Evil (Encarnação do Demônio) (2008, Brazil, dir Jose Mojica Marins).
Exam (2009, UK, dir Stuart Hazeldine).
Exorcist, The (1973, USA, dir William Friedkin).
Farmhouse (2009, USA, dir George Bessudo).
Final, The (2010, USA, dir Joey Stewart).
Flesh, TX (2008, USA, dir Guy Crawford).
Forced Entry (1973, USA, dir Shaun Costello).
Friday the 13th (1980, USA, dir Sean Cunnigham).
Friday the 13th: A XXX Parody (2010, USA, dir Gary Orona).
Frontier(s) (2007, France/Switzerland, dir Xavier Gens).
Frontline: American Porn (2002, USA, dir Michael Kirk).

Frozen (2010, USA, dir Adam Green).
Fuckenstein (2012, USA, dir Joanna Angel).
Funny Games (2007, USA/France/UK/Austria/Germany/Italy, dir Michael Haneke).
Gag (2006, USA, dir Scott Mckinlay).
Girl Next Door, The (2007, USA, dir Gregory Wilson).
Gnaw (2008, UK, dir Gregory Mandry).
Graphic Sexual Horror (2009, USA/Sweden, dirs Barbara Bell and Anna Lorentzon).
Great American Snuff Film, The (2003, USA, dir Sean Tretta).
Great Ecstasy of Robert Carmichael, The (2005, UK, dir Robert Clay).
Grindhouse (2007, USA, dirs Quentin Tarantino and Robert Rodriguez).
Grotesque (Gurotesuku) (2009, Japan, dir Koji Shirashi).
Gruesome (Salvage) (2006, USA, dirs Jeff Crook and Josh Crook).
Halloween (1978, USA, dir John Carpenter).
Hamal_18 (2004, USA, dir John G. Thomas).
Hard Candy (2005, USA, dir David Slade).
Hardcore (2000, UK, dir Stephen Walker).
Header (2006, USA, dir Archibald Flancranstin).
High Lane (Vertige) (2009, France, dir Abel Ferry).
Hike, The (2011, UK, dir Rupert Bryan).
Hills Have Eyes, The (2006, USA, dir Alexandre Aja).
Hills Have Eyes 2, The (2007, USA, dir Martin Weisz).
Hills Run Red, The (2009, USA, dir Dave Parker).
History of Horror, A (2010, UK, dirs John Das and Rachel Jardine).
Hoboken Hollow (2006, USA, dir Glen Stephens).
Horseman, The (2008, Australia, dir Steven Kastrissios).
Hostel (2005, USA, dir Eli Roth).
Hostel: Part II (2007, USA, dir Eli Roth).
Hostel: Part III (2011, USA, dir Scott Spiegel).
House of 1000 Corpses (2003, USA, dir Rob Zombie).
House of 9 (2005, UK/Romania/Germany/France, dir Steven R. Monroe).
Human Centipede (First Sequence), The (2009, Netherlands, dir Tom Six).
Human Centipede II (Full Sequence), The (2011, Netherlands/USA/UK, dir Tom Six).
Human Sexipede, The (2010, USA, dir Lee Roy Myers).
Hunger (2009, USA, dir Steven Hentges).
Hush (2009, UK, dir Mark Tonderai).
I Know Who Killed Me (2007, USA, dir Chris Sivertson).
I Saw the Devil (Akmareul boatda) (2010, South Korea, dir Jee-woon Kim).
I Spit on Eli Roth (2009, USA, dir Devi Snively).
I Spit on Your Grave (1978, USA, dir Meir Zarchi).
I Spit on Your Grave (2010, USA, dir Steven R. Monroe).
Inside (A L'interieur) (2007, France, dirs Alexandre Bustillo and Julien Maury).
Invitation Only (Jue ming pai dui) (2009, Taiwan, dir Kevin Ko).
Irreversible (2002, France, dir Gaspar Noe).
Jackass Number Two (2006, USA, dir Jeff Tremaine).
Keepsake (2008, USA, dir Paul Moore).
Kidnapped (Secuestrados) (2010, Spain/France, dir Miguel Ángel Vivas).
Kill Theory (2009, USA, dir Chris Moore).
Killer Inside Me, The (2010, USA/Sweden/UK/Canada, dir Michael Winterbottom).

Killing Room, The (2009, USA, dir Jonathan Liebesman).
Killing Words (*Palabras encadenadas*) (2003, Spain, dir Laura Mañá).
Last Exorcism, The (2010, USA/France, dir Daniel Stam).
Last House on the Left, The (2009, USA, dir Dennis Iliadis).
Law Abiding Citizen (2009, USA, dir F. Gary Gray).
Live Animals (2008, USA, dir Jeremy Benson).
Live Feed (2006, Canada, dir Ryan Nicholson).
Louis Theroux: Twilight of the Porn Stars (2012, UK, dir Jason Massot).
Louis Theroux's Weird Weekends: Porn (1998, UK, dir Geoffrey O'Connor).
Loved Ones, The (2009, Australia, dir Sean Byrne).
Madness (2010, Sweden, dirs Sonny Laguna, David Liljeblad, and Tommy Wiklund).
Manhunt (*Rovdyr*) (2008, Norway, dir Patrik Syversen).
Maniac (1980, USA, dir William Lustig).
Martyrs (2008, France/Canada, dir Pascal Laugier).
Maskhead (2009, USA, dirs Scott Swan and Fred Vogel).
Matchdead (*The Abducted*) (2009, USA, dir Jon Bonell).
Meat Grinder (*Cheuuat gaawn chim*) (2009, Thailand, dir Tiwa Moeithaisong).
Meatholes 2 (2005, USA, dir Khan Tusion).
Meatholes 3 (2005, USA, dir Khan Tusion).
Meatholes 5 (2005, USA, dir Khan Tusion).
Meatholes 6 (2006, USA, dir Khan Tusion).
Megan Is Missing (2011, USA, dir Michael Goi).
Missing (*Sil-jong*) (2009, South Korea, dir Sung-Hong Kim).
Ms. 45 (1981, USA, dir Abel Ferrara).
Mum and Dad (2008, UK, dir Steven Sheil).
Murder Collection V.1 (2009, USA, dir Fred Vogel).
Murder-Set-Pieces (2004, USA, dir Nick Palumbo).
Nailed Down (2012, USA, dir Harley David Morris).
Naked Fear (2007, USA, dir Thom Eberhardt).
Neighbor (2009, USA, dir Robert Masciantonio).
Night of the Living Dead (1968, USA, dir George Romero).
Nightmare on Elm Street, A (1984, USA, dir Wes Craven).
Nine Dead (2010, USA, dir Chris Shadley).
Oral Fixation (2009, USA, dir Jake Cashill).
Ordeal, The (*Calvaire*) (2004, Belgium/France/Luxembourg, dir Fabrice Du Welz).
P2 (2007, USA, dir Franck Khalfoun).
Panic Button (2011, UK, dir Chris Crow).
Paranormal Activity (2007, USA, dir Oren Peli).
Paranormal Activity 2 (2010, USA, dir Tod Williams).
Passion of the Christ, The (2004, USA, dir Mel Gibson).
Peeping Tom (1960, UK, dir Michael Powell).
Pelt (2010, USA, dir Richard Swindell).
Penance (2009, USA, dir Jake Kennedy).
Pig Hunt (2008, USA, dir James Issac).
Pit and the Pendulum (1961, USA, dir Roger Corman).
Porn of the Dead (2006, USA, dir Rob Rotten).
Porn Shutdown (2005, UK, dir Richard Sanders).
Poughkeepsie Tapes, The (2007, USA, dir John Erick Dowdle).

Psycho (1960, USA, dir Alfred Hitchcock).
Razor's Ring (2008, USA, dir Morgan Hampton).
Re-Animator (1985, USA, dir Stuart Gordon).
ReGOREgitated Sacrifice (2008, Canada/USA, dir Lucifer Valentine).
Re-Penetrator (2004, USA, dir Doug Sakmann).
Rest Stop (2006, USA, dir John Shiban).
Rest Stop: Don't Look Back (2008, USA, dir Shawn Papazian).
Resurrection County (2008, USA, dir Matt Zettell).
Ring, The (2002, USA/Japan, dir Gore Verbinski).
Roadkill (Joyride) (2001, USA, dir John Dhal).
Rogue River (2012, USA, dir Jourdan McClure).
Rosemary's Baby (1968, USA, dir Roman Polanski).
Rough Sex 2 (1999, USA, dir Khan Tusion).
Saw (2004, USA/Australia, dir James Wan).
Saw 3D (Saw: The Final Chapter) (2010, Canada/USA, dir Kevin Greutert).
Saw II (2005, USA/Canada, dir Darren Lynn Bousman).
Saw III (2006, USA/Canada, dir Darren Lynn Bousman).
Saw IV (2007, USA/Canada, dir Darren Lynn Bousman).
Saw V (2008, USA/Canada, dir David Hackl).
Saw VI (2009, Canada/USA/UK/Australia, dir Kevin Greutert).
Saw: A Hardcore Parody (2010, USA, dir Hef Pounder).
Scar (2007, USA, dir Jed Weintrob).
Scarce (2008, Canada, dirs Jesse Cook and John Geddes).
Scream (1996, USA, dir Wes Craven).
Scream 4 (2011, USA, dir Wes Craven).
Scream Bloody Murder (1972, USA, dir Marc B. Ray).
Senseless (2008, UK, dir Simon Hynd).
Serbian Film, A (Srpski film) (2010, Serbia, dir Srdjan Spasojevic).
Sex and the City 2 (2010, USA, dir Michael Patrick King).
Shadow (2009, Italy, dir Federico Zampaglione).
Shaun of the Dead (2004, UK, dir Edgar Wright).
She's Crushed (2009, USA, dir Patrick Johnson).
Shock Cinema Vol. 2 (1991, USA, dir Robert Hayes).
Shortbus (2006, USA, dir John Cameron Mitchell).
Shrek the Third (2007, USA, dirs Chris Miller and Raman Hui).
Sixth Sense, The (1999, USA, dir M. Night Shyamalan).
Slaughtered Vomit Dolls (2006, USA, dir Lucifer Valentine).
Slave (2009, Spain, dir Darryn Welch).
Slow Torture Puke Chamber (2010, USA/Canada, dir Lucifer Valentine).
Snuff (1976, Argentina/USA/Canada, dirs Roberta Findlay and Michael Findlay).
Somebody Help Me (2007, USA, dir Chris Stokes).
Spiderhole (2010, Ireland, dir Daniel Simpson).
Splat Pack, The (2011, USA, dirs Mark Henry and Frank H. Woodward).
Squealer (2004, USA, dir Jack the Zipper).
Standard Operating Procedure (2008, USA, dir Errol Morris).
Stash (2007, USA, dir Jacob Ennis).
Steel Trap (2007, Germany, dir Luis Camara).
Stockholm Syndrome (2008, USA, dir Ryan Cavalline).
Stoning of Soraya M., The (2008, USA, dir Cyrus Nowrasteh).

Storm Warning (2007, Australia, dir Jamie Blanks).
Straightheads (2007, UK, dir Dan Reed).
Stranded (2005, USA, dir Laume Conroy).
Strangers, The (2008, USA, dir Brian Bertino).
Sutures (2009, USA, dir Tammi Sutton).
Switchblade Romance (*Haute Tension*) (2003, France, dir Alexandre Aja).
Sympathy (2007, USA, dir Andrew Moorman).
Task, The (2010, USA, dir Alex Orwell).
Territories (2010, France/Canada, dir Oliver Abbou).
Texas Chainsaw Massacre, The (1974, USA, dir Tobe Hooper).
Texas Chainsaw Massacre, The (2003, USA, dir Marcus Nispel).
Texas Chainsaw Massacre: The Beginning, The (2006, USA, dir Jonathan Liebesman).
Texas Chainsaw Massacre: The Shocking Truth, The (2000, UK, dir David Gregory).
Texas Vibrator Massacre (2008, USA, dir Rob Rotten).
Them (*Ils*) (2006, France/Romania, dirs David Moreau and Xavier Palud).
Timber Falls (2007, USA, dir Tony Giglio).
Tortura (2008, Germany, dirs Michael Effenberger and Marcel Walz).
Torture Me No More (2005, USA, dir Francis Xavier DeGennaro).
Torture Room (*Pledge of Allegiance*) (2007, USA, dir Eric Forsberg).
Tortured (2008, USA/Canada, dir Nolan Lebovitz).
Tortured, The (2010, USA/Canada, dir Robert Lieberman).
Torturer, The (2008, USA, dir Graham Green).
Train (2008, USA, dir Gideon Raff).
Trunk (2009, USA, dir Straw Weisman).
Truth, The (2010, USA, dir Ryan Barton-Grimley).
Turistas (*Paradise Lost*) (2006, USA, dir John Stockwell).
Unforgiving, The (2010, South Africa, dir Alastair Orr).
Unthinkable (2010, USA, dir Gregor Jordan).
Untraceable (2008, USA, dir Gregory Hoblit).
Vacancy (2007, USA, dir Antal Nimrod).
Vacancy 2: The First Cut (2008, USA, dir Eric Bross).
Walled In (2009, USA/France/Canada, dir Gilles Paquet Brenner).
Watermen, The (2011, USA, dir Matt Lockhart).
Wet Dream on Elm Street, A (2011, USA, dir Lee Roy Myers).
Wicked Lake (2008, USA, dir Zach Passero).
Wilderness (2006, UK, dir Michael J. Bassett).
Wire in the Blood (2002–present, UK, dir Andrew Grieve et al.).
Wolf Creek (2005, Australia, dir Greg McLean).
Woman, The (2011, USA, dir Lucky McKee).
Would You Rather (2012, USA, dir David Guy Levy).
Wrong Turn (2003, USA/Canada/Germany, dir Rob Schmidt).
Wrong Turn 2: Dead End (2007, USA, dir Joe Lynch).
wΔz (*The Killing Gene*) (2007, UK, dir Tom Shankland).
XXXorcist (2006, USA, dir Doug Sakmann).
Zombie Strippers! (2008, USA, dir Jay Lee).

Index

Printed and bound by CPI Group (UK) Ltd, Croydon, CR0 4YY